JOHN FREDERICK KENSETT

An American Master

John Paul Driscoll

John K. Howat

with contributions by

Dianne Dwyer

Oswaldo Rodriguez Roque

Edited by Susan E. Strickler

JOHN FREDERICK KENSETT

An American Master

WORCESTER ART MUSEUM
in association with
W. W. NORTON & COMPANY
NEW YORK   LONDON

EXHIBITION ITINERARY:

Worcester Art Museum
March 24 – June 9, 1985

Los Angeles County Museum of Art
July 11 – September 8, 1985

The Metropolitan Museum of Art
October 29, 1985 – January 19, 1986

John Frederick Kensett (1816–1872): *An American Master*
is made possible through the generous support of Norton
Company, Worcester, and the National Endowment for
the Arts.

Published simultaneously in Canada by Stoddart,
a subsidiary of General Publishing Co. Ltd,
Don Mills, Ontario.

ISBN 0–393–01934–9

First Edition

Printed in Great Britain by Balding + Mansell

Typeset in Monotype Fournier
by Michael & Winifred Bixler

Designed by Homans/Salsgiver

W. W. Norton & Company, Inc.
500 Fifth Avenue, New York, N. Y. 10110

W. W. Norton & Company Ltd.
37 Great Russell Street, London WC1B 3NU

1 2 3 4 5 6 7 8 9 0

Frontispiece:
Kensett
Shrewsbury River, 1858
oil on canvas
15 x 27 in. (38.1 x 68.6 cm.)
Erving and Joyce Wolf

Cover illustration: Kensett, *Forty Steps, Newport, Rhode
Island*, 1860. Jo Ann and Julian Ganz, Jr. See Plate 25.

CONTENTS

LENDERS TO EXHIBITION   6

FOREWORD   7

ACKOWLEDGMENTS   9

KENSETT'S WORLD   *John K. Howat*   12

FROM BURIN TO BRUSH: THE DEVELOPMENT OF A PAINTER   *John Paul Driscoll*   46

THE LAST SUMMER'S WORK   *Oswaldo Rodriquez Roque*   136

JOHN F. KENSETT'S PAINTING TECHNIQUE   *Dianne Dwyer*   163

APPENDIX   181

NOTES   184

BIBLIOGRAPHY   194

EXHIBITION CHECKLIST   199

INDEX   204

LENDERS TO THE EXHIBITION

Susan and Herbert Adler

The Art Institute of Chicago

The Century Association, New York

Cornell Fine Arts Center, Rollins College,
　　Winter Park, Florida

Babcock Galleries, New York

The Baltimore Museum of Art

The Brooklyn Museum, New York

Museum of Art, Carnegie Institute, Pittsburgh

The Cleveland Museum of Art

Corcoran Gallery of Art, Washington, D.C.

Cummer Gallery of Art, Jacksonville, Florida

Mr. and Mrs. Stuart P. Feld

Dan Flavin, New York

Dia Art Foundation, New York

Jo Ann and Julian Ganz, Jr.

High Museum of Art, Atlanta

Hirschl and Adler Galleries, Inc., New York

Mrs. Alice M. Kaplan

Mr. and Mrs. Maurice N. Katz, Naples, Florida

Los Angeles County Museum of Art

James Maroney, New York

Mead Art Museum, Amherst College, Amherst,
　　Massachusetts

The Metropolitan Museum of Art, New York

Milwaukee Art Museum, Wisconsin

Montclair Art Museum, New Jersey

Museum of Fine Arts, Boston

National Academy of Design, New York

National Gallery of Art, Washington, D.C.

National Museum of American Art,
　　Smithsonian Institution, Washington, D.C.

The Newark Museum, New Jersey

The New-York Historical Society

The Saint Louis Art Museum, Missouri

Santa Barbara Museum of Art, California

Mr. and Mrs. W. Knight Sturges

The Toledo Museum of Art, Ohio

Wadsworth Atheneum, Hartford, Connecticut

Wellesley College Museum, Wellesley,
　　Massachusetts

Erving and Joyce Wolf

Worcester Art Museum, Worcester,
　　Massachusetts

Jane Voorhees Zimmerli Art Museum, Rutgers,
　　The State University, New Brunswick,
　　New Jersey

Private Collections

FOREWORD

THE ONGOING REAPPRAISAL OF THE WORKS OF AMERICAN ARTISTS remains one of the most
exciting responsibilities currently being undertaken by museums. Not only do we reassess careers of
artists and their works of art, but we also find new opportunities to look into the American past, both
historically and visually. Despite his undisputed position as a successful and admired painter and
prominent artistic figure during his own day, Kensett has only relatively recently been reintroduced
to today's art audience, chiefly by John K. Howat, the Lawrence A. Fleischman Chairman of the
Departments of American Art at the Metropolitan Museum of Art, New York. In 1968 Mr. Howat
organized an important exhibition of Kensett's paintings, which circulated to five cities across the
country. A decade later John Paul Driscoll, guest Curator for this exhibition, brought to light further
details about Kensett's career and his talents as a draftsman through an exhibition and catalogue of his
drawings. These two scholars, along with an advisory committee chaired by Susan E. Strickler, Curator
of American Art at the Worcester Art Museum, and ably assisted by Dianne Dwyer, Conservator,
Oswaldo Rodriguez Roque, Associate Curator of Decorative Arts, and Lewis Sharp, Curator and
Administrator of the American Wing, all at the Metropolitan, have assembled the most extensive
exhibition of Kensett's oeuvre since the Memorial Exhibition held at the National Academy of Design
in 1873, shortly after the artist's death. Together, this book—the first monograph on Kensett—
and the exhibition present the most significant visual and written documentation of the artist's life and
work to date.

It is appropriate that the Worcester Art Museum and the Metropolitan Museum of Art collaborate
on this study. Worcester is close to so many of the New England sites that were interpreted by
Kensett's hand, and the museum has long been a center for the study of American art. Kensett was
also a founder and trustee of the Metropolitan, which holds the most extensive collection of his paintings, many of which were given in 1874 by the artist's brother, Thomas. In a way, the exhibition's
showing at the Los Angeles County Museum of Art—one of the primary repositories of American art
on the West Coast—asserts yet another facet of the expansiveness of the American continent that
Kensett and his contemporaries loved. Although he never traveled as far west as California, certainly
Kensett would be gratified by the reception his work has since received by the numerous collectors in
Los Angeles who now prize his paintings as their own.

While purposely small in the number of works it presents, this exhibition nevertheless reveals the
breadth and range of Kensett's extraordinary achievement, from his early exploratory paintings inspired by such masters as Constable and Claude to his mature, innovative, and breathtaking coastal
views. For the first time in recent years, a significant group of his final paintings—traditionally referred

to as "The Last Summer's Work"—have been displayed together following conservation treatment. The historical and aesthetic importance of these hauntingly poetic works, many of which are not well known to either the historian or the general viewer, is fully discussed for the first time by Oswaldo Rodriguez Roque. Dianne Dwyer, who restored these works, has contributed the first study of Kensett's materials and techniques, which adds not only new perspective to this artist's working methods but also a new chapter to the practices of his fellow painters.

A congenial yet modest man, Kensett unfortunately wrote relatively little about his aesthetic principles. However, the quality of the paintings and drawings in this exhibition conveys an underlying poetic sensibility for the American landscape that was not only in concert with literary and artistic expression of the day but that also revealed a unique vision that set Kensett apart from his contemporaries as a quiet innovator. His untimely death at age fifty-six seems all the more tragic as his last works appear to herald a new direction that may well have influenced succeeding generations of painters. While we are consequently deprived of following this exciting avenue of his work to its full conclusion, Kensett may, ironically, have been spared the cruel fate of neglect that so many of his contemporaries and friends suffered in their mature years as their art fell out of fashion. Thus this exhibition and monograph end on a note of celebration of Kensett's successes and accomplishments while he was at the height of his full powers.

We are indebted to the team of scholars from Worcester and the Metropolitan who organized this exhibition, and to their colleagues Michael Quick, Curator of American Art, and Myrna Smoot, Assistant Director for Museum Programs, at the Los Angeles County Museum of Art. We extend our gratitude to the various lenders who so selflessly parted with their paintings and drawings for such an extended period of time, and to the Norton Company, Worcester and the National Endowment for the Arts for support of this project. Funds for research travel for the staff from the Metropolitan and photography of their paintings were provided by the William Cullen Bryant Fellows of the American Wing of the Metropolitan, and the Worcester Art Museum contributed seed money to initiate this project. W. W. Norton & Company has been a most congenial and receptive partner in producing this handsome publication. Perhaps it is most appropriate, however, to express our appreciation to the artist whose vision continues to inspire a new generation of viewers with its poetry.

Tom L. Freudenheim
Director, Worcester Art Museum

Philippe de Montebello
Director, Metropolitan Museum of Art

Earl A. Powell, III
Director, Los Angeles County Museum of Art

ACKNOWLEDGMENTS

THE GRACIOUS AND GENEROUS ASSISTANCE of many individuals and institutions has made this exhibition and publication possible. Special acknowledgments are due to Linda Ayers, National Gallery of Art; Jeffrey R. Brown; Georgia B. Bumgardner, American Antiquarian Society; Andrew Zaremba, The Century Association; Richard J. Ulrich, Cheshire Historical Society; Ruth Gleeton, Cheshire Public Library; Geoffrey Clemens; Roy Davis, Davis and Langdale; Elaine Evans Dee, Cooper-Hewitt Museum; John Dobkin, Abigail B. Gerdts, and Barbara Krulick, National Academy of Design; Joseph O. Endriss, Jr.; Stuart Feld and M. P. Naud, Hirschl and Adler Galleries; Linda Ferber and Kathie Manthorne, The Brooklyn Museum; Dan Flavin; Robert Foley, Fitchburg State College Library; Catherine Gordon; Thompson R. Harlow; D. Roger Howlett, Childs Gallery; C. M. Kaufman, Victoria and Albert Museum; Thomas Dunnings and Mary Alice Kennedy, The New-York Historical Society; Mark Piel, New York Society Library; Donald Keyes; Nancy Kreig; and Sandra L. Langer, University of South Carolina; Robert P. MacDonald, Louisiana State Museum; Edward Morris, Walker Art Gallery, Liverpool; Betty Monkman, The White House; Milo M. Naeve, Art Institute of Chicago; Edward Nygren and Judy Riley, Corcoran Gallery of Art; Nancy Kessler Post, Museum of the City of New York; Helen Allen, The Union Club; Jane Reed, The Union League Club; Norman S. Rice, Albany Institute of History and Art; Michael St. Clair, Babcock Galleries; Robert Schlageter, Cummer Gallery of Art; Johanna Van Hazinga; Charles Vogel; and Robert C. Vose, Vose Galleries.

The staffs of the following institutions all provided assistance in making their collections available: Archives of American Art, Detroit; Cape Ann Historical Society; Connecticut Historical Society; The Frick Art Reference Library; Massachusetts Historical Society; The National Archives, Washington, D.C.; New Haven Colony Historical Society; New York Public Library; New York State Library; The Witt Art Reference Library, London; and the Worcester Public Library. Descendants of John F. Kensett, Mr. and Mrs. Frank Sprower and Mr. and Mrs. David Evans, were especially hospitable in opening their homes and their records to provide invaluable information. Very special thanks also go to Jeanne Baker Driscoll and Anne H. Howat for their assistance and support.

The cooperation of the staffs of both the Worcester Art Museum and Metropolitan Museum of Art was crucial to the success of this project. In Worcester special thanks go to Gaye Brown, Robert Coleman, Sally R. Freitag, Anne Gibson, Roberta Waldo, Ron White, and Beverly Willson. Susan E. Strickler, who helped to conceive and shape this project, also directed the many facets relating to the production of the exhibition and catalogue.

We also extend our appreciation to Nancy Gillette, David Kiehl, Patricia Pellegrini, Kristine Schassler, and Natalie Spassky at the Metropolitan. Their colleague Lewis Sharp deserves a special round of applause for his agile administrative assistance.

The conservation departments of both museums provided technical information and prepared works for the exhibition. We wish to thank John Brealey, Maryan Ainsworth, Rene de la Rie, Chiyo Ishikawa, and Laura Juszczak from the Metropolitan, and their associates in Worcester, Paul Haner and David Findley.

The production of the monograph could not have been accomplished without the nimble editorial skill of Janet G. Silver, and the enthusiasm and expertise of James L. Mairs and his assistant Jeremy Townsend of W. W. Norton & Company, Inc.

Finally, a special debt of gratitude is owed to all the lenders who helped to make possible this exhibition of one of America's great masters.

JOHN PAUL DRISCOLL
JOHN K. HOWAT
DIANNE DWYER
OSWALDO RODRIGUEZ ROQUE

As we at Norton Company celebrate our one hundredth anniversary, we are pleased to join the Worcester Art Museum in presenting an exhibition of the works of the influential nineteenth-century American artist John Frederick Kensett. Some of these works have never before been publicly displayed, and we are proud to sponsor the first complete documentation of his life and work.

Norton Company was founded as a grinding wheel manufacturer in Worcester, Massachusetts, in 1885. The Worcester Art Museum opened its doors less than fifteen years later. The history of the museum and the history of Norton parallel each other. Since the very beginning, Norton people have been active in the affairs of the museum, as individuals and as representatives of a company with a long tradition of community service, including support for the arts.

Norton is now a diversified manufacturer with operations in twenty-eight countries, but its headquarters are still in Worcester and its roots are in nineteenth-century America. So it is appropriate that we celebrate our centennial by helping to present the works of a nineteenth-century artist who is an important part of America's cultural heritage. Although Kensett traveled throughout the United States, his favorite subjects were the White Mountains in New Hampshire, the Berkshires in Massachusetts, the Adirondacks in New York, and the New England seashore, which once circumscribed the Norton world.

As we look forward to Norton's second hundred years, we are glad that, through our efforts and those of the Worcester Art Museum, many Americans will be able to enjoy the works of John Frederick Kensett.

DONALD R. MELVILLE
President and Chief Executive Officer, Norton Company

KENSETT'S WORLD

John K. Howat

JOHN FREDERICK KENSETT (Fig. 1) WAS BORN ON 22 MARCH 1816 in Cheshire, Connecticut. He was the second child of an English father, Thomas Kensett, and a New England mother, Elizabeth Daggett Kensett, who were married in 1813.[1] Cheshire, located some thirteen miles north of New Haven, was then a small and close-knit rural township of several thousand inhabitants devoted almost wholly to farming, as indeed was most of Connecticut, except for the active coastal region where maritime commerce thrived. Connecticut's intermittent industrial development in the major river valleys and along the coast was in its infancy, but Connecticut could pride itself on being the home of numerous diligent farmers and creative mechanics. Cheshire, which later developed manufacturing (especially ivory combs, buttons, and metal stampings) and mining (copper and barite), in 1838 was still, according to John Warner Barber, "a pleasant village of 40 or 50 dwelling houses, three churches and an Academy. . . . The Township is pleasantly diversified by hills and valleys, and the prevailing soil is a gravelly loam, generally rich and fertile."[2] In 1816 Connecticut was dominated politically and socially by the Congregational Church and the state's only college, Yale. In 1819 Jedidiah Morse, father of the soon-to-be famous Samuel F. B. Morse, noted that the citizens of Connecticut were "almost to a man, of English origin."[3] Connecticut adopted a new and more liberal Constitution in 1818, disestablishing the Congregational Church, after which the state's Episcopalian minority agitated for their own college to receive graduates of the Cheshire Episcopal Academy and other schools who chose not to attend Yale. The General Assembly complied and in 1823 chartered Washington College, Hartford, which later became today's Trinity College.

It was through his parents—their families and activities—that John Kensett entered the larger world beyond Cheshire and crossed the threshold of his artistic career. Elizabeth Kensett was the first of eleven children born in New Haven to Ezra Daggett and Eunice Tuttle Daggett.[4] The Tuttle family name was well established in New Haven and Cheshire. Captain Lucius Tuttle had manufactured the bricks that built the Episcopal Academy in 1796.[5] Probably of greater genealogical and social import, however, in the "Congregational Republic" of Connecticut, was the fact that Elizabeth was a granddaughter of Naphtali Daggett. Daggett was already well known to Connecticut history as the Congregational cleric, prolific religious author, professor, and controversial president of Yale (removed upon petition of the students), who ardently supported the American revolutionary cause and joined local resistance against the attack of Tryon's British raiders at New Haven in July 1779.[6]

Thomas Kensett was of less eminent social background than his wife. Born at Hampton Court, near London, in 1786, he and his brother John left England for the Americas before 1806.[7] By January of 1806, when Thomas would have been nineteen, there was published "a plan of New Haven with all the Buildings in 1748 taken by the Hon. Gen. Wadsworth of Durham," commissioned by "William Lyon" from "T. Kensett, Engraver."[8] This is believed to be the earliest engraved map of New Haven. Thus presumably began a career of engraving, painting, and publishing which Thomas was pursuing both in New Haven and Cheshire by 1810.[9] From his hand came other maps of the United States and Canada, scenes depicting events of the War of 1812, allegorical and biblical scenes, engraved invitations, and masonic aprons, all of which are attractively quaint, almost primitive in design.[10] Much of this work was done in concert with the now far-better-known Amos Doolittle, a Cheshire native also married to a Daggett, who had settled in New Haven. In 1813 Thomas Kensett established the Cheshire firm of Shelton and Kensett with Dr. Charles Shelton, a Yale graduate, physician, and local entrepreneur. Thomas' brother John, who had been living in Jamaica, also moved to Connecticut and provided Thomas with funds for his firm.[11] He returned to Hampton Court in the 1830s and later was to be an important family tie for his nephew during the young artist's travels.

The active Shelton and Kensett firm, located on the banks of the Quinnipiac River, employed local women to color the prints produced by Kensett, Doolittle, and Ralph Rawdon.[12] One historical account describes how

> *Mr. Kensett who afterwards became a skilled painter had charge of the work, that is: the practical part of employing several assistants. . . . It is said the pictures that were painted represented Napoleon the French Conqueror, the Devil, the Arch enemy of the human race. Also that animals, like the Horse-ox, rhinoceros etc., were among the paintings here produced and were Common Articles of traffic among the School Children.*[13]

Though the Shelton and Kensett association lasted only until 1817, it probably was Connecticut's first printmaking firm and certainly could be credited as a pioneer of Connecticut industry, even if only of the "cottage" variety.[14]

As a small boy John Kensett briefly attended the Cheshire Episcopal Academy, from 1820 to 1821, when the founding principal, Reverend Tillotson Bronson, was still alive and Reverend Asa Cornwall was the instructor (Fig. 2).[15] Jedidiah Morse described the academy in 1819 as having "60 students and is flourishing."[16] Although no contemporary record attests to it, we may assume that, thanks to his surroundings, young Kensett learned something, however rudimentary, of engraving, coloring, and painting in the years before he is known to have entered the engraver's profession in the late 1820s.

Engraving was a large, thriving, and growing industry at that time, and Connecticut boasted a large number of engravers who either worked in the state or had begun there. Before the invention of photography and the revolution in the mass reproduction of images, engraving along with lithography and woodcut provided the only printed images available. Because engraving was far more precise than woodcut and lithography, it monopolized the printing of currency, stock certificates, and fine-art reproductions at a time when American banks, industry, and art concerns were expanding rapidly and requiring greater service—in both quantity and quality—from engravers.

Under pressure of these demands, the craft of engraving underwent revolutionary changes in the early nineteenth century. Charles Toppan, one of the pioneer engravers, later wrote a "History and Progress of Bank Note Engraving" which appeared in 1855 in *The Crayon*, the most important Ameri-

FIGURE 2.
View of Episcopal Academy
at Cheshire, Connecticut
*a wood engraving illustration
from John Warner Barber,
Connecticut Historical
Collections, New Haven,*
1837

Episcopal Academy, at Cheshire.

can art magazine of mid-century.[17] Prefacing his "History" with the comment that bank-note engraving in America had "of late years become legitimately entitled to rank as a branch of the fine, as well as the useful arts," Toppan gave a brief but specific description of the mechanical changes that occurred in American commercial engraving during his own lifetime. He noted that in 1791, when the first Bank of the United States was founded, American engravers were "few in number and 'mediocre' in talent," which subsequently made the excellent and less easily forged products of his own Philadelphia firm, Murray, Draper, and Fairman, welcome and successful after its establishment in 1810.

More essential than gifted engravers to the growth of the industry, however, were the inventions of Jacob Perkins of Newburyport, Massachusetts, the first of which was patented by him in 1799. Perkins' inventions allowed the combination of engraved vignettes (small decorative and figurative scenes), lettering, and geometric designs—altogether as many as sixty-four separate engraved steel dies—in one matrix from which the Perkins Stereotype Steelplate was made. In 1804 Perkins made a further essential innovation, a method of using steel transfer rolls and heat to reproduce engraved steel plates. Perkins' process, which displaced the use of softer and shorter-lived copper plates, allowed, according to Toppan,

> *transfers of fine engravings from hardened steel plates to steel cylinders, and re-transfers to flat plates; thus enabling the engraver to multiply his finest work, preserving the original, and yet repeating it on other plates to any extent, so that labor of months and years even may be re-engraved as it were in a few minutes. This invention may be justly considered as the first great improvement in the art, as it enabled the engravers to bestow much more time on the execution of the originals, and thus led to the excellence of the work now to be seen on all the notes executed in this country.[18]*

Another technical advance, the invention of the geometric lathe by clockmaker Asa Spencer of New London, allowed the mechanical engraving of complicated linear patterns in the backgrounds of plates. William Rollinson, Cyrus Durand (Asher B. Durand's elder brother), and Christian Gobrecht

FIGURE 3.
*Attributed to Kensett, vignette
for a bank note, 1830s, engraving, 2⁵⁄₁₆ x 3⁹⁄₁₆ in. (5.9 x
9.1 cm.), sheet size, Prints
Division, The New York
Public Library, Astor, Lenox
and Tilden Foundations.*

FIGURE 4.
*Kensett, engraved frontispiece
for* Autumn Leaves,
*1837, 1⁹⁄₁₆ x 2 in. (4 x
5.1 cm.), image size, American Antiquarian Society,
Worcester, Massachusetts.
This vignette for a literary
annual is the earliest of
Kensett's works to be
identified and dated.*

(of Murray, Draper, and Fairman, and after 1840 head of the United States Mint)[19] invented methods of mechanically engraving extremely complex but regular linear patterns which have ever since made the forger's life more difficult and facilitated the growth of the American engraving industry.

Kensett was probably working for his father and uncle Alfred Daggett in their New Haven engraving shop by 1828, doing minor jobs. At some point, possibly in 1829, when he would have been a mere thirteen, Kensett went to New York to work in the shop of Peter Maverick, America's best-known engraver. There he met John Casilear (1811–1893), five years his elder, who became a leading engraver and landscape painter and Kensett's lifelong friend. A letter of 1833 from Casilear in New York to Kensett in New Haven casts a jolly light on those New York apprenticeship days: "I wish you was here that we might make merry over a good glass of whisky punch and a good cigar and talk over old times: it is not seldom I assure you when indulging in the latter with my feelings a little heightened, that my thoughts wander back to the old office of 'Uncle Peter' where we first became acquainted, and passed many happy hours."[20] Cigars and punch helped chase away the tedium of engraving, something which afflicted almost every engraver, and Kensett in particular. The benefits of increased speed that technical innovations provided applied to the engravers who ran the machines and lathes and assembled the engraved elements, but not to the artists like Kensett who toiled at length on bed-piece vignettes, small graphic scenes which could not be reduced to mechanical formulas (Figs. 3 and 4). Far from being a dour Connecticut Calvinist, Kensett was by nature a most convivial creature. His correspondence and later descriptions of his way of life highlight his delight in social gatherings, singing, talk, pretty

FIGURE 5.
Thomas P. Rossiter (1818–1871), New Haven Green, c. 1850–53, oil on canvas, 17 x 28 in. (43.2 x 71.1 cm.), The New Haven Colony Historical Society, Gift of E. K. Rossiter.

women, club life, committee work, and, of course, cigars and whisky. A decade later his uncle John complained that his nephew was apt to be too playful and dilatory.

Thomas Kensett died in June of 1829, after which young John returned to New Haven, where he rejoined his uncle Alfred Daggett's firm of Daggett and Ely. In those years, New Haven was a small but growing city of just over eight thousand inhabitants, which a decade before had impressed the stern and orthodox reverend Jedidiah Morse, a New Haven resident at the end of his life, as being particularly neat, clean, and attractive (Fig. 5). It was dominated by the handsome Yale buildings, well-kept white clapboard houses, elm trees, and a new Egyptian-style cemetery. In addition, said Morse, "The state of society in this town is enormously agreeable. Few towns of this size can boast as large a collection of citizens possessing refined manners and cultivated minds."[21] Local society was led by such distinguished figures as Professor Benjamin Silliman, the poet James A. Hillhouse, the architect Ithiel Town, the engraver and painter Nathaniel Jocelyn, and his clergyman-engraver-abolitionist brother Simeon Jocelyn.

At this time Kensett established his warm friendship, which was to be lifelong, with Thomas P. Rossiter (1818–1871) of New Haven, who had studied painting with Nathaniel Jocelyn. New Haven thus could have been a happy residence for Kensett; but the young man was bright and quite ambitious, intent on learning all he could about art in order to advance himself in it. Casilear corresponded regularly with Kensett, repeatedly giving him advice and perceptive criticisms of his engravings:

My dear friend Kensett,
The little specimen of your work you sent me I have been much gratified with and sincerely think it does you much credit—you expressed a desire in your last that I would mention a few of the faults. . . . your

foliage is improperly managed and considerably too open in the distance; when copying an engraving I think it's best to restate it as near as possible, I mean the style. . . . The next deficiency of your piece is perhaps, a want of cleanup in the cutting; this is a deficit of no small importance which I trust you will endeavor to guard against in the future. . . . In engraving drapery you must be very particular not to make square crosses, the diamon [sic] squares being much the handsomest.

Casilear later wrote commending him for his "eager desire to acquire a knowledge of his art," despite the dull work of Daggett and Ely which kept Kensett "eternally digging at maps and labels," and offering advice on how to improve his drawing by using casts.[22] Soon after, Casilear gave Kensett a set of plaster hands and feet for the purpose.[23]

Kensett's hopes led him in 1832 to apply unsuccessfully for a position with Asher B. Durand, who had succeeded his master and subsequent partner Peter Maverick as America's greatest engraver. So Kensett continued to work quietly in New Haven, engraving for his uncle's new firm, Daggett and Hinman and Company, until early in 1835, when he had a falling out with Daggett and removed to New York to work for the Jocelyn firm.[24] He was still working in New York in 1837 and enjoying membership in the informal Waconsta Club, a group of men who jointly owned a small sailboat. Through his younger sister Sarah, who attended boarding school in Burlington, New Jersey, Kensett met the charming Caroline Mayland, with whom he was much taken. In a letter to Sarah he spoke coyly of possibly moving to Burlington because of "some very particular object of attraction in that quarter." The evening before, he had attended the wedding of a mutual friend and

had a pleasant time—had Miss Caroline M[aylan]d been present my happiness would have been nearly complete. I send you by the morning boat some of the cake. . . . It is accompanied with a peice [sic] which John F. Kensett forwards to Miss Mayland with his love and esteem and trusts that at her wedding he may be present and enjoy himself. I enclose a small billet to Miss M—, and if you see her fail not to hand it to her—as it contains the ring.[25]

Nothing came of Kensett's ardor, and not long after he removed to Albany, where he worked for the engraving firm of Hall, Packard, and Cushman from 1838 until early in 1840 (Fig. 6). His life there was similar to the one he had led before in New Haven and New York in that he had a pleasant circle of friends and a growing sense of frustration with his situation. He apparently disliked Albany from the start, prompting Casilear to write: "I regret to learn that you find Albany so little to your taste."[26]

Despite his discontent in Albany, Kensett's work at Hall, Packard, and Cushman may have held some interest for him thanks to the technical innovations instituted there. On 21 June 1838 the *Daily Albany Argus* reported:

Mr. J. H. Hall, of the firm of Hall, Packard, and Cushman of this city, have been for some time engaged in perfecting machinery for tracing dies on bank note plates, and we are gratified to say, has succeeded in bringing out combinations and forms altogether new and inimitable, except by the machinery itself. The modus operandi is similar to that heretofor practised, but infinitely more diversified in its application, producing what we are informed has been hitherto considered impossible, rectangular, as

FIGURE 6.
Thomas Cole (1801–1848), Albany—Taken from the East Side of the River, *c. 1844, pen and pencil on paper, 9 x 11¾ in. (22.9 x 29.8 cm.), Albany Institute of History and Art.*

well as circular and oval dies now so common on bank notes. The intricacy and yet perfect accuracy of the process by which this result is accomplished, by one continuous line, and the beauty and perfect finish of the work, reflect the highest credit on the mechanical skill and science of our fellow-citizen.[27]

Later the same year, the *Daily Albany Argus* complimented the firm on a new series of bank notes, praising their "beauty, simplicity, and inimitable finish. As engravings, they are creditable to the progress of the arts in this country, and to the ingenuity and skill of our townspeople, Messrs. Hall, Packard, and Cushman."[28]

That Kensett left behind an admiring group of friends when he left Albany early in 1840 is made clear in a warm letter from one of his closest companions, Stephen Johnson Field, who later became a United States Supreme Court justice. Field, too, had just left Albany, but reminisced particularly about the attractive girls: "The girls—how many pleasing associations cluster around the manner of some of them. . . . By the bye, do you know what an impression you made upon Miss van Valkenberg? She makes many inquiries of her absent friend?—May I not say . . . absent lover? . . . and let me add the rememberance of you is cherished by a numerous circle in Albany." In a later letter, Field upbraided Kensett for "not paying more attention to that girl. So said Mrs. Robinson to me a few days since, adding at the same time that you could not have failed to win the prize."[29] Perhaps memories of Miss Mayland interfered or, more likely, Kensett's lively ambition prevented him from turning to marriage.

One of Kensett's closest friends in Albany was the managing partner of Hall, Packard, and Cushman, Thomas H. Cushman. Cushman died shortly after Kensett left Albany, the result, according to the Albany papers, of "impaired health growing out of the anxieties of managing an extensive concern. . . . [H]e unfortunately engaged in daguerrotyping, then an embryo art, which he introduced onto this place, in connection with Prof. E. N. Horsford. His experiments were made under exposure to the unhealthful fumes of the necessary materials . . . [which] laid the foundation for the total ruin of his health."[30]

Although Kensett was dissatisfied with engraving as a career, something he made clear in correspondence with Casilear and others, he used his craft as a crutch to support himself. Yet, beyond all else he wanted to become a painter of whom his country, family, and friends could be proud. His departure for England on 1 June 1840 aboard the *British Queen*, accompanied by the much older Durand and his friends Casilear and Rossiter, marked his most important step toward the achievement of his goal: to explore the European world of travel, languages, and history and the seductive riches of European art, in the service of advancing his own career. Like almost every aspiring American artist of that time, Kensett saw travel and study in Europe as central to his professional happiness, since that rested so much upon developing both a trained eye for artistic beauty and the technical dexterity necessary for transcribing the artist's vision into physical and aesthetic reality. America's largest cities, including New York, possessed, in limited numbers, art schools, academies, and teachers who could introduce hopeful youths to the basic techniques of draftsmanship and painting. Nowhere in America, however, could an artist immerse himself in firsthand experience of recognized masterpieces of art. That was only to be had in the artistic capitals of Europe. The remarkable accumulation of great objects of art which has been a central feature of American culture is essentially a post-Civil War phenomenon, marking, in part, the coming of age of the nation. In 1840 America had no great collections, private or public. Kensett and his contemporaries knew that a European sojourn—a great adventure in any event—was essential to their knowledge, artistic growth, and success. Some responded by eagerly embracing Europe, becoming expatriates like sculptors Thomas Crawford, William Wetmore Story and Hiram Powers and painters George Loring Brown and Christopher Pearce Cranch. Others, the majority, did as Kensett, absorbing as much as possible from the various "shrines" of history and art, and usually working very hard at it, before returning to the United States to resume an art career or to launch themselves in one. Kensett, always alert and hard working, made the most of what stretched into seven years in England and Europe, and he returned to America greatly changed, a successful painter, a knowledgeable traveler, and blessed with a large circle of new friends who, to a great extent, provided him easy entry to the top level of America's cultural elite. Kensett's European experiences yielded pleasures and happy results, but these were not gained without attendant labors and difficulties.

When Kensett arrived in England he immediately set off to meet his grandmother and uncle John at Hampton Court. It was an emotional occasion:

I arrived here safely . . . after a days excitement such as I never before experienced—fraught as it was with emotions strange yet overpowering—arising from the interview with those to whom I am so nearly allied. . . . Could I have believed that hardly three weeks should elapse between the period of my treading the soil of my native land and that of my forefathers—it seems even now but a dream. . . . My reception was all my fondest hopes could have wished—and thank god that the privilege and happiness of seeing you both was granted me.[31]

Not one to dawdle, Kensett had already visited the National Gallery in Trafalgar Square—"feasting on the glorious works of the Old Masters"—later visited and made notes on the Dulwich College collection, and resumed the distasteful business of engraving for his American employers, work which was to support him for several years to come.

Despite the pleasures and temptations of family and the artistic attractions of London, Hampton Court, and Windsor, Kensett and his companions pursued their purposes and continued on to Paris. There, rooming with Rossiter and agog with anticipation, Kensett entered an intense period of study and discovery. He immediately wrote somewhat breathlessly to his uncle that

> the advantages held out here to the artist are incalculably great—Here he may find what his heart most craves. The finest specimens of art extant here present themselves—and the student and lover of art will discover here food for gratifying that appetite that grows by which it feeds on. We discover the necessity of the most constant and indefatigable exertions in order to arrive even to mediocrity. . . . The wonders of Paris are now before me, and I shall take the opportunity before getting into my rooms to reconnoiter and take a few brief glances of them—I shall remain in Paris should nothing occur to change my resolution from four or five months perhaps six—for getting once settled down to work it will not be a matter of policy to break up in the middle of winter and take our departure.[32]

The Paris which Kensett found in 1840 was quite different from that of today, although the majority of the monuments sought by today's tourists were staples on "the tour" of that time: the Louvre, the Tuileries, the Palais Royal, the place Vendôme, the Cathedral of Nôtre Dame, the Invalides, and so on. The recently rearranged garden and palace of the Tuileries and place de la Concorde, and the newly completed Church of the Madeleine and Arc de Triomphe were specially brought to the visitor's attention, as were the new palaces, on the left bank, of the Quai d'Orsay and École des Beaux-Arts (Fig. 7).

The majority of English-speaking visitors to Paris, like Kensett, relied upon *Galignani's New Paris Guide*, frequently reissued during the nineteenth century as a handbook of tourist information. The 1839 edition gives a precise image of the Paris Kensett first saw. Prior to the construction of the railroads, which brought an immense influx of foreigners, its population, "exclusive of strangers and troops" was 909,126, of whom half were workers and half tradesmen, professionals, and *rentiers*. This was the Paris of Louis-Philippe, long before the radical changes wrought upon it by Napoléon III and Baron Haussmann between 1848 and 1870 that transformed it into the familiar "City of Light," belted and interconnected by the *grands boulevards*. The Paris of 1840, despite the eighteenth- and nineteenth-century improvements like the avenue de Champs Elysées and the rue de Rivoli, was still essentially medieval in character. According to Galignani, the streets were "formed, more or less, upon the model of those which existed in the older parts of town long before coaches were invented, or carts and waggons ever traversed the city. . . . Hence Paris is inferior to most of the other capital towns of Europe as far as the width, cleanliness, and general appearance of most of its streets are concerned."[33] Despite the recent improvements to the city—"widening and embellishing the roadways"—Galignani still thought that "the mud and black unwholesome gutters of the greater part of central streets of this capital will still offend the sense of the visitor."[34]

In his interesting book *An Englishman in Paris (Notes and Recollections)* of 1892, A. P. Van Dam

described the physical, intellectual, and artistic character of the city at the time. The Latin Quarter on the Left Bank (where Kensett and Rossiter settled) was "almost entirely sacred from the desecrating stare of the deliberate sightseer." According to Van Dam, "Even in those days 'the Boulevards' meant to most of us nothing more than the space between the present Opera and the Rue Drouot."[35] The Latin Quarter then was host to numerous youthful students, writers, artists, doctors, lawyers, and other would-be *savants* who were to provide the cast for Henri Murger's *Scènes de la vie de bohème*, which appeared serially between 1847 and 1849. Contrary to Murger's account, Van Dam, who lived among the bohemians, reported "there was a good deal of roystering and practical joking, and short-lived liaison, [but] there was little of deliberate vice, of strategic libertinism."[36] Such indeed became the case with Kensett and the friends he soon brought about him.

Kensett and Rossiter settled right in, after shifting rooms once, and began their studies. At the same time Kensett ventured into painting landscapes for exhibition at the National Academy of Design in New York. Writing to his uncle John, who was unhappy with Kensett's lapses as a correspondent, he said he was active

> *painting and engraving alternately. . . . R[ossiter] and self are drawing every night in the week of the Ecole Préparation des Beaux Arts from the Antique and life—and are carrying on our studies briskly.*

FIGURE 8.
View of the Grande Galerie of the Louvre *as illustrated in Jules Janin's* The American in Paris During the Summer, or Heath's Picturesque Annual for 1844, *London*, 1844. *This is a scene that the young artist Kensett would have recognized immediately.*

. . . You will readily perceive every moment of time I can devote to my studies is so much gained and yet only fulfilling a paramount duty—the day being devoted to painting or engraving—the evening until 10 o.c. to drawing—French till 12½—the only portion then remaining not occupied by any pursuits is Sunday which I devote to letter writing and not a Sunday passes but I am obliged to write four or five letters."[37]

All this activity took place in the face of the tempting urgings of Casilear for Kensett to join him in Italy in keeping with an earlier plan.[38]

The facilities offered to an art student in Paris in 1840 were probably the best in the world. The history, the city, the collections, the schools—and access to them—provided a wealth of opportunity. Kensett, Durand, Casilear, Rossiter, and the aging John Vanderlyn (1775–1852), who had first come to Paris in 1796 and had returned in 1803, were only a few among an army of artists who had special access to the galleries of the Louvre, which was subdivided into separate sections: Musée des tableaux, Musée des tableaux de la galerie espagnole, Musée des desseins, Musées des antiques, and the Musée égyptien (Fig. 8).[39] Once a year the main picture galleries of the Louvre were given over to the Salon for contemporary works hung in front of the permanent collection. Here one saw "an immense crowd. [A]mongst the admirable rapins, (an emphatic word to designate great but unknown artists) you will see long beards, long hair, long teeth, long hands appearing beneath coats which are too short. There is a brilliant, animated, above all sarcastic, conversation. . . . Nothing is spared, neither name, nor sex, nor age."[40]

This was the Paris of Baudelaire, Delacroix, Ingres, and their argumentative partisans. Yet one may search Kensett's correspondence with greatest care and not detect a whiff of smoke from the art-theory battles between the Classicists and Romantics which preoccupied European artists. Kensett's interests and art pursuits were limited in scope, confined to working hard, learning draftsmanship, and making friends. His artistic intellect was not lacking but was of a less intensely argumentative and more idealistic, or indeed transcendentalist, sort than that of his French contemporaries. We may judge this by his words written in 1842 after a brief sketching trip in the English Midlands:

> It is a beautiful characteristic of genius, that whatsoever receives its touch is gifted with its immortality. It is by mixing up intellectual and spiritual associations with things, and only so that they have any importance to our minds; Things are nothing but what the mind constitutes them. Nothing, but by an infusion into them of the intellectual principle of our nature tis thus this humble habitation becomes a shrine . . . and thus the most indifferent, and of itself undervalued thing—be it but a fragment of a rock, a broken weapon, a torn raiment, a decayed branch, or a simple log.[41]

Constantly afflicted by financial problems, Kensett and his artist-friends, Rossiter, Casilear, Benjamin Champney (1817–1907), and Thomas Hicks (1823–1890), mutually lent money when they had it and borrowed it when they had none. Early in 1841, as he wrote his uncle, Kensett concluded an arrangement by mail with Samuel Carpenter of the firm Toppan, Carpenter, and Company of Philadelphia (where Casilear became a partner in 1849).[42] The arrangement provided Kensett's support for a time: "A ready compliance to the proposition I make to them—which was vis.—giving me a commission for the engr[aving] of 12 vignettes during the year at 50$ each—or allowing me 18 months to eng[rave] them in and retaining the right of commanding my services for the two following years."[43] Still hard-pressed, Kensett also borrowed money from his uncle and later proposed that the funds be raised on his expectations of trust inheritance upon his grandmother's death.[44]

Until he returned to England in mid-1843, when his grandmother died, Kensett's financial importunings, which included requests for money that would allow him to leave Paris for Italy, caused a definite coolness between him and his uncle. Uncle John felt that his nephew was not applying himself to his main source of income—engraving—and he was correct in noting Kensett's drifting away from it. The young artist's life at that difficult time was ameliorated by his friendships, especially that with Champney, whom he met in 1841 (Fig. 9). They took rooms together at 19, rue de l'Université not far from the Quai d'Orsay and the Ministry of War. The best source for descriptions of their life in Paris is Champney's memoirs, in which he succinctly captured Kensett's artistic, and thus financial, predicament:

> Kensett was at heart a painter, and it was hard for him to stick to his burin when he saw me busy at painting, and before many months he had thrown down his engraving tools, and taken to brushes and paint. He showed a great deal of imagination and poetic feeling in his first essays, and finished a half dozen sound canvases full of feeling for delicate color and suavity of line. I was surprised and delighted, too.[45]

FIGURE 9.
*Kensett, Self-portrait, 1840,
watercolor and pencil on
paper, 5⅜ x 4⅜ in. (13.7 x
11.2 cm.), Private Collection.
Kensett drew this somewhat
self-conscious likeness as an
aspiring artist in Paris.*

Although help was not forthcoming from Hampton Court, Kensett and Champney managed
to patch things together in Paris, receiving occasional loans from, among others, a very kind retired
English guardsman of means—a Captain Hanky, "a bluff soldierly man," according to Champney.
Hanky, a lifelong friend of the author William Makepeace Thackeray, was a social anchor for
Thackeray whenever he visited the city. Through Hanky, Champney many times met and supped
with Thackeray, not then famous but always "very genial, brilliant and witty, the leading spirit
of the dinner table."[46] Kensett probably joined in some of these festivities; he certainly socialized
with Thackeray later, both in New York and London.

For the historian of American art, aside from Kensett's and Champney's description of art life in
Paris, perhaps most interesting is these young Americans' connection with the elderly Vanderlyn, the
painter of *Marius Amidst the Ruins of Carthage*, *Ariadne*, and *The Landing of Columbus*, on which he
was laboring when Champney and Kensett were with him. "Broken in spirit and health, . . . he was
alone in the world, discouraged and disheartened. We [Vanderlyn and Champney] used often to dine
in company with Kensett and Casilear at a modest little restaurant in the Rue Ste. Marguerite, where we
listened with pleasure and profit to his memories of other times, his experiences in pursuit of art, and

his early history."[47] Champney, paid five francs a day, became a studio assistant and "almost a pupil" of the kindly Vanderlyn as he worked on the immense *Columbus* picture, which now hangs in the United States Capitol. Kensett recorded his gratitude for Vanderlyn's openhandedness in a long and possibly pointed letter to his uncle:

> *Mr. John Vanderlyn the distinguished American painter . . . is making great efforts to assist the young American artists by the establishment of a small society for copying the works of the great masters. He is a gent[leman] whose generosity exceeds the limits of his purse and is consequently seldom in a situation to do much more than give his advice, which he is always ready and happy to give out to those who desire it, and it is invaluable to us, as coming from a man who has occupied a distinguished rank at home and abroad.*[48]

Kensett made other friendly artistic connections in Paris, including Thomas Cole (1801–1848), for whom he performed various small personal services while Cole was on his subsequent trip to Italy. Kensett met and began a long-standing friendship with Francis William Edmonds (1806–1863), characterized by Kensett as "a distinguished member of the Banking fraternity of New York . . . now cashier of the Mechanics Bank, one of the largest and finest Institutions in the Country and is a most excellent man as well as an amateur painter which gives him a rank equal to any professional artist we have among us."[49] An accomplished genre painter, Edmonds was a leader in New York art politics by virtue of his membership in the National Academy of Design (he was later its recording secretary and treasurer) and a founder and officer of the committee of the Apollo Association for the Promotion of the Fine Arts in the United States, which later was renamed and reorganized as the American Art-Union. Between 1840, when he sent some "specimens of engraving" to the Apollo Association, and 1852, when the Art-Union ceased operation, Kensett sold a total of forty-eight pictures to that organization, eleven of them while he was in Europe.[50] Without the financial boost provided by the sale of those pictures, Kensett probably would have been forced to return to New York without enjoying his extended stay in Italy.

Kensett's friendship with Edmonds was a vital link in his current and later success. Evidence of this comes from Casilear in a letter to Kensett in London, sent shortly after Casilear had returned to New York in 1844: "The Apollo Association is in a very prosperous condition—Bryant of the Post has been elected its president and Edmonds still continues in the Committee of management, so you may count as heretofore on his influence."[51] Extraordinarily important as an art sales and distribution organization, the Art-Union indeed was a beneficial, even revolutionary, force during its mushroomlike growth and popularization of the American art scene of mid-century. Fully aware of this, and not given to modesty, the Art-Union *Bulletin* of October 1849 accurately enough praised the organization for having "brought into notice a considerable number of men of decided ability, who would have remained entirely unknown or, at any rate, advanced with much less rapidity excepting for this assistance." Leutze, Deas, Bingham, Cropsey, Inness, Stearns, and Casilear were among the recipient artists cited, as were "Baker, Church, and Kensett [who] owe their present distinguished position in great part to the encouragement bestowed by the committee."[52]

Kensett's letters to his uncle at Hampton Court were composed almost entirely of descriptions of his artistic endeavors, his difficulties, and the discomfort of poverty. They do not dwell upon the great good time that Kensett was having with a jolly circle of friends. To Champney we owe an intimate view of the robustly happy group which gathered regularly at "the island of Bougival, six or eight miles below Paris, and surrounded by the waters of the Seine . . . our favorite resort, as well as that of many artists from the city."[53] There they enjoyed sketching under umbrellas and many picnics with the Osbornes, an English family which included two very attractive daughters, Sarah and Caroline. There also was the family of Benjamin Laroche, a poet "after the manner of Beranger" and a regular contributor to the *Courier français*, an opposition paper. Laroche, "a delightful man, full of wisdom and knowledge," who had sought exile in England during the reign of Charles X, had an English wife and a daughter Henrietta, who gave regular Thursday evening receptions.

> *The unpretentious home was always filled with pleasant people, a judicious mingling of French and English and other nationalities. There were musicians, literary people and artists, and we had singing, recitations and conversation in different tongues. There was always a sprinkling of pretty English girls, who had come over from London for a few months residence in Paris to be polished off, and there was always plenty of fun with plays and charades, closing with a merry dance in the salle à manger.*[54]

That Kensett was an active and possibly intimate part of the Osborne and Laroche salons is suggested in a letter from Champney to Kensett in London: "Mr. Laroche, Madame, and Henrietta (in particular) wish to be remembered and begged I would on no account forget it. We have been quite often to the Osbornes. Sarah looks sad. I am afraid she takes your absense too much to heart."[55]

In 1843 Kensett went to Hampton Court to help settle his grandmother's estate, an undertaking that developed into a two-year legal snarl that kept him in England much to his and his friends' dismay. Kensett thus missed the pleasure of being a regular member in the OMC or Out of Money Club, a group of Americans in Paris led by Benjamin Perley Poore, later famous as a prolific Washington author and journalist. William Morris Hunt and Rossiter were among the members who gathered to eat, drink, tell jokes and stories, and sing. As Champney recalled, "our meetings were always closed by my singing the Star Spangled Banner, while all hands joined the chorus."[56] The members jointly drew a caricature of the group, which was lithographed and distributed to the members. Kensett requested a copy, claiming an "honorable seat in that distinguished fraternity." Thus ended the varied, happy, and profitable Parisian chapter in Kensett's life.

The two years Kensett was obliged to spend in England, from June 1843 to June 1845, are fairly well recorded in his correspondence, and it is clear that he passed much of the time in and around London with his uncle, who took lodgings at 77 Newman Street. From that vantage point Kensett was able to sally forth into the clutches of the lawyers as agent for his relatives in America, or into the London art world, centered in Newman Street, and into the verdant countryside in search of scenery.

London in 1843, despite its Dickensian slums, was still a city of livable proportions but was beginning to expand rapidly as a result of the burgeoning railroads. It became an easy matter to escape into the neighboring countryside, where great parks were the favored resorts of the poor and middle class (Fig. 10). In 1834 Hyde Park was "situated at the western extremity of the metropolis."[57] During the late 1830s and early 1840s, remarkable developments transformed London and the life of its citizens

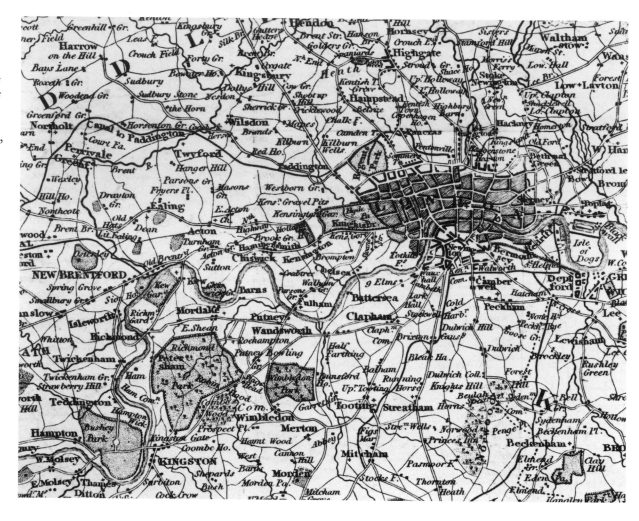

and visitors. In 1838 the National Gallery opened in Trafalgar Square and the Great Western Railroad opened as far as Maidenhead. In the next seven years, the expansion of the railway from London to the suburbs and as far as Cambridge permitted "thousands of pleasure-seekers" to escape "from the dense and dusty vastness of London . . . at a cheap rate, through a delightful country."[58] Except for the West End parks, the city was not well supplied with amusements for the poorer classes, so on weekends out-lying resorts like Hampton Court and its surrounding parks acted as huge magnets for humanity. As an American traveler commented of Hampton Court in 1853, "I have seen thirty thousand people there at one time, nearly all of whom were London mechanics and their families, and not once did I notice a single improper act."[59]

It took little time for Kensett to settle into a regime dedicated to country sketching, painting for the New York market, and occasional engraving. Kensett sold a *Scene on the Wye, England*, done after his trip to England and Wales late in 1841, to the American Art-Union in 1843. In the next two years he completed three English scenes which he sold to the Art-Union in 1845 (*Outskirts of Windsor Forest; Footpath in Burnham Forest;* and *A Peep in Windsor Forest*) and three more which he sent to the 1845 National Academy exhibition (*A View Near Richmond, England; An Avenue in Hatfield Park, the Seat of the Marquis of Salisbury;* and *The Mountain Stream*, which may have been a Welsh scene).

As we could expect, the sociable Kensett had several close friends in London, particularly the artists Edward John Cobbett (1815–1899) and William Parrott (1813–1869), neither of whom are known today outside of a circle of specialists in Victorian art. Cobbett, better known than Parrott, was a genre and landscape painter, a member of the Royal Society of British Artists, and a regular exhibitor of rustic scenes.[60] Parrott was a topographical painter who worked in watercolor and lithography, later producing popular views of Rome, as well as a set of lithographs of *Paris et ses environs*. It should be noted that Kensett's friends were minor figures in the British art world, not apt to divert him into new stylistic pathways. The Pre-Raphaelite Brotherhood had not yet appeared to redirect Britain's artistic future.

Kensett's long and chatty letter of 11 February 1844 to Rossiter in Rome summarizes his London life:

> *Since I last wrote you [three months before] I have removed with my uncle to . . . [77 Newman Street] . . . and as you will perceive, am in the very center of the artistic atmosphere of the metropolis—where I am very comfortably located and waiting with all due patience the termination of the troubles and an- noyances incident to things of the like nature when once in the hands of the law doctors—Spring will open before I shall have closed the vexatious business. Until then I shall be devoting myself to engraving and painting alternately, but after this month most likely wholly to the latter, as I have determined upon sending a couple of pictures to the National Academy, N.Y. Landscapes, of course! . . . I have accom- plished little during my sejour in England having had many, many drawbacks. The mind unsettled and in a state of constant suspense. I hope however ere long to be relieved from this thraldom of uncertainty.*

Kensett sounded a happier note talking of meeting Rossiter's friend the famous genre painter William Frith (1819–1909), seeing George Catlin's exhibition of "Indian Curiosities . . . and bona fide examples of Nine Nations indians fresh from the north western shore of Lake Huron," and the arrival of "funds arising from the pictures sold."[61]

Not long after writing Rossiter, whom he planned to join in Rome as soon as possible, he sent a letter to his brother Thomas in New York, anticipating that their legal problems would be finished shortly. He admitted that "I have long set myself down as a confirmed old bachelor, beyond the hope of redemption—I am wedded to the arts and they must be my bride, and a more charming mistress I could not hope to win."[62] He also sketched out an itinerary he wished to follow in Europe beginning in May: back to Paris for a brief stay, then to Naples for the summer, winter in Rome, then through northern Italy, Switzerland, the Rhine, and then home. It was the broad outline for the trip he did take beginning a year later, which then grew into a two-year stay in Italy.

For unrecorded reasons Kensett left his uncle's Newman Street quarters in mid-1844, since letters were subsequently sent to him first at 41 Robert Street, off Hampstead Street, near Regent's Park, and then at 9 William Street (now William Road) in the same neighborhood. With Cobbett and Parrott, he made outings to search out, as he wrote his uncle from Windsor, "the true elements of the pictur- esque beauty—being covered with lichen—rich moss—the ivy and the vine. . . . The studies I am making will be invaluable to me as references, independent of the use I may make of them as subjects for larger pictures."[63]

Knowing now what we do about Kensett's previous life and how he had devoted himself so diligently to his art studies, it seems clear that at Windsor he first felt the surge of confidence that comes with artistic competence, if not maturity. Toward the end of his stay in London,

> *he exhibited a view of Windsor Castle in the exhibition of the Society of British Artists. . . . It is the custom of this Association to have a lottery at a guinea a head, and the holders of the two lucky numbers are allowed to choose a picture as a prize. The winner of the first prize on this occasion selected Kensett's picture, which was admitted by every one to be the best landscape painting in the collection.*[64]

When Kensett set off for Paris in mid-1845, he was complimented by Champney for doing "those old oaks of Windsor—that kind of scenery that is your forte."[65] So despite his original loneliness in London, and the morass of legal affairs that held him there, Kensett left England a changed man, an artist in his own right.

Kensett arrived in Paris by June 1845[66] and remained there briefly with Champney (the two men "making a few sketching excursions to Fontainebleau and other places")[67] before setting out for Rome in July, following a route across the Alps through Germany, Switzerland, and Italy. Kensett entered Rome in October 1845 and joined the sizable band of artists of many nations who made up the local art community. Germans were the largest non-Italian group, but French, English, Russian, Polish, and other nationalities were represented. The American contingent was considerable, having grown rapidly since the Napoleonic Wars, from several dozen to several hundred in the 1850s, by one estimate.[68] The artists and other foreigners tended to congregate and live, as they had for centuries, in the area around the Spanish Steps and the Piazza di Spagna, giving that locale an international flavor which it preserves to this day. In 1821 Theodore Dwight, the diligent American travel writer, stayed in the neighborhood, "the principal resort of strangers, and we soon were seated at tables in a trattoria [no doubt, Lepre], among a very agreeable company, principally English travellers and resident artists, but including individuals of taste and limited fortunes from most of the countries of Europe."[69]

The attractions of Rome to artists were quite different from those that drew Kensett to Paris and London, and certainly Rome fell far short of Paris in offering teaching and copyist facilities to the artist. When one reads the ample literature of different artists' recollections of life in Rome, one is struck by the emphasis upon the camaraderie and friendly mixing of this cosmopolitan group. Nathaniel Hawthorne later put it well, writing in his journal for 15 February 1858, some two years before his Roman romance *The Marble Fawn* appeared:

> *This is a strange fascination that Rome exercises upon artists—there is clay elsewhere and marble enough, and heads to model; and ideas may be made sensible objects at home as well as here. I think it is the peculiar mode of life, and its freedom from the enthralments of society, more than the artistic advantages which Rome offered; and then, no doubt, though the artists care little about one another's works, yet they keep each other warm by the presence of so many of them.*[70]

George Stillman Hillard (1808–1879), a Massachusetts lawyer and author, and a friend of Hawthorne's, visited Rome for several months beginning in September 1847. Noting that Rome then seemed

FIGURE II.
*Albert Bierstadt (1830–
1902), The Portico of Octav-
ia, 1858, oil on canvas,
28½ x 37 in. (72.3 x 94 cm.),
The Fine Arts Museums of
San Francisco, Gift of Mr.
and Mrs. John D. Rocke-
feller, 3rd. Although Kensett
preferred to paint the countryside outside of Rome, such
historic ruins as this were
familiar to Kensett and his
fellow artists.*

politically dead and futureless, and thus of little interest to most people as a home, Hillard praised the city as a resort for artists, being "full of the picturesque; which is seen not only in its well-known ruins, its renowned churches, its sparkling fountains, its obelisks, its arches, and its columns—in those objects which are described in guide-books and sit for their pictures in sketch-books" (Fig. 11). For Hillard, as an American, Rome was particularly attractive for "the absence of that dingy red brick which predominates so tyrannically over all our cities. . . . This glaring color is quite unknown in Rome."[71]

Hillard and numerous other writers of the 1840s and 1850s found especially notable in the Roman art world the important role played by sculptors, particularly the Englishman John Gibson (1790–1866) and the American Thomas Crawford (1813–1857). These men, as well as most of the Roman sculptors, were, in artistic essence, the neoclassical progeny of Antonio Canova (1757–1822) and the Dane Bertel Thorwaldsen (1768–1844), who left Rome in 1838 after forty-one productive years there. According to Hillard, there were no painters to compare in importance with the sculptors, excepting Friedrich Overbeck (1789–1869), the leader of the German Nazarenes, a band of medievalizing religious painters. Overbeck and the Nazarene Brotherhood occupied the monastery of Saint Isidore, located on the Pincian hill near the French Academy, not far above the Spanish Steps and the artists' quarter. As for local painting, things seemed quite in a bad way to Hillard, who reported, "There was an exhibition of the works of native artists in the spring of 1848, most of which were incredibly bad—to which England seemed to have contributed the drawing; Germany, the color; and France, the sentiment."[72] Despite this, the attractions of Rome to the artist, combining the ideal elements of art, history, light, and atmosphere, were immense.

Hillard, gifted with cool perception and a sense of distance, was a far more critical observer of Rome than Kensett or his circle of American friends in Rome. Later they recalled not that the level of art was miserable but that they had had a wonderful and constructive time together. Champney listed some of the young men whom they discovered in Rome: Hicks, Rossiter, George A. Baker (1821–1880), Louis Lang (1814–1893), and others, "all more or less distinguished in after years. . . . This made a jolly crowd, full of fun and life. But while they all liked gaiety and amusement, there was a serious and working side to them, and almost to a man, they were a studious set."[73] Kensett's "set" grew, during the year and a half of his stay, to include Thomas Crawford's family, James E. Freeman (1808–1884), an artist and the author of "Gatherings from an Artist's Portfolio" which describes life in Rome for artists, Christopher Pearse Cranch (1813–1892) and his wife, and George William Curtis (1824–1892) and his brother James Burrill Curtis.

When he first arrived in Rome, Kensett suffered a prolonged rheumatic illness, through which Hicks nursed him, and which prevented him from sketching and painting. Champney wrote Kensett late in the following spring, commiserating, "Accept my sympathy for your misfortune in being ill during so long a period. For to say nothing of the suffering you went through with the fact of your having been so long debarred the privilege of using your palette and brushes at a moment when you felt that much depended upon hard work and study was enough to render your situation anything but agreeable."[74]

Kensett and Hicks had, in succession, two particularly agreeable studios in the Via Margutta, near the Spanish Steps, where sociable gatherings provided regular amusement for a sizable group. Bachelor tea parties, providing refreshments and lots of good talk, were regular events in the Hicks-Kensett studios. The nearby trattoria Lepre, priced for the impecunious, the Caffè Greco, dingy and smoky enough for any bohemian, and a local billiard room on the Piazza di Spagna provided basic sustenance and additional innocent social pleasures. William Wetmore Story (1819–1875), the sculptor, writer, and Boston intellectual who arrived in Rome late in 1847, some months after Kensett had departed, described the atmosphere of the Caffè Greco in lively and precise detail:

> *Artists meet and discuss subjects of art, pictures and statues, read the French newspapers and Galignani's, and fill the air of the crowded little rooms with tobacco-smoke. There you may see every night representatives of art from all parts of the world, in all kinds of hats, from the conical black felt, with its velvet-ribbon, to the still French stove-pipe; and in every variety of coat from the Polish and German nondescript all befrogged and tagged, to the shabby American dress-coat, with crumpled tails; and with every cut of hair and beard, from that of Peter the Hermit, unkempt and uncut, to the mustache and pointed beard of Anthony Vandyck.*[75]

Mrs. Cranch, writing in her journal, recorded several happy times meeting "Mr. Freeman, Mr. Hicks, and Mr. Kensett [who] are interesting young artists whom we like very much. Altogether life here is very pleasant, apart from the great attractions of the place." Cranch, who arrived in Rome a

FIGURE 12.
Kensett, Standing Female Figure, *c. 1845–47, water-color and pencil on paper,* 13¼ x 9⅞ *in. (33.6 x 25.1 cm.), Maurice and Carol J. Feinberg.*

year later than Kensett, "soon joined a night-school where students drew and painted in watercolor from costumed models. The cost was about a dollar and a half per month!" as Mrs. Cranch noted. This school, whose models would have been collected from the Spanish Steps where they daily displayed themselves in peasant clothing, was attended every evening beginning at eight o'clock by thirty or forty artists, among whom may have been Kensett, if his numerous Italian costume sketches are acceptable testimony (Fig. 12). In a nearby apartment permeated by the international sounds of "three guitars, one grand piano, a violin cello, two flutes, and an accordian," the Cranches also provided occasional entertainment. Mrs. Cranch recalled a lovely walk outside Rome's walls: "That same evening [18 November 1846] Kensett and Hicks came to see us, and I had prepared for them some good, strong tea, and some American apple sauce, and we had a merry time around our table, that night."[76]

By artistic tradition winter in Rome was the season for study, studio work, and socializing, while the summer season was the time to leave the shimmering heat of Rome and hike through the mountains and hills to the south and east. Kensett and two friends left Rome on 1 June 1846, but soon he was left to his own devices. Albano, Ariccia, Gensano, Lake Nemi, Velletri, Olevano, Subiaco, Civitella, and Tivoli made up his itinerary through country that still bore a reputation as the picturesque haunt of bandits.[77] Later Kensett wrote his sister far away in Ithaca, New York, "I commenced my studies from nature without delay and up to the 15th of Aug. had the most delightful weather so far as light and cloudless skies went, but the heat was of the most oppressive character."[78] Hicks joined him in July for several months, and the summer ended successfully as Kensett, unmolested by bandits, returned to Rome laden with "some thirty odd studies in oil, some quite large, all made with care and attention to nature."[79] Kensett's return to Rome for the winter of 1846–47 was apparently a pleasant resumption of a semibohemian life made happier by the increasing sale of pictures to occasional collectors and, more vitally, to the American Art-Union.

Kensett's career, up to this point, was the product of a good and sunny character, hard work, sociability, and acquaintance with leading American artists. When the Curtis brothers appeared in Rome in early 1847 and became Kensett's intimates, a great door—both intellectual and social—opened for him. George and James Curtis were New Englanders (from Providence, Rhode Island) who had both recently spent several years at Brook Farm, that seedbed and academy of transcendentalism. The Curtises, especially George, formed a lasting friendship with Ralph Waldo Emerson and other intellectuals, which helped determine the robust combination of idealism and nationalism that characterized George Curtis' influential writings and orations during his years as editor of *Harper's Weekly*. Before the Civil War, he was a friend and leader of the many authors from the North who campaigned vigorously against slavery: "The services of Curtis in the four or five years that were to pass before the Civil War disrupted the country, and the influence of his voice during the war period, can hardly be overestimated."[80]

George Curtis' friendship with Kensett became close, lasting until Kensett's death, and through him Kensett came to know intellectual leaders like Emerson and to share in their attitudes and enthusiasms. There indeed may have been in Kensett's studio some hot debates over the Sage of Concord, judging by a letter to Kensett from Curtis sent from Germany a year after they left Rome, reporting on a recent party in that city: "A brother of Leafy's [nickname for an artist friend] . . . gave a spree on which occasion, to T's [Hicks] and my entire delight it seems this brother smashed into Macpherson and Freeman and all the misunderstanders and *therefore* slanderers of Emerson with whom you remember I used to head a lance now and then."[81] His friendship with Curtis was subsequently the connecting element for Kensett with a long list of distinguished literati, among them Charles A. Dana, Thomas G. Appleton, Charles Eliot Norton, James Russell Lowell, Henry Wadsworth Longfellow, and John Field, all of whom attracted Kensett to Newport, Nahant, and Cambridge for repeated visits in later years.

Kensett's last months in Italy were spent traveling south of Rome with the Curtis brothers, visiting such famous sites as Naples, Amalfi, Pompei, and Sorrento. After returning to Rome, they then went on a month-long Italian tour, via Florence to Venice, where for another month they took lovely rooms. George Curtis later recalled to Kensett "those breakfasts in a 'salon' over the Canale Grande with the door open that looks upon the flowered and [illegible] balcony with peaches, grapes, and pears upon the table, with Checo and Beppo awaiting us at the river with the gondola and our slight drooping Hebe. How could I ever eat again?"[82] This happy time, full of discovery and hard work, "with wonderfully little waste,"[83] came to an end in September, when Kensett left the Curtises in Verona and returned through Switzerland to Paris, and then to London, and finally, in November, home to New York after seven years' absence.

George Curtis wrote of Kensett's return "to a series of noiseless victories" and described the rapid success he enjoyed: "He was a recognized master of landscape, all his pictures are biographical, for they all reveal the fidelity, the tenderness, and the sweet serenity of his nature. Universally beloved, he was always welcome."[84] Kensett's character—quiet, thoughtful, and diligent, unfailingly kind and well mannered—guaranteed his easy acceptance into the leading artistic and intellectual society of New York, Boston, and elsewhere. In those first years back in the United States, before the Civil War, his art gained national recognition, while his personal nature opened every door.

Kensett's reliability and calmness were in marked contrast to the whirlwind of change around him. In those thirteen pre–Civil War years, the United States ended its brief but highly successful agitation against Mexico, adding Texas, California, and most of the southwestern region to the Oregon Territory. The California gold rush and the increasing political controversies between North and South over the dividing of the new territories into slave and nonslave areas disrupted American life.

New York City was the primary beneficiary of the Erie Canal, the development of the railroads, and a rapidly growing international ship traffic, as well as the general national expansion, and it mushroomed in population from 312,710 in 1840 to 813,669 in 1860.[85] This upsurge also had its negative consequences, and in 1850 New York possessed some of the worst slums in the Western world, particularly the Five Points area, famed for its criminal gangs, gambling halls, and houses of prostitution.[86] In a city like New York, never far removed from national events and debates, no time is "ordinary," but those years were extraordinary for their physical, financial, political, and sociological turmoil. In 1840 Kensett had left a "knickerbocker" New York where all the social leaders knew one another and artists were few in number; it was a unique situation never to be recaptured. Fostered by urban growth, many new organizations were established to absorb the activity and interests of the burgeoning population and to represent those interests and activities to the larger public.

Kensett's mature life, beginning in New York in 1847, revolved almost wholly around his art and accompanying social activity. He was keenly devoted to his work and was a copious producer, as a glance at the exhibition records of the American Art-Union and the National Academy of Design, and at the approximately six hundred pictures left unsold in his studio at his death, amply attests. Kensett's studio, which he shared for almost a quarter-century with Lang, became a constant resort for artists, continuing a pattern established by Kensett in Rome, which allowed him the pleasures of work and sociability in easy proximity. The voluminous Kensett correspondence, involving scores of people, also offers a clear picture of his life outside the studio, where he quickly settled into the life of clubman and art-world celebrity.

Central, perhaps key, to his career at this time was his membership in the Century Association in New York, to which he was elected 12 May 1849.[87] The Century, so named because of the originally intended number of its membership, had been founded two years previously on 13 January 1847, at a meeting held "in the Rotunda of the New York Gallery of Fine Arts in the Park," next to City Hall.[88] The association was to be composed of "authors, artists, and amateurs of letters and the Fine Arts, residents of New York City and its vicinity; its objects, the cultivation of a taste for letters and the arts, and social enjoyment." The founding members, forty-two in number, included several friends of Kensett's (John Gadsby Chapman, Asher B. Durand, Francis Edmonds, Daniel Huntington, and Thomas Rossiter) and many others who were to become his intimates (William Cullen Bryant, Reverend Henry Bellows, A. M. Cozzens, Reverend Orville Dewey, John Gourlie, Charles M. Leupp, Jonathan Sturges, and Henry T. Tuckerman). These men were unanimous in the opinion that founding such a club was "a measure both expedient and practicable, one promising mutual advantage to its members, as being calculated to draw closer the bonds of social intercourse between those who should be better known to each other and one that may do much to promote the advancement of Arts and Letters which is in accordance with the progressive Century in which we live."[89] The establishment of the Century, whose rooms immediately became the center of New York's literary and artistic world, and which grew rapidly in membership, is symbolic of the growth of New York from a small cohesive city into a large diverse metropolis containing multitudes of independent groups and societies. Previously New York had small literary and art clubs, like the Columb and The Bread and Cheese (founded in 1824 by James Fenimore Cooper), the latter of which evolved into the Sketch Club in 1829.[90]

The Sketch Club, strictly limited to twenty-five members, was a distinguished group of writers, artists, and amateurs of the arts who met biweekly during the fall, winter, and spring months to eat, drink, sing, compose poems, and make sketches to a set theme. The meetings were invariably delightful, and it became the club for the artistic set, who, if not members, eagerly accepted invitations to attend as guests. One member had to die before another could be selected, and the situation was thus delicate, with much social pressure felt on all sides. Thomas S. Cummings, longtime treasurer of the National Academy of Design and member of the Sketch Club, commented that "the difficulty of admission into the Sketch Club [was] such as almost to amount to 'prohibition.'"[91] Chapman was the Sketch Club member who first proposed that a larger club be established to answer the problem, and thus the Century was born. The Sketch Club, however, remained active as a separate organization, with membership still avidly sought after by many, including Kensett. Sketch Club minutes record that he first attended as a dinner guest at Cozzens' on 11 December 1850. It was not until four years later, on 8 December 1854, after attending many such meetings as a guest, that Kensett was finally "unanimously elected a member of the Club."[92]

Kensett became deeply involved in the affairs of the Century, and in 1857 he was one of seven Centurions, Bryant and Durand among them, who were "Incorporators" in a special act of incorporation passed by the New York State legislature.[93] Kensett's devotion to the Century was warmly reciprocated, for in May 1861, just before he departed for Europe, a testimonial dinner was given in his honor at the Century. The dinner was arranged by Kensett's friends Lang, William H. Appleton, and Edward Slosson, and included his companions Hicks, Durand, Huntington, Jasper Cropsey, Jervis McEntee, and George A. Baker.[94]

In May of 1864 Kensett received a letter from George Bancroft, president of the Century, commissioning a painting on behalf of "several of your fellow members." Kensett was to receive the remarkable sum of five thousand dollars for a landscape subject of his choice. Bancroft complimented Kensett, saying, "The subscribers make their request animated by a just admiration of your talent as an artist, by an affectionate regard for you as an early and faithful member of the Century and by a desire to promote one of the great objects for which the Association was chartered."[95] As requested, Kensett completed the picture within two years. The members of the Century and the Sketch Club, many of whose names are not readily recognizable today, were the prime movers in the art activities of the city (Bryant, Cummings, Durand, Edmonds, Gray, Huntington, Ingham, and Sturges being among the best known), who could effect great changes in the cultural world and beyond.

At the Century, and particularly at the Sketch Club, Kensett made friendly acquaintance with guests like Emerson and renewed his friendship with Thackeray. Thackeray's American tour in 1852–53 included receptions at both clubs. Eyre Crowe, Thackeray's traveling companion, revealed that "among the friends of student-time in Paris I now met at the 'Century' Club was a clever landscape painter, Kensett, who had grown as stout as he was formerly the reverse, and who didn't recognize me in the least, owing to come facial change of the same nature. We met at an artistic gathering called the 'Sketch Club,' the assembled company coming together with no other design than to chat, smoke, and last, not least, eat oysters of the usual huge size."[96] Thackeray's trip, like Dickens' before him, was a great cultural event that survives in the historical and literary record of the period. James Grant Wilson, himself a well-known author, described the great throng of twelve hundred listeners, "an unusual number of artistic, literary, and professional celebrities," that filled Reverend Bellows' Unitarian Church on 19 November 1852 to hear Thackeray lecture: "Besides an imposing array of society leaders, the writer recalls Bancroft and Bryant, Hallock and Irving, Verplanck and Willis, President King and Professor Morse; Durand, Hicks and Kensett, Daniel Lord, and O'Conor, with the editors Bennett, Greeley, Morris and Webb."[97]

Kensett and Thackeray also met at social dinners, one given by Frederick Cozzens, a popular wine merchant and amateur man of letters, and another given by Hicks in his studio. The Hicks party was exceedingly jolly, including readings and songs by Thackeray, who possessed a fine singing voice, songs by George Curtis, and many stories.[98] Neither Kensett nor Thackeray let the seriousness of their art interfere with social gaiety. Nor did Thackeray's connection with Kensett cloud his vision of the nature of his friend's work. Thackeray, writing to an English lady friend in 1855 during his second and last American tour, provided a friendly yet penetrating appreciation of Kensett's work, which speaks clearly both of Thackeray's Englishness and the difference between English and American art:

> *I had been looking at sketches (by an excellent artist Kensett) all in the morning of New England wood and sea-shore scenery—and the character of them seemed to me shaggy wan melancholy like an American beauty of 35. I like the English style best from habit and education—a great buxom elm tree, a jolly green sward, a fair sonsy lady of what age shall we say?—better than these lean trees haggard landscapes and shrivelled matrons.*[99]

Kensett's Century friends dominated the committees that ran the National Academy of Design, the organization which, by and large, determined the success of American artists through its popular exhibitions and the award of the coveted "N.A." (National Academician) or "A.N.A." (Associate National Academician). The close-knit nature of this group and their organization was demonstrated by the list of those invited to the Twenty-second Annual Exhibition of the Academy in 1847: "Members of the Sketch Club, Century, Society Library, Mercantile Library, American Art-Union, City Gallery, Columbia College and New-York University."[100]

FIGURE 13.
Richard Morrell Staigg
(1817–1881), John F. Ken-
sett, 1858, *watercolor on
ivory,* 4⅜ x 3¾ *in.* (11.1 x
82 *cm.*), *Private Collection.
Staigg was active in Newport
and he may well have painted
Kensett during one of the
many summers his subject
visited the resort town.*

Kensett was quickly elected an Associate Academician in 1848 and full Academician in May of 1849. He immediately wrote acknowledging his election with characteristic modesty: "In accepting the honorary distinction conferred I beg leave cheerfully to subscribe to the requirements of membership as well as a duty all ways to contribute my humble efforts to the furtherance of the objects for which the Institution was founded."[101] The National Academy at mid-century numbered just less than fifty Academicians, plus many more associate and honorary members, providing a goodly number to act as officers and to sit on committees. Except for its top officers, the academy diligently rotated membership on its Council and other committees. Kensett, however, was soon identified as a particularly sage and businesslike person and from 1850 onward was repeatedly placed in important committee positions, on the Council or otherwise (Fig. 13). Perhaps because he was too shy, he never served as an academy officer although he was on the Council in 1850, 1859, 1861, 1862, 1864, 1865, and 1866. As a Council member he was automatically on the Committee of Arrangements, which selected and installed the annual exhibition, obviously a position of great power since the hanging of a picture often determined how well it looked and, thus, whether it sold. In 1855 and 1856 he was also on this committee while not on the Council.

Kensett's most important contribution to the academy was as a member and then treasurer of the Fellowship Fund, established in January of 1863 to raise funds to erect a new academy building. The

FIGURE 14.
National Academy of Design, *a wood engraving illustration from* Scientific American, 16 *February* 1867. *American Antiquarian Society, Worcester, Mass. Kensett helped to raise funds for this building designed by Peter B. Wight.*

academy membership, bursting with cultural boosterism and a New Yorker sense of competition, voiced its needs thus:

> *The interests of the City of New-York require that the Fine Arts should be provided for on more solid foundation. Other cities of the Union have Art Institutions jointly established and endowed, with spacious buildings, galleries and collections of casts from the Antique etc., while in this city, though we have our Academy of Design, it has no permanent Edifice, and therefore lacks completeness and energy. . . .* We need, and must have, a Building. *Should one be erected of striking and beautiful Architecture, the various Societies of Art would cluster around it, and the schools of design and collections of models might be so amply provided as to stimulate the zeal of students, and tend to raise American Art to the highest excellence."*[102]

Kensett and his fellow committee members raised the required hundred thousand dollars in a surprisingly short period, Kensett successfully leading the way by landing the first contribution of one thousand dollars from twenty-four-year-old Robert Hoe, a wealthy manufacturer of newspaper presses and later a founder of both the Metropolitan Museum of Art and the Grolier Club.[103] Construction on Peter B. Wight's colorful neo-Venetian gothic structure, at the corner of Twenty-third Street and

Fourth Avenue (now Lexington Avenue) began 18 April 1863, and the cornerstone was laid with great ceremony on 21 October that same year (Fig. 14). Invocations, addresses, and remarks, all interspersed with music, were offered by a long list of luminaries, including Parke Godwin, William Cullen Bryant, Samuel F. B. Morse, Wight, Bancroft, and the ever-present Reverend Bellows.[104] It was seen as a great day for New York, which for the first time had a sizable building with proper—even grand—public spaces for the creation and display, both temporary and permanent, of works of art.

On a more personal level, Kensett always stood ready to help young artists who needed money and the opportunity to sell pictures. The Morgan Collection of manuscripts contains letters exemplifying his many kindnesses. Kensett allowed artists, Samuel Coleman and Charles Henry Moore among them, to use his studio, something of an artistic crossroads in New York, to display their work for possible sale. He also bought their works and on occasion did very well indeed: in 1859 he bought the now-famous *Negro Life in the South* from the young Eastman Johnson for the considerable sum of twelve hundred dollars.[105] Kensett also lent money to his childhood friend Rossiter, who fathered nine children and found it difficult to support such a large family solely with his painting. The artists remembered these kindnesses vividly, as their demonstration of grief at Kensett's death made clear.

Kensett's close association with the National Academy of Design and his solicitude for the well-being of fellow artists led him to become involved during the late 1850s and afterward with two other important activities which combined artistic with public interests. The first was the Artists' Fund Society of New York, founded in 1857 to benefit widows and children of deceased artists through the exhibition and sale of works contributed by living artists. The Artists' Fund Society was, in effect, a life-insurance society, the first beneficiary of which was the family of William Ranney, painter of frontier genre scenes, who died in 1857 leaving a sizable mortgage on his home. Thanks to the Fund Society, the mortgage was retired and five thousand dollars invested for the survivors' benefit. Kensett probably was brought into the society's counsels by his old friend and protector Edmonds, who was a founder of the group. In later years Kensett became president of the society and worked closely with John M. Falconer (1820–1903), an artist of many skills, who served as manager of the society's affairs. An arrangement of the annual exhibition of contributed pictures and the handling of resulting funds claimed much of their time over the years.

In 1859 Kensett found himself thrust onto the national political stage. In recent years considerable controversy had arisen in the American art community over the use of supposedly non-American artists to decorate the United States Capitol building. The ire of some was directed at the Roman Constantino Brumidi (1805–1880), who came to this country in 1852 as a political refugee, fleeing repression in Italy, and had obtained United States naturalization papers. Shortly thereafter, he received the large commission to paint frescoes in the Capitol Extension. The final insult for the artists, it seems, was the decision by Congress in 1857 to commission the famous Parisian history painter Horace Vernet (1789–1863) to paint a "large battle scene for one of the grand staircases of the addition to the Capitol."[106] A congress of over one hundred native artists met in Philadelphia on 22 March 1858 to protest and to demand of the government "the most judicious patronage of American Artists, in reference to the decoration and adorning of the public buildings at Washington with Works of Art."[107]

The proposal to establish a presidentially selected art commission of three artist members to supervise the Capitol decorations was hotly debated in the houses of Congress during the spring of 1858, and finally two acts establishing an Art Commission were voted upon on 12 June 1858 and 3 March 1859. On 15 May 1859, President James Buchanan approved and appointed as commissioners Kensett, the portrait painter James R. Lambdin (1807–1889), and the sculptor Henry Kirke Brown (1814–1886), with Brown as president of the commission. In Buchanan's words, the commission was to review "all designs for sculpture or paintings for the decoration and embellishment of the United States Capitol Extension," which in fact gave the commission little more than advisory power since the acts allowed expenditures to be made only by the Joint Congressional Committee on the Library of Congress.[108] In addition, the Capitol "regulars," especially Captain Montgomery C. Meigs, superintendent of the Capitol Extension, objected to this legalized meddling by outsiders who were considered an impediment to completion of the works. Meigs grumbled that "now with the commission of artists, and various other obstructions, I do not know when, if ever in my lifetime it will be completed."[109] The commissioners met in Washington on the following 15 June to begin their surveys and planning.

The result of their work was a report dated 23 February 1860, which the three commissioners signed and submitted to President Buchanan, who forwarded it to the House of Representatives after review by the secretary of the interior and the secretary of war. The eight-page report was a general lecture complaining of past aesthetic errors ("we find but little . . . which relates to our history, or in which the American mind will be interested") and recommending a much simpler, less brightly colored decorative approach emphasizing American birds, plants, and history. Vernet (and other benighted foreign artists) was dismissed chauvinistically with the comment that "it is morally impossible that he should wholly adopt his style or form of expression to ours. The expediency therefore, of inviting even the most distinguished foreign artist to paint on the walls of the Capitol may well be questioned."[110] Flat color schemes, reduced use of stucco ornaments, employment of carved wood and stone, and cast bronze architectural elements were advocated, as was the direct award of commissions to artists rather than the use of competitions, to which successful artists would object. A specific list of pictures, statues, busts, architectural finishes, painting, and decorating, with total cost estimates of $166,900, completed the report. In the body of the report, the commissioners unwisely went beyond their mandate to criticize at length the inferior design of United States coinage.

The response of Congress on 20 June 1860 was not surprising: it voted funds for the building, but none for paintings or sculpture, and abolished the Art Commission immediately. *The Crayon* published an angry reaction and rebuke, saying,

> *We are not surprised of it . . . the causes of the repeal of the law providing for the Art Commission are characterized with the coarseness, ignorance and cunning which are always brought into play in all matters when Government aid and protection are sought. They are due both to the craft of politicians and to the impassive state of opinion in relation to the art that prevails throughout the country.*[111]

The three commissioners were not entirely subdued by defeat, and following the lead of Brown they hotly pursued the Congress for recompense for their time and expenses incurred in Washington. Brown wrote Kensett in April 1862, in one of many letters between them, that "I have never spent a winter of such anxiety, doubt, and discouragement. The only thing which has sustained me was the justice of my cause."[112] They each finally received the sizable sum of three thousand dollars for their efforts as commissioners, putting an end to a particularly undistinguished chapter in America's cultural history.

Unless a landscape painter confined himself to depicting unspecific locations or details of nature, his business usually required considerable travel, especially if he lived in a large city, as did Kensett. Like Frederic Church (1826–1900), Sanford Gifford (1823–1880), and Albert Bierstadt (1830–1902), Kensett was an avid traveler, as his oeuvre shows. During his career, in hundreds of pictures, he depicted the changing faces of Europe, the British Isles, and the large expanses of the United States, ranging from Maine to Colorado and Montana. Often he traveled alone on his painting excursions, but usually he was in the company of friends, which allowed for fun and occasional highjinks. With Champney and others he socialized and painted in New Hampshire and Maine; with Church he hiked across central Maine to climb and paint Mount Katahdin; with Francis Blackwell Mayer and a flock of artists, photographers, and railroad men he painted along the scenic path of the Baltimore and Ohio Railroad between Baltimore and Saint Louis; with the fur trader Pierre Chouteau he steamed up and painted the Missouri River as far as eastern Montana; and with Gifford and Worthington Whittredge (1820–1910) he went into the Colorado Rockies back of Denver.

These picturesque outings, though less dramatic than those of Church to the Andes or the Middle East or of Bierstadt to the Wind River Mountains, were not the placid but thoughtful stuff of which most of Kensett's pictures were made. The shores of Nahant and Beverly, Massachusetts, Newport and Narragansett, Rhode Island, and of Connecticut, Long Island, and New Jersey, along with the Catskills, Berkshires, Adirondacks, and Green and White Mountains, were the scenes of Kensett's best work, calling forth his characteristic linear and coloristic clarity. These works are the product of a concentrated mentality which did not require the grandness of vast mountain chains to find great expression. Kensett did indeed travel for his art, but he did not need to travel far.

The advent of the Civil War, the greatest political and military trauma suffered by the United States in its history, had its impact as well on the quiet Kensett, who had returned from Washington to his comfortable New York studio and former way of life in 1860. He was a strong backer of the Union effort to stop secession, as were most of his friends, who closely followed the lead of Curtis, Godwin, Bryant, Longfellow, and others of his literary companions. Kensett and the ardently pro-Union elements were a minority in New York. Both the city and state had considerable Copperhead biases in their executive leadership. In 1861 the mayor of New York, Fernando Wood, paraded the idea of secession of the city from the Union. Governor Horatio Seymour, elected in 1862, was an anti-abolitionist whose temporizing language was blamed partly for the spread of the murderous 1863 draft riots that scarred the city. "If Jeff Davis had been running against Abraham Lincoln in 1862 he would have won New York City by 60,000 votes," according to Colonel George Bliss of the New York militia.[113]

One important countermove for the Unionists was the establishment of the Union League Club of New York City early in 1863, some months before the July draft riots. Kensett became an early member of the club, which was first tentatively named the National Club, and was established by and for men who demonstrated "absolute and unqualified loyalty to the government of the United States, and unwavering support of its efforts for the suppression of the rebellion." Their object was to "discountenance and rebuke by word and social influences all disloyalty and to that end the members [would] use every proper means in public and private."[114] Born of alarm at the election of Seymour, the club was the idea of Dr. Wolcott Gibbs, medical professor of the Free Academy (later the City College of New York), and his colleagues on the United States Sanitary Commission (forerunner of the American Red Cross), Frederick Law Olmsted, who was already famous as co-planner of Central Park and was then general secretary of the Sanitary Commission, and Reverend Bellows, who had conceived of and established the commission. An early move of the Union League Club, in the aftermath of the riots in which numerous blacks were lynched, was to recruit and equip two "colored" regiments (the Twentieth and Twenty-sixth) of the United States Infantry. This was done partly under the leadership of the painter Vincent Colyer (1825–1888), a close friend of Kensett's. Colyer, an employee and member of the club, also brought the club into a successful campaign against the long-standing practice of "denying colored people the unrestricted use of our city railroad cars, following the forcible removal from a car of the widow of a Sergeant of the 26th Regiment."[115]

In November 1863, possibly at the urging of Colyer, Reverend Bellows, president of the Sanitary Commission, brought together at the clubhouse "about a hundred of the most patriotic women in New York to consider the best method for starting the plan of a Metropolitan Fair."[116] Bellows was convinced that a large fair would be the most effective way to raise funds to support the commission's humanitarian and patriotic activities. In his usual broadly and carefully reasoned manner, he set forth a preamble that the fair should be "on a National scale. . . . It must be Universal; enlisting all sympathies, from the highest to the lowest—democratic, without being vulgar; elegant, without being exclusive; fashionable, without being frivolous; popular, without being mediocre. In short, it must be inspired from the higher classes, but animate, include, and win the sympathies and interest of all classes."[117] Bellows and his Union League Club colleagues quickly organized an extremely complex group of associations and committees which made arrangements for what became an immense and somewhat bewildering extravaganza.[118] The committees organized displays that dealt with seemingly every aspect of American life and activity: art, clothing, farm products, finance, flowers, furs, machinery, metals, music, police, plumbing, schools (private and public), saddlers, thread and needles, and wines, among others. Bierstadt, Kensett's friend and the most famous painter of the Far West, was chairman of the Indian Department, while Kensett undertook the much more complicated task of chairing the Art Committee, as well as sitting on the Men's Executive Committee.

The Art Committee was charged with bringing together the single largest display of the fair, an exhibition of some 360 American and European paintings, many of which were contributions and were to be sold to benefit the Sanitary Commission (Fig. 15). The Art Committee members were almost all close friends of Kensett's and included Bierstadt, Huntington, Whittredge, Sturges, Hicks, Cranch, William Tilden Blodgett, A. M. Cozzens, Emanuel Leutze, and Matthew Brady.[119] Kensett and his associates had the difficult job of arranging for loans and contributions of pictures, shipping them, framing many of them, and, finally, installing them. Kensett's correspondence bulges with dozens upon dozens of notes to and from him dealing with all such matters.

The result—the opening of the fair and its art exhibition on 4 April 1864—was a huge success. Housed in the Twenty-second Regiment Armory and in a series of large buildings erected on Union

FIGURE 15.
Picture-gallery of the Fair,
Fourteenth-Street Building,
*a wood engraving illustration
from* Harper's Weekly, 16
April 1864. *American Antiquarian Society, Worcester,
Mass. The crowd is viewing
the exhibition of American
and European paintings
assembled by Kensett's Art
Committee for the Metro-
politan Fair.*

Square, the fair was seen by hundreds of thousands of eager visitors by the time it closed on 23 April (Fig. 16). The paintings exhibited caused quite a stir, calling forth loud praises but also some criticism from pro-Ruskinian quarters. On balance, however, it was recorded that

> *the little world of picture-lovers in New York was charmed and delighted. . . . There was a large, pleasant room, high and well lighted, and filled with works bearing, for the most part, the most honored names in American art. Everybody admitted that the pictures were generally well hung, unusually well hung, . . . and the only drawback to seeing them well, was the crowd that constantly filled the Gallery, and made it impossible to see any painting on the line at a greater distance from it than six feet.*[120]

Financially the fair succeeded far better than anticipated. Despite high expenses for the art exhibition—over ten thousand dollars—it returned a clear profit, and, according to Reverend Bellows' later recollection, the fair as a whole raised free and clear over one million dollars, an immense sum for that time.[121] Kensett's efforts were recognized and applauded warmly by his fellow organizers of the fair, who sent him this resolution the week after the fair's end: "Among the many agreeable reminiscences of our arduous labors during the past winter, stands out in bold relief your untiring devotion to the enterprise which has just resulted so successfully, and in communicating to you the . . . resolution of our committee . . . the spontaneous and enthusiastic expression of our appreciation of your ability and courteous zeal in furthering the cause of patriotism and humanity."[122]

FIGURE 16.
Metropolitan Fair Buildings, on Union Square, *a wood engraving illustration from* Harper's Weekly, 9 *April* 1864. *American Antiquarian Society, Worcester, Mass.*

Another fortunate result of the fair, and not an indirect one, was the founding of the Metropolitan Museum of Art in 1870. In 1867 Tuckerman wrote in his influential *Book of the Artists* that "the surprise and delight exhibited by the thousands of all degrees, who visited the Picture Gallery of the Metropolitan Fair, has suggested to many, for the first time, and renewed in other minds more emphatically, the need, desireableness, and practicality of a permanent and free Gallery of Art in our Cities. The third metropolis of the civilized world [New York] should not longer be without such a benign provision for and promoter of high civilization."[123] Tuckerman and Kensett were but two of those involved in the Metropolitan Fair who were to become founding trustees of the Metropolitan Museum. The fair thus inspired both the idea and probably the name of the museum. The idea was eagerly taken up next by a group of Americans in Paris who in 1869 sent a memorial to John Jay, urging the establishment of such an institution. Jay, a friend of Kensett's, was then American minister to Austria, as well as president of the Union League Club. Jay referred the proposal to the Art Committee of the Union League Club, on which Kensett sat from 1865 to 1869. That committee, chaired by George P. Putnam, also had as members Whittredge, Colyer, Baker, John Quincy Adams Ward, and Samuel Putnam Avery. Heartily endorsing the idea, the committee submitted a report to a general meeting of the club on 14 October 1869 asking, "May we not look forward to a reasonably early dedication of an ample structure, worthy in all respects of this great metropolis where the A. collection and the B. collection, and the L. collection and the S. collection, and many others, will some day be combined in one harmonious and magnificent national gallery?"[124]

The report was adopted and invitations were sent by the Art Committee to "members of the National Academy of Design, other artists, the Institute of Architects, the New-York Historical Society, the Century, Manhattan and other clubs" to attend a preliminary organizational meeting on 23 November.[125] At that meeting and later ones the basic nature and structure of the museum was decided upon. Not the least important of these meetings was a supper party held at the club directly after the 23 November general gathering, where twelve men, including Kensett, discussed the evening's activities. Alfred J. Bloor, an architect, recalled that "there was a free exchange of opinion as to the prospects of the new-born institution and as to available methods for carrying it to success, to which and to the chief workers so far toasts were pledged."[126]

Kensett was in his element in that era of great public meetings and large committees, acting as a cheerful force behind the scenes. On 17 January 1870 he was elected along with twenty-six other men to the first Metropolitan Museum Board of Trustees, where he served on the Executive Committee until his death in 1872.[127] Because the fledgling museum had as yet no collection and no staff, the trustees themselves performed all functions of conceiving policy and structure, raising money, inventing programs, and implementing them. They did so with great gusto and within a year had purchased the museum's first two collections. Kensett's unexpected death, which came in the same week as that of fellow trustee Putnam, moved the Metropolitan's Board of Trustees to issue a public resolution which cited their work as founders and as members of the Executive Committee: "Mr. Kensett from the outset has contributed to us not only the aid of his distinguished name, but also his wise counsels and his untiring personal labors."[128] Kensett was a notable member of a memorable group of founders. A great museum, the child of the joint efforts of philosophers, poets, artists, and philanthropists, was born.

Kensett's death was the result of pneumonia and heart disease contracted while heroically trying to retrieve the lifeless body of Mrs. Vincent Colyer from a chilly ocean inlet at Contentment Island, Connecticut, where she had fallen from her carriage and drowned. If we can rely upon the voluminous newspaper reports, his death became a considerable public event. The leading New York papers—the *Times*, the *Evening Post*, and the *Daily Tribune*—carried a series of articles, some quite complete and lengthy, which described the tragedy.[129] Kensett had been thought to be on the mend, but he suffered an attack in his studio on Saturday, 14 December, and died immediately. By tradition in New York, on Saturdays artists held open house in their studios. And so it happened that within minutes of Kensett's death a group of artists and friends—T. Addison Richmonds, Huntington, Avery, Hunt, and others—arrived on the scene and

> *were soon collected about the sofa where lay all that remained of their dear dead friend, and they could not restrain their tears as they gazed upon the lifeless clay. They tenderly composed the limbs and closed the eyes, not without many heartfelt sobs, for Kensett had been throughout a long artistic life a man with as much kindness as genius, of the sweetest amiability of character, and without one drop of envious blood. To artists of his own standing he was as a brother; to his juniors he was ever a patient teacher and generous friend, quick to discern merit, quicker still in aiding it.*[130]

Kensett's dear friend and early and constant patron, Robert M. Olyphant, made arrangements for the funeral. On the following Wednesday morning, a snowy day, Kensett's open rosewood coffin, with silver handles and bearing a silver plate reading "JOHN F. KENSETT, Born March 23, 1816, Died December 14, 1872," was laid in state in the flower-banked library of the National Academy of Design. Baker's bust portrait of Kensett, now owned by the National Academy, hung on the wall above the head of the casket. Until one o'clock, when the coffin was moved to the Fifth Avenue Presbyterian Church at Nineteenth Street for the service, the room "was thronged with the friends of Mr. Kensett. Almost every prominent artist in this city was present and the deepest sorrow was manifested as they viewed the face of their late fellow-worker who was so warmly beloved by all."[131] The Union League Club, the Century, the Artists' Fund Society, and the Metropolitan Museum of Art sent delegations to join the many dozens of artists in attendance, and they all followed the solemn procession on foot led by carriages to the church. Colyer, Huntington, Whittredge, Casilear, Gifford, Hicks, R. W. Hubbard, Jervis McEntee, Henry Kirke Brown, John Falconer, Robert Hoe, and George Talbot Olyphant were pallbearers. The large church was full for the Masonic service, which was accompanied by organ music, a quartet who sang parts of Beethoven's Seventh Symphony, and, at the end, the congregation singing "Nearer My God to Thee," one of Kensett's favorite hymns. Kensett at a later date was buried at Greenwood Cemetery, Brooklyn.

Kensett had begun his life somewhat humbly in a small Connecticut town, and ended it in a remarkable position of power and respect, both within and without the world of art. He along with Cole, Durand, Huntington, Crawford, Powers, Church, Bierstadt, and others had helped raise the status of the artist to the highest level yet achieved in America. The work, purposeful character, and individualism of these men won them a new and enviable role in a different and rapidly changing society. American society and the world of art, of course, continued the processes of evolution even more rapidly after Kensett's death, thrusting the accepted style of art aside and, to some extent, swallowing up the individual artist in the ever-expanding economic and social scene. Kensett died relatively young, but he was thus spared the anxiety of seeing his art hidden away from public view and almost forgotten in basements and attics across the nation, an experience both Church and Bierstadt suffered. We are now long past that intermediate stage of perception and can better appreciate the discerning yet selective beauty of Kensett's pictures and the thoroughly creative nature of this beguiling man's life.

FIGURE 17.

Thomas P. Rossiter (1818–
1871), A Studio Reception,
Paris, 1841, *oil on canvas,*
32 x 39⅝ in. (81.3 x 100.6
cm.), Albany Institute of
History and Art, Gift of
Miss Ellen W. Boyd.
Rossiter conveys the convivi-
ality of fellow American
artists in the Paris studio he
shared with Kensett. Rossiter
sits before the easel next to
Thomas Cole. Behind them
stands Kensett holding a
palette and mahlstick; Asher
B. Durand leans towards him.
Daniel Huntington rests
against the mantel; G.P.A.
Healy is on the far right.
Others who may be depicted
are Robert Cook, Benjamin
Champney, John Casilear,
and James Deveaux.

FROM BURIN TO BRUSH: THE DEVELOPMENT OF A PAINTER

John Paul Driscoll

I. The Artist in Europe, 1840-1847

There is a certainty of my always being assured of a respectable living at my present occupation, whereas at the art to which my thoughts and feelings most tend, there is an uncertainty that weakens the energy of my resolutions, leaving me like a leaf between two currents of wind, now blown by this until caught by the opposing one and carried back to its starting place to tremble lifelessly between the two.

—KENSETT, 31 DECEMBER 1841[1]

AS THE DECADE OF THE FORTIES BEGAN, Kensett could see no escape from his unhappy life engraving plates at Hall, Packard, and Cushman in Albany. Early in the spring of 1840, however, he learned that his friend John Casilear had booked passage for England, to depart New York City in June in the company of the eminent engraver Asher B. Durand. During the next few months, Kensett discussed his friend's approaching departure with Thomas Rossiter, his friend since boyhood and also an aspiring artist. Suddenly, and perhaps impetuously, the two decided that they also would go to Europe.[2] The circumstances surrounding their decision may never be known, but when the steamship *British Queen* set sail for London on 1 June, Kensett and Rossiter were on board with Casilear and Durand.

Kensett's arrival in London marked the beginning of seven and a half years of work and study in Europe. It was to be an important formative period in his career, a time filled with the excitement of living in London, Paris, and Rome, of visiting the famous scenery and hallowed ruins of England, France, the Rhine Valley, Switzerland, and Italy, of meeting colleagues and making new friends, and of viewing the fine paintings and drawings of Old Masters. It was also a time of self-doubt and poverty for the young artist. He was constantly plagued by a chronic lack of funds, which confined his travels to England and France for five years while his companions Rossiter, Casilear, and Durand were able to go to Rome. During this time, Kensett was required to eke out an income as an engraver, which often tested his fortitude. Yet he never faltered in his resolve to pursue his ambition to become a painter. Although engraving occupied much of his energy, he reserved time to make studies of Old Master works, practice drawing, and go on sketching expeditions during the summer months. In 1845 he finally put his engraving tools aside for good and went to Rome, where, near the end of his stay in Europe, he produced the painting that established his reputation in the United States.

Among the most enriching experiences of Kensett's travels was the contact he had with other artists. Kensett's genial nature and eager receptivity to diverse ideas and personalities made him a favorite among these acquaintances. He, in turn, revelled in the artistic milieu they provided. "We are now surrounded by most of the . . . celebrated artists of Paris. . . . just the spot for us artists,"[3] he cheerfully noted in his journal. In Paris he shared rooms with Rossiter at 3, rue de Savoie, which he described as a "tabernacle for the followers of the burin and brush."[4] Rossiter's painting *A Studio Reception, Paris* (1841; Fig. 17), pictures the room, showing Rossiter and Kensett in the midst of an amiable gathering that includes Thomas Cole, Daniel Huntington, and G. P. A. Healy. In Paris too Kensett also met the Boston landscape painter Benjamin Champney, whom he often joined for dinner with the aging John Vanderlyn. Later, in Rome, Kensett enjoyed a similar confraternity in the rooms he shared with Thomas Hicks. George W. Curtis recalled that one evening their spacious quarters became the site of a "symposium" where Luther Terry, James Freeman, Christopher Cranch, Henry Willard, and other American artists gathered for conversation, song, and feasting. Curtis also remembered late-night socializing at the Caffè Greco and wondered if "among all the famous loiterers at the Greco was there ever a kinder, simpler, sweeter companion than Kensett?"[5]

Kensett's enthusiasm for life in Europe was tempered only by his meager financial circumstances. He was troubled by the lack of critical attention his endeavors as an engraver attracted and equally concerned about the uncertain prospects America offered to painters. Diligence with his burin, he knew, would repay him with a life that would be comfortable, though wholly lacking in aesthetic appreciation. With a sense of despair he wrote, "The engraver must fag away for weeks and months . . . and even then no one or at least very few can or will justly appreciate the performance," and he bemoaned the fact that he was "debarred from those enjoyments which I might receive were my time devoted to the more fascinating yet no more difficult department of the brush, instead of the burin."[6] Kensett was also discouraged by the volatile economic situations of colleagues like George Catlin, whom he met in London in 1840, and John James Audubon, whom he met in Paris, also in 1840. Vanderlyn, too, offered unhappy accounts of life with insufficient patronage. Kensett once made sympathetic inquiry if Vanderlyn had "yet received any substantial marking of favor from any of our monied countrymen in Paris?"[7] and worried that his own endeavors as an artist would never provide even a basic income. He had already, on various occasions, been "without a shilling I can call my own" and "without funds—3300 miles from home!"[8]

Kensett's determination consistently overcame his discouragement, however. In 1842 he wrote to his kindly uncle John R. Kensett, who lived in London, declaring his resolve to succeed as a landscape painter:

> *With 250 dollars or 300 including materials, I can support myself by the most severe and strait economy for a year. . . . Higher motives than personal considerations [illegible] influence me in my projects for the future—I hope to effect something that will reflect credit on my native place and upon my family. . . . I am determined to accomplish something before I return home, something that will introduce me to a consideration above the mass. Whether I shall realize any hope I know not. But thus I know the prospect fires every nerve and my motto is and shall be Onward! Still Onward.*[9]

FIGURE 18.
Claude Lorrain (1600–1682),
Seaport with the Landing of
Cleopatra at Tarsus, 1642,
46¹⁄₁₆ x 58¹⁄₁₆ *in.* (117 x
147.5 *cm.*), *Louvre.*

FIGURE 19.
Kensett, Scaport with the
Landing of Cleopatra at
Tarsus, *c.* 1842, *oil on canvas,*
23 x 32 *in.* (58.4 x 81.3
cm.), *Private Collection.*

Kensett's primary resource in working toward the accomplishment of his goal was the study of paintings and drawings by Old Masters, which he saw in museums, galleries, and private collections. On his first full day in London, joined by Durand, Casilear, and Rossiter, he visited the National Gallery. Here for the first times in their lives these Americans could gaze "without skepticism of authenticity" upon the paintings of Raphael, Giulio Romano, Claude Lorrain, Salvator Rosa, Titian, Veronese, Ostade—in short, a pantheon of Old Master works that could not then be seen anywhere in the United

States.[10] Further expeditions took the companions to the British Institution, Royal Academy, Royal Watercolour Society, Hampton Court, Dulwich, and several private collections.

Of the Old Masters, Claude Lorrain (1600–1682) made the strongest impression on Kensett. After a year of looking at fine paintings in London and Paris, he headed his list of favorite artists with Claude's name.[11] In Paris he copied "a delicious little Claude"[12] entitled *Seaport with the Landing of Cleopatra at Tarsus* (1642; Figs. 18 and 19). Later, in Claude's beloved Rome, Kensett created an original composition, *The Shrine—A Scene in Italy* (1847; Plate 2), which in its pastoral theme, measured sense of space, and warm light recalls the French master's romantic landscapes. After returning to America, Kensett adapted these Claudian devices to his views of the New World, such as *The White Mountains—From North Conway* (1851; Plate 4) and *Camel's Hump from the Western Shore of Lake Champlain* (1852; Plate 7).

Kensett frequently named Titian as one of his favorite artists and made a particular note of the Venetian's use of "rich color."[13] Although no evidence proves that Kensett copied paintings by Titian, in Rossiter's *Studio Reception, Paris* a copy of the Venetian's *Deposition* (c. 1625) hangs prominently on the back wall, an indication of the admiration for Titian's work among the American artists in Paris during the early 1840s.[14] It also raises the possibility that either Kensett or Rossiter had made a copy of the *Deposition* at the Louvre. Kensett's admiration of Titian's color anticipates the important role his own study of hues would have. Kensett also admired the work of another Venetian, Canaletto, and he noted in his journal one of that artist's views of Venice, which he saw in London.[15] Kensett's later work suggests to us that he was probably attracted to Canaletto's pure coloring, glassy atmosphere, cool light, precise detailing, and even his topographical subjects.

Prominent on Kensett's list of favorite artists are the names of seventeenth-century Dutch painters: David Teniers, Paulus Potter, Jacob van Ruisdael, Jan Vermeer, Willem van de Velde, and Meindert Hobbema. He also wrote of Adriaen van Ostade's "glowing color" and the "sunlight effect" in a painting by Jan Both. He noted of Gerard Dou's work that it "possesses the most important requisites for a picture—truth, expression and the most elaborate finish."[16] The bright sunlight in such later works as *View of the Beach at Beverly, Massachusetts* (1860; Plate 24) and the subtle, glowing color and smooth surfaces of *Shrewsbury River* (1858; frontispiece) and *Coast Scene with Figures* (1869; Plate 27) suggest an affinity with the Dutch masters Kensett had admired as an aspiring artist.

The English landscape artists John Constable and James Mallord William Turner also interested Kensett. He owned a painting by each and may have met Turner as early as July or August 1840. Although Constable's work was not generally on view in London in the early 1840s, several private collectors welcomed visits from Kensett and his companions. C. R. Leslie invited them to see his collection of Constable's sketches, and he provided Kensett, Durand, and Rossiter with an introduction to the collector John Sheepshanks.[17] At Sheepshanks' Durand found a "picture by Constable evincing more of simple truth and naturalness than any English landscape I have ever met with."[18] Constable's effect on Kensett is evident in *View from Richmond Hill* (c. 1843–45; Plate 1), which shows a debt to the English master's vision and technique in its on-the-scene immediacy, vigorous brushwork, liquid line, chiaroscuro, and sympathy for the quiet river valley scene. In Kensett's later work, for example the fine Niagara Falls sketch of c. 1851–52 (Plate 13), the energetic brushwork and focus on the subtleties of the locale rather than on the falls itself indicate the continued influence of Constable's paintings. *Bash*

Plate 1. Kensett

View from Richmond Hill

c. 1843–45

oil on canvas, 13 x 19⅛ in. (33 x 48.6 cm.)

Private Collection

FIGURE 20.
Kensett, Tintern Abbey,
1841, *pencil on paper,* 10⅛ *x*
13½ *in. (25.7 x 34.2 cm.),*
Babcock Galleries, New York.

Bish Falls (1855; Plate 10), one of Kensett's finest woodland scenes, also evokes dramatic lighting effects, rich and vigorous paint surfaces, and an immediacy reminiscent of Constable.

The painters from whom Kensett drew inspiration in the early 1840s suggest a lineage which provided the context for Kensett's own efforts to establish himself as a landscape painter: from Claude, Titian and Canaletto, and the Dutch landscape painters, to their descendant, Constable. The tradition of painting this lineage established provided a basis from which Kensett composed many major works of the 1850s.

Kensett supplemented his study of Old Masters with his dedication to drawing. He often drew from nature in the woods near Windsor Castle and frequently sketched at Fontainebleau. In Paris he took classes at the Ecole Préparation des Beaux-Arts where he spent evenings drawing from plaster casts and from life. At the Louvre he found affirmation of his devotion to drawing:

> *In the rooms where the drawings are collected—I have thus far experienced more pleasure in the examination of these splendid trophies of the genius of bygone spirits—here exhibiting itself in all their native vigour and freshness—than in many of their most finished compositions—Rubens-Michael Angelo-Veronese-Claude Lorrain-Titian.*[19]

Some months later he wrote of "devoting my time evenly to drawing. . . . I have made some progress in that very important department of art."[20]

In September 1841 Kensett and Casilear returned to England from Paris for a month-long sketching tour, the first significant expedition of that kind in Kensett's career and the prototype for his activity of thirty summers to come. Summer tours of country locales resulted in sketches and studies that could be used during winter months as sources for paintings. Today several hundred of his pencil sketches, some of them signed, attest to the value he placed on them.

The sketching tours Kensett undertook were important to him, not only because they provided an opportunity to hone his drawing skills and accumulate subject matter, but especially because they afforded the artist regular contact with nature. Early in his career, Kensett dedicated himself to "carrying on a steady course of study from nature."[21] He believed that the closer one was to nature, the closer one would be to truth, and he judged the work of other artists according to its fidelity to nature.[22] This belief had a religious foundation. Kensett was a Romantic to the extent that he viewed nature as the embodiment of divinity; he was a transcendentalist insofar as he had confidence in man's power to perceive the holiness of Creation. Kensett's belief in a tripartite union of God, nature, and man is symbolized by a small packet of pressed flowers he picked at the tomb of Jean-Jacques Rousseau on 22 September 1847 and preserved for the rest of his life.[23]

The itinerary of Kensett's 1841 tour of England included Kenilworth and Warwick Castles, Stratford upon Avon, Cheltenham, Tintern Abbey, Salisbury, and Netly Abbey, all sites associated with the romantic images of earlier times. The ruin in his *Tintern Abbey* (1841; Fig. 20) is covered with ivy and overgrowth, a sentimental evocation of man's past in the eternal cycle of nature. The architecture is the focus of attention, presented as a vignette isolated in the center of the page and delineated with the sharp detail expected of an engraver. Kensett was still treating his pencil as a burin, but in the next several months his drawing hand would loosen considerably. The spare use of outlines to indicate the presence of the surrounding hills in *Tintern Abbey* places emphasis on shape over form and strikes an important note for Kensett's future work.

In 1843 Kensett returned to locales he and his companions had sketched earlier: Richmond, Hampton Court, and Windsor Castle. His sketches from this year of *Eton School* (Fig. 21) and *Windsor Castle from the Park* (Fig. 22) now confidently cover the entire page with a livelier and more fluid line, indicating the artist's greater self-assurance. The drawings' Claudian compositional design, which balances lateral tree groups and central coulisse, augurs that of Kensett's major landscape paintings of the early 1850s. A strong sense of composition, as seen in *View from Richmond Hill,* is evident in the sophisticated manner in which foreground, middle ground, and distant elements effectively balance form and weight. Freed from the unforgiving metal plate, Kensett revelled in the graphic richness and variety possible on the soft and tactile paper of his sketch pad. These drawings were a revelation even to Ken-

FIGURE 24.
Kensett, Capri, 1847, *pencil on paper*, 11¾ x 18⅜ *in.* (29.8 x 46.7 cm.), *Dan Flavin, N.Y.*

sett, as he later recalled: "My real life commenced there, in the study of the stately woods of Windsor, and the famous beeches of Burnham and the lovely and fascinating landscape that surrounds them."[24]

After five years in Europe, Kensett's financial woes were alleviated somewhat by his receipt of a small inheritance from the estate of his grandmother, Sarah Kensett Newbury. This allowed him to make his long-awaited trip to Rome. On 26 July 1845, in the company of Champney, he departed Paris by diligence and reached the Rhine at Remagen four days later. From there they traveled upriver to Basel, passed through Switzerland, and eleven weeks after leaving Paris Kensett arrived in Rome. The trip had been both exhilarating and exhausting. He arrived in Rome suffering from a severely inflamed arthritic condition that confined him to bed for several weeks. Thomas Hicks, a young portrait painter recently come from America, attended him until the malady subsided. They shared a studio on the Via Margutta and thereafter were lifelong friends.

Kensett's plan for his journey to Rome had been "to sketch and paint scenery from nature, fill our portfolio with valuable materials and once snugly located either in Florence or Rome [make] choices of the best to paint for exhibitions at home, or for such travellers as may be disposed to purchase on the spot."[25] And indeed, the sketchbook studies he accumulated reveal the fresh and vital draftsmanship he had developed. *Stolzenfels* (1845; Fig. 23) is typical of these sketches. Here the vigorous handling of foreground motifs dissipates to a faint articulation of distant hills. Foreground lines in all these sketches are clean and lively, while the engraver's stipplelike technique is fluently employed to delineate the background. Kensett later would adapt this approach to the touches of paint that form the edges of hills in his Shrewsbury River paintings.

Kensett's drawings of 1845 articulate the assertion of shape over three-dimensional form evident in his earliest drawings and so important in his later paintings. This tendency in his drawings culminated in the fine *Capri* in 1847 (Fig. 24). The spacious areas of water and sky, silhouettelike motifs, and strong linear character of this fine drawing anticipate Kensett's *Beacon Rock, Newport Harbor* (1857; plate 20), *View from Cozzens' Hotel near West Point* (1863; plate 32), and *Lake George* (1869; plate 33).

In Rome Kensett was at last in the recognized center of the art world. His friend George Curtis

FIGURE 25.
Kensett, Standing Artist, *c. 1845–47, pencil and water-color on gray paper, 11⁵/₁₆ x 8⅝ in. (28.6 x 21 cm.), National Museum of American Art, Smithsonian Institution, Washington, D.C.*

FIGURE 26.
Kensett, Standing Monk Holding a Staff, *c. 1845–47, pencil on gray paper, 9⅞ x 6¾ in. (25 x 17.2 cm.), Susan and Herbert Adler.*

FIGURE 27.
Kensett, Huntsman with Rifle, *c. 1845–47, pencil and watercolor on tan paper, 11½ x 8½ in. (29.2 x 21 cm.), Babcock Galleries, New York.*

recounted that Kensett enjoyed visits to historic sites such as the Colosseum and Villa Borghese gardens and often watched "the sun setting and St. Peter's steeped in rosy light."[26] But the city's rich architecture did not move him to paint it, as it did his colleagues Cole, Brown, Cropsey, and Gifford. His studies of plants and landscape scenery in which ruins are present always subordinate the architectural subject to its surroundings.[27]

As he had in Paris, Kensett attended art classes in Rome, where he made pencil and watercolor studies of live models in authentic provincial costumes. His fellow artists may also have served as subjects (Fig. 25). These popular evening classes provided the thirty or forty artists in attendance with a source for types and costume designs.[28] *Standing Monk Holding a Staff* (c. 1845–47; Fig. 26) and the so-called *Huntsman with Rifle* (c. 1845–47; Fig. 27) exemplify Kensett's efforts from this class. Their subsequent use in his painting *The Shrine—A Scene in Italy* (1857; Plate 2) demonstrates how Kensett crystallized his motifs and technique in studies before committing them to form in an oil painting. The fact that pencil studies do exist for a number of his paintings from the 1850s, including a sketch for *Camel's Hump from the Western Shore of Lake Champlain* (1848; Fig. 52), indicates that Kensett later continued to rely on this process.

The Shrine—A Scene in Italy is a kind of *veduta ideata*, or imaginary view, in which the classical composition conveys religious and philosophical sentiments. The reverent woman and child kneeling before a roadside shrine, the monk, and the shepherd with his flock are symbolic of the inherent religious conviction Kensett brought to his landscape painting. The ruins of a pagan civilization, Christian shrine, and distant hilltop villa signal the Romantics' belief in man's continuity in a harmonious natural setting.

Claude Lorrain was the inspiration for Kensett's compositional design. The large mass of trees on the left countered by a smaller and more fragile arboreal grouping on the right, and the dissipation of forms in an aerial perspective of atmospheric light and palpable haze, are standard Claudian devices. The ruins punctuating the middle ground, as well as the shepherd and flock, also recall Claude's *Land-*

FIGURE 28.
Claude Lorrain (1600–1682),
Landscape with Narcissus and
Echo, 1644, *oil on canvas,*
37⅜ x 46½ in. (94.5 x 118
cm.), National Gallery of Art,
London.

scape with Narcissus and Echo (1644; Fig. 28), which Kensett had seen at the National Gallery in London.

The delicacy of finish, reserved palette, and schematic use of browns, greens, and blues to suggest, respectively, foreground, middle ground, and background areas are Dutch influences. In the foreground, the detailed representation of the stones, broadleaf plants, and thin dead branches just touched by highlights recall the lively contrasts Constable registered in the interaction of foreground details and more generalized panoramic views. This detailing gave the viewer a starting point at which to enter the broad expanse of space and scenery represented in the painting.

The Shrine was the fulfillment of all that Kensett had hoped to achieve as a result of his European studies. In July 1847, after a spring sketching tour to Naples, he left Rome for Florence, Venice, and Verona and then made his way back to London through Geneva and Paris. In England he learned that the 1847 edition of the *London Art Union Annual* bore an engraved illustration of his painting *A Peep at Windsor Castle from St. Leonard's* (now unlocated). News soon followed that a Mr. S. Taylor, one of the Art Union's prize holders, had acquired the painting. These events, along with three commissions Kensett had received while in Italy, boded well for the future, and he eagerly anticipated his return home. On 3 November 1847, he boarded a steamer bound for New York, almost exactly seven and a half years to the day of leaving America.

Any lingering doubts Kensett may have harbored for his future as an artist were quickly dissipated by the enthusiastic reception accorded him in New York. The ready sales of his paintings, critical approval of the press, and his election to the National Academy of Design constituted what his good friend George Curtis called "a series of noiseless victories"[29] that established Kensett's reputation. Kensett exhibited five paintings at the spring 1848 National Academy exhibition, and two of them, including *The Shrine*, were purchased by a Mr. Ives of Providence. At the same time the New York press acclaimed his pictures:

Plate 2. Kensett

The Shrine—A Scene in Italy

1847

oil on canvas, 30⅜ x 41⅝ in. (77.1 x 105.7 cm.)

Mr. and Mrs. Maurice N. Katz, Naples, Fla.

FIGURE 29.
Kensett, Winter Sports, 1848,
*oil on canvas, 18 x 24 in.
(45.7 x 61 cm.), Chase Manhattan Bank, New York.*

Mr. Kensett has benefited much by foreign study. His landscapes have surprised us by their excellence, and we do not hesitate to pronounce them the best in the exhibition. This is high praise when the pictures of so many older hands hang upon the walls, but it is sincere. He has his faults, doubtless, and in many particulars, the landscapes of Mr. Durand are superior—in drawing, in handling, in the rotundity of foliage, and perhaps in practical conception, but in general excellence, we think Mr. Kensett has surpassed him, for his pictures savor less of mannerism and the conventionalities of art, and more of the unstudied freedom and largeness of nature.[30]

These overt manifestations of his public success were followed by a growing self-confidence that permitted the luxury of turning down some sales. Kensett wrote J. W. Moore of the American Art-Union, "The offer of $250. for my picture Distant View of the Mansfield Mountain, Vermont, I must beg leave respectfully to decline ($300. with frame affording me but a fair remuneration)."[31] In 1848 he sold at least twelve paintings ranging from $25 to $250. The following year he sold two paintings in England, recorded nearly a dozen sales to collectors in America, and placed several with the Art-Union, including *Winter Sports* (1848; Fig. 29) and *Lake Nemi* (unlocated) for which he received $200.[32] Kensett clearly had gained recognition as one of the most promising landscape painters in America. He was to be among the most prominent artists in New York for the next quarter century.

II. Kensett's Landscapes: A Decade of Change

I long to get amid the scenery of my own country for it abounds with the picturesque, the grand, and the beautiful—to revel among the striking scenes which a bountiful hand has spread over its wide-extended and almost boundless territory.

—KENSETT, 16 DECEMBER 1844[33]

THE AMERICA TO WHICH KENSETT RETURNED IN 1847 was steeped in the spirit of Jacksonian Democracy, transcendentalism, and a program of territorial expansionism—Manifest Destiny—under the determined leadership of President James K. Polk. At the heart of this consciousness was a belief, summarized by William Cullen Bryant's "A Forest Hymn" and Ralph Waldo Emerson's "Nature," in the American wilderness as the source and embodiment of the country's deepest spiritual and demo-cratic values. Manifest Destiny legitimized the concept that God had granted Americans the solemn responsibility of impressing "the likeness of your moral character" upon the land.[34] The historian Frederick Jackson Turner perceived the American belief that the land, abundant in provisions for a wise people, was the source of democracy and harmonious society.[35] Implicit in this ideology was a confidence in the amiable rapport between the "wide extended and almost boundless" land and the enlightened individuals who civilized it.

The leading landscape painters of the period, Cole and Durand, were committed to the idea that the unspoiled landscape, if contemplated with sufficient devotion, had the power to convey religious, philosophical, didactic, and even therapeutic meaning. Peter Marzio has shown that many painters felt compelled by a moral imperative, that "art crusaders" viewed the natural scenery of America as the "source for democratic art," and that there was a "serious attempt by professional artists to educate the untrained populace . . . of a political democracy . . . to build an artistic democracy of citizen artists."[36]

Embedded in these artists' belief in the religious and moral content of the landscape was a notion of the sublime informed by intellectual and artistic writings of the period. This was a sublime of peace, quiet, and harmony. The transcendentalist philosophy inspired by Emerson and Thoreau, combined with the works of authors such as Bryant, Washington Irving, and John Ruskin, contributed to perva-sive attitudes that were to influence a generation of thinkers before the Civil War. Irving had declared in his *Sketch Book* that "Never need the American look beyond his own country for the sublime and beautiful of natural scenery," and Ruskin stated in *Modern Painters* that "God is not in the earthquake, nor in the fire, but in the still small voice."[37] An article in the *New York Mirror* of 4 May 1837 neatly summarized the spirit of the generation:

There are times when the gentle influences of the country more strongly impress us; there are days, . . . when the woods and fields possess a hallowing, tranquillizing power, which banishes every unholy thought, obliterates care, subdues the passions, and as it throws a Sabbath over the mind, causes us to bless with gratitude the love that made the earth so fair.[38]

Kensett was deeply sympathetic to such an idealistic love of nature, and his paintings express a confidence in democracy and a fundamental belief in "that beautiful harmony in which God has created the universe."[39] Harmony is central to Kensett's notion of the sublime. His desire was to immerse himself in what he called the immortal influence of God's bountiful hand to be found in "great nature's handiwork," America.[40] Concurrently, the decade following his return from Europe was a period of growth, experimentation, and change for Kensett, a prelude to the final years of his career in which he would define a personal and evocative style.

In 1826, Robert Gilmore, Jr., one of Cole's patrons, had expressed his preference for "real American scenes,"[41] and by 1850 that preference had become pervasive among patrons and public alike. Kensett had by this time developed his technical and artistic skills to the point where they served his need to portray the sublime harmony between America's landscape and its inhabitants, and his own need matched popular demand for pictures of native American scenery (see Plate 3).

In the summer of 1850 Kensett and his friends Champney and Casilear made a sketching tour of the White Mountains. Champney recalled that in the vicinity of Bridgeton and Fryberg, Maine, "we caught our first view of the air-drawn lines of the Mount Washington Range."[42] On 8 July Kensett made his first known sketch of Mount Washington and began formulating his ideas for the most ambitious painting he had yet undertaken, a canvas of 40 by 60 inches that would embody his philosophical and artistic beliefs.

The White Mountains—From North Conway of 1851 (Plate 4) cogently summarizes Kensett's ideas about landscape painting, in particular the consonant relationship between man and nature. In the next few years, Kensett stepped from the sphere of influence of the Old Masters and of Cole and Durand. His ideas about painting underwent changes demonstrated by the dramatic differences between the stagelike, narrative composition and bright palette of *October Day in the White Mountains* of 1854 (Plate 5) and the simplified, almost abstract design and cool palette of *Shrewsbury River* of 1856 (Fig. 61). His attitudes about nature and man did not undergo significant alteration, however, but only became more refined as he sought to express himself in an increasingly personal idiom. As one of the most powerful expressions of the sublime harmony between nature and man to come from the ranks of American landscape painters at mid-century, *The White Mountains—From North Conway* looms as a keystone in the development of ideas expressed through landscape painting in America.

The North Conway painting has a conventional Claudian tripartite composition, in which the viewer looks down a low, gently sloping foreground hill into the flat plain of the middle ground valley flanked by stands of trees and mountain ridges. In the background stands the tall, massive peak of Mount Washington. This arrangement suggests a natural amphitheater in which the scene's activity occurs. Kensett supplemented this compositional design with a traditional Renaissance perspective system, enhanced by tonal gradations in which lighter values imply greater distance. The spectator's entry into the scene is facilitated by a series of *repoussoir* devices in the foreground: a diagonally placed log, arrangements of rocks, shadows, and a path set with framing trees. These foreground elements give the viewer a sense of direct contact with the scene. Taken as a whole, the composition of *North Conway* reveals Kensett's thorough understanding of Claude's compositional symmetry.

As the specificity of the painting's title suggests, the scene so perfectly embodied the ideas Kensett wished to express that he felt he could paint it without improving upon the view before him. It exem-

Plate 3. Kensett

A Holiday in the Country

1851

oil on canvas, 21 x 30 in. (53.3 x 76.2 cm.)

On extended loan to the Columbus Museum of Art, Ohio,

from the collection of Mr. and Mrs. W. Knight Sturges

Plate 4. Kensett
The White Mountains—From North Conway
1851
oil on canvas, 40 x 60 in. (101.6 x 152.4 cm.)
Wellesley College Museum, Wellesley, Mass.,
Gift of Mrs. James B. Munn (Ruth C. Hanford, '09) in the name of the class of 1909

FIGURE 30.
Frederic E. Church (1826–1900), Intervale at North Conway, c. 1856, oil on canvas, 13½ x 19¾ in. (34.3 x 50.1 cm.), Private Collection.

plified what Champney called "the beau ideal of a certain kind of scenery—a combination of the wild and the cultivated, the bold and graceful . . . the quiet beauty of the little village. . . . The inhabitants are sober—pious—well disposed and have all gone to church. . . . Not even a bird dare sing."[43] Benjamin Willey said of the scene that "One feels, in standing on the green plain . . . that he is not in any country of New Hampshire . . . but in a world of pure beauty—the adytum of the temple where God is to be worshipped as the infinite artist, in joy."[44] Five years after Kensett, Durand visited the site and wrote that the scene formed "a beautiful composition without need of change or adaption,"[45] and it was to have a similar effect on Church, who painted a nearly identical view, *Intervale at North Conway*, about 1856 (Fig. 30).

Kensett's perception of the site's natural perfection and tranquility is conveyed through technical means. The smooth brushwork—nearly imperceptible in the sky—subtle tonal modulations, and compositional balance are the visual equivalents of stopped motion, silence, and stability. Kensett carefully selected the setting, time of day, and meteorologic conditions to portray the scene isolated in time and space. All elements, actions, and feelings radiate unanimity and tranquility. Traditional signs of civilization's contact with nature—tree stumps, axes, plows, railroads—are absent from his scenes because they were not compatible with his peaceful and passive vision. This vision, clearly expressed in the North Conway picture, would be consistently reiterated in subsequent works throughout Kensett's career.

The notion of man's "civilizing effect" on nature—the idea that the American people could chop down trees, clear fields, and build roads, factories, and cities without doing harm to the primordial nature they proclaimed divine—was a paradox central to the age. Unlike many of his peers, Kensett portrayed an American Eden, where nature and civilization interact in perfect harmony. In *The White Mountains—From North Conway*, a cultivated garden is set at the periphery of the wilderness, with fields in the intervale, sheep in the meadows, and a contemplative figure lounging on the hillside. The fine, neat houses indicate man's prosperity in the midst of this inspiring, benevolent scene. The spire of

FIGURE 31.
*James Smillie (1807–1885)
after Kensett*, Mount Washington from the Valley of Conway, 1851, *engraving,
7 x 10⅜ in. (17.8 x 26.4
cm.), American Antiquarian
Society, Worcester, Mass.*

the Baptist church rises adjacent to the tower of the academy, testifying to the endurance of religion and learning even in this remote country setting. As Alexis de Tocqueville had noted, "The man you left behind in New York you find again in almost impenetrable solitude: . . . you enter this cabin which seems the asylum of all miseries, but the owner wears the same clothes as you, he speaks the language of the cities. On his rude table are books and newspapers."[46]

Kensett's portrayal carries the conviction of the American people's unique destiny in the new land, unencumbered by the ideas and environment of the Old World. An anonymous reviewer of the 1852 exhibition of the National Academy of Design, in praising Kensett's landscapes, noted that

> *American landscape must by its very nature be very different from that of any other country . . . the artist in [America] looks to the free, unbroken wilderness for the highest expression of the new world motive, and thence with some mingling of human sympathy to the clearing and the log-cabin; . . . the strongest feeling of the American is to that which is new and fresh—to the freedom of the grand old forest—to the energy of the wild life. He may look with interest to the ruins of Italy, but with enthusiasm to the cabin of the pioneer; to that in which our country excels all others, the grandeur of its natural scenes—its boundless expanses and the magnitude of objective.*[47]

The nationalistic element comes through quite clearly in *The White Mountains—From North Conway*. Rising in patriarchal glory above the scene is the image of the great snow-covered mountain that bears the name of the *pater patria* of the United States: Washington.

Thus, in this topographically correct depiction, nature assumes the role of a religious and national shrine, infused with the self-confident spirit of democracy. This was new in American landscape painting, and it extended Kensett's reputation to a broad and sympathetic public. The American Art-Union acquired the painting and had it engraved for its more than thirteen thousand subscribers by James Smillie with the title *Mount Washington from the Valley of Conway* (1851; Fig. 31). Later the view

Plate 5. Kensett
   October Day in the White Mountains
   1854
   oil on canvas, 31⅜ x 48⅜ in. (80 x 123.5 cm.)
   The Cleveland Museum of Art,
   John L. Severance Fund and gift of various donors

Plate 6. Kensett

Hudson River Scene

1857

oil on canvas, 32 x 48 in. (81.3 x 121.9 cm.)

The Metropolitan Museum of Art, New York,

Gift of H. D. Babcock, in memory of S. D. Babcock, 1907

reached an even wider popular audience through a Currier and Ives print. In 1893 Champney said that Kensett's picture "interested artists and others in our mountain scenery. So much so that the next season many artists followed in our wake."[48]

The artistic concerns Kensett expressed in the North Conway painting remained important to him throughout the early 1850s and presaged the development of his personal style in the later part of the decade and into the 1860s. The artist experimented with various subject matter, compositions, and techniques, but certain elements already evident in *North Conway* continued to occupy him. Subtle tonal modulations, smooth paint surface, and linear balance, for example, also function together to isolate time and action and submerge discordant factors in *Hudson River Scene* (1857; Plate 6), *View from Cozzens' Hotel near West Point*, and *Mount Chocorua* (1864–66; Plate 15). In these paintings, as well as *October Day in the White Mountains*, leisurely society is set in charming arcadian vistas cast in a bell jar world. Kensett's refined technique, bucolic scenery, and tranquil figures permeate his work with a serenity that signals the poetry of his vision.

A noticeable change in Kensett's landscapes of the 1850s was the movement toward a distillation of fully rounded forms into more thoroughly abstract shapes. The progression of this change is evident in three important paintings of the 1850s: *North Conway, October Day in the White Mountains*, and *Hudson River Scene*. The hardness and substantiality of Mount Washington in the 1851 North Conway picture gave way in *October Day* of 1854 to a sense of a physical presence, suffused with soft light, hovering in the mist. Laden with moisture, the atmosphere loses the transparency of the earlier picture and gains a tactile or, as Durand put it, "palpable" quality. By 1857 the atmosphere in Kensett's painting was once again transparent. In *Hudson River Scene*, the atmosphere assumes a clarity reminiscent of *North Conway*. The atmospherically diffuse light of Kensett's 1854 and 1855 paintings becomes bright and hard in works of 1856 and 1857. This sharp clarity emphasizes the preference for hard edges over ample volumetric form. In *North Conway*, two mountain ridges enter the composition from the right side and are painted as flat overlapping shapes with crisp contours. This establishes not only Kensett's method for defining spatial relationships through parallel planes, but also his tendency to distill landscape forms to their basic emotive shapes.

From the time Kensett returned to the United States from Europe in 1847, until 1856 when he again went back to England, his primary frame of reference for American landscape painting was the work of Cole and Durand, and their successors Frederic Church, Jasper Cropsey, George Inness, and Sanford Gifford. Church was ten years younger than Kensett, but still of the same artistic generation. He had worked under Cole's tutelage for a time, and during the mid- to late 1840s was gaining his own reputation as a landscape painter. Two of his paintings, *West Rock, New Haven* (1849; Fig. 32) and *New England Scenery* (1851; Fig. 33), had attracted considerable notice. The former met with critical success at the 1849 exhibition of the National Academy of Design, and the latter at the 1852 American Art-Union auction.

West Rock, New Haven shares with Kensett's North Conway painting a fidelity to a specific locale and a stable composition, and also conveys Kensett's concern with the coexistence of American industriousness and nature's divine bounty. These factors figured in the painting's popular reception and suggest a possible predecessor for Kensett's *North Conway*. But there are critical differences between the two works. Kensett's painting is imbued with a sense of tranquility, optimism, and harmony;

FIGURE 32.
*Frederic E. Church (1826–
1900), West Rock, New
Haven, 1849, oil on canvas,
26½ x 40 in. (66.7 x 101.6
cm.), New Britain Museum
of American Art, Conn.,
John Butler Talcott Fund.*

FIGURE 33.
*Frederic E. Church (1826–
1900), New England Scen-
ery, 1851, oil on canvas, 36 x
54 in. (91.4 x 137.1 cm.),
George Walter Vincent
Smith Art Museum, Spring-
field, Mass.*

Church's image is less certain in its evocation of man's relationship to nature. The resourcefulness of the farmers laboring in the fields in Church's picture is compromised by the shadow of a large cloud that virtually encompasses the field, threatening rain and the spoilage of the crop. Nature is not always accommodating, in Church's view. Kensett's meadows, by contrast, typically are drenched in munificent sunshine and figures are never seen toiling. When human figures appear in Kensett's pictures, as in *North Conway*, they are finished with their work, engaged in recreation, or contemplating nature. The church spire in Church's picture suggests the religiousness of civilization, but Kensett indicates a more diverse blend of religious and intellectual ideals. The serenity of his scenes is intended to stimulate not only a reverence for Creation but also a heightened sense of the high intellectual and moral

principles it embodied. The concept of civilization in the wilderness suggested by Kensett's rendition of the village houses integrated into the natural setting suggests a confidence not even hinted at by Church. Kensett and Church held similar convictions about nature and the American people, but Kensett possessed a breadth of thought that Church, brilliant but young, was yet to match.

Church's *New England Scenery*, painted the same year as *North Conway*, also suggests a kinship between the two artists in its title, rural setting, and panoramic view. Each artist employed a precise drawing technique to convey a clarity of vision and presentation, and each produced paintings which celebrated nature, the individual, and the new nation's expansion into the virginal land. Both paintings depict "a pristine Yankee Arcadia, a thriving agrarian paradise."[49] However, Church's *New England Scenery* differs from Kensett's *North Conway* in one crucial aspect: it is an invented scene, a composite of several different places. *New England Scenery* was a popular painting and possessed superior technical qualities, but it nonetheless lacked the kind of authenticity and fidelity to nature central to Kensett's art. Precocious Church had yet to step away from the imaginary, allegorical mode of Cole, just as Kensett was yet to step entirely out of the shadow of an equally important mentor, Asher B. Durand.

Like *New England Scenery*, Jasper Cropsey's *American Harvesting* (Fig. 34), also of 1851, portrays a bucolic landscape while at the same time indicating the artist's ambivalence regarding civilization's relationship to the wilderness. The verdant woods are in deep, forbidding shadow, while the cultivated wheat field is enshrined in sunlight. Furthermore, the woods are separated from the fields by a man-made rail fence, which separates the civilized landscape from the wilderness. The tree stumps indicate that man has already begun to transgress the border. This painting, like those of Church, stands in contrast to the harmonious integration of man and nature in Kensett's *North Conway*.

In a similar manner, Inness' *Lackawanna Valley* (1855; Fig. 35) and Gifford's *Twilight on Hunter Mountain* (1866; Fig. 36) demonstrate further that Kensett's unambiguous vision was not universally shared by his fellow landscape artists. In Inness' picture, as in Kensett's, a reclining, contemplative figure is identified with a small stand of trees. However, the countless foreground tree stumps, the partitioning of the scene by fences, and the steamy activity of trains and factories present the figure, and the viewer,

with a much less congenial image of progress than Kensett. Gifford's poignant view of Hunter Mountain, painted in the middle of the next decade, documents the price progress extracts from the wilderness, making similar use of tree stumps and fences, and penetrating the scene with a spectral twilight that haunts the image. The ragged tree stumps and dim light of Gifford's work are far removed from the cultivated fields and bright noontime light Kensett preferred. If, as James Jackson Jarvis said, "Gifford . . . saw the landscape through stained glass,"[50] then Kensett saw it through clear panes set in a Palladian frame.

At this point in his career, Kensett still felt the pull of Cole's influence. He shared with Cole a belief in art as an instrument for conveying the fundamental link between beauty and morality. Cole had expressed this belief in several "real American scenes" such as *The Ox Bow* (1836; Fig. 37) and *The Notch of the White Mountains* (1837; Fig. 38). But from the late 1820s until his death, "it was landscape painting of a more overtly allegorical, literary, and moralizing sort that . . . occupied his thought and

FIGURE 37.
Thomas Cole (1801–1848),
The Ox Bow, 1836, *oil on
canvas, 51½ x 76 in. (130.2 x
193 cm.), The Metropolitan
Museum of Art, New York,
Gift of Mrs. Russell Sage,*
1908

FIGURE 38.
Thomas Cole (1801–1848),
The Notch of the White
Mountains, 1837, *oil on can-
vas, 40 x 61 in. (101.6 x 156
cm.), National Gallery of Art,
Washington, D.C., Andrew
W. Mellon Fund,* 1967.

time,"[51] and he had little interest in painting landscape per se. Cole was ambivalent regarding the bal-ance of real and ideal in man's moral character, and this forced his hand toward imaginative expressions. In such allegorically conceived scenes as *Expulsion from the Garden of Eden* (1827–28; Fig. 39), or his series pictures *The Course of Empire* (1836; New-York Historical Society) and *The Voyage of Life* (1839–40; Munson-Williams-Proctor Institute), landscape plays an important but supporting role in relation to the narrative.

Kensett was at once more optimistic and more introspective than Cole, regarding both the future of nature's bounty and the enlightened nature of the individual. He was more comfortable with the dual pull of the real and ideal and was able to move back and forth with some equanimity between such realistic images as *Camel's Hump from the Western Shore of Lake Champlain* of 1852 (Plate 7) and the

FIGURE 39.
Thomas Cole (1801–1848),
Expulsion from the Garden
of Eden, 1827–28, *oil on
canvas, 39 x 54 in. (99 x
137.2 cm.), Museum of Fine
Arts, Boston, M. and M.
Karolik Collection.*

FIGURE 40.
Kensett, White Mountain
Scene, 1853, *oil on canvas,
48 x 72½ in. (121.9 x 184.2
cm.), Virginia Steele Scott
Foundation, Henry E. Hunt-
ington Library and Art
Gallery, San Marino, Calif.*

idealized *White Mountain Scene* of the next year (Fig. 40). Where Cole saw grandeur in the dying limb, decaying trunk, or lightening-blasted tree stump, Kensett venerated the perfectly formed tree, standing regally as an exemplar of its kind.

Plate 7. Kensett

Camel's Hump from *the Western Shore of Lake Champlain*

1852

oil on canvas, 31 x 45 in. (78.7 x 114.3 cm.)

High Museum of Art, Atlanta,

Gift of Virginia Carroll Crawford

Plate 8. Kensett

Conway Valley, *New Hampshire*

1854

oil on canvas, 32¾ x 48 in. (81.2 x 122 cm.)

Worcester Art Museum, Worcester, Mass.

Kensett's technical approach also differed from Cole's. As a matter of practice, Cole composed a painting from a variety of sketches, sometimes taken from different sources, until he achieved the thematic spirit for a scene. For Kensett the landscape itself evoked its specific sentiment, and his scenes are more literal. In composing his thematic paintings, Cole employed restless yet fluid and facile brushwork, a colorful palette, nervous, broken line, selective light of dramatic contrasts, and fully rounded forms to express the universality of the American landscape. Kensett, by contrast, painted quite specific scenes, which in comparison with Cole's landscapes are more taciturn, the brush strokes more technically proficient than facile, the muted palette more reserved in its hues and values, and the light more pervasive. The sense of quiet and inwardness conveyed in these scenes are indicative of the personality of the artist who painted them.

Cole's influence on Kensett is most visible in his 1854 painting of *Conway Valley, New Hampshire* (Plate 8), which is reminiscent of Cole's *Ox Bow* of eight years earlier. Kensett appropriated from Cole the device of a rotting tree limb in the foreground, as well as the ominous cloud moving in above the hills, the high, windswept prospect overlooking a placid, light-filled valley, and the animated foreground tree. Most important is the mood of the picture: Kensett here captures the same sense of impending change in nature that Cole loved so much and painted so often. Kensett departed from Cole chiefly in his palette. Cole's painting contains a wide range of hues which vigorously assert the contrasts of light, weather, form, and distance. Kensett, on the other hand, developed rich browns, greens, and grays according to their range of values and saturations. Such exploration of color was to take him beyond the influence of both Cole and Durand to his own discoveries and practices.

Kensett's landscapes of the early 1850s, especially *North Conway*, *White Mountain Scene*, *Adirondack Scenery* (1854; Plate 9), and *Bash Bish Falls* (Plate 10) reveal that his closest artistic and spiritual tie at that time was with Durand. Yet Kensett was more interested in the confluence of man's will and nature's purpose than was Durand, who believed that a landscape "will be great in proportion as it declares the glory of God, by representation of his works, and not those of man."[52] Durand's paintings focus on nature's role in expressing the character and will of God to man, "in revealing the deep meaning of the real creation around and within us."[53]

Durand did at times use human figures and activites in his landscape views, as can be seen in *The Beeches* (1845; Fig. 41), and *Sunday Morning* (1860; Fig. 42). However, in *The Beeches* the lush vegetation, moss-jacketed trees, and warm yellow light of closing day combine to convey a declaration of the glory of God. Durand, like Church, was less certain of man's role. The shepherd passes through the scene and is caught midway between the church spire rising amid the background trees and the tree stump in the foreground. These monuments to, respectively, man's reverence for and plunder of nature indicate an equivocation not generally found in Kensett's work.

The affinity between the two artists is displayed in Kensett's *White Mountain Scene* and Durand's *Landscape with Birches* (c. 1855; Fig. 43). Kensett wrote of the "striking scenes which a bountiful hand has spread over [America]," revealing his own belief in the divine inspiration of nature.[54] It was paralleled by Durand's idea that the beauty and grandeur of nature was God's doing: "The Great Designer of these glorious pictures has placed them before us as types of the Divine attributes."[55] These paintings share a pious appreciation of natural forms. Their focus upon the broad expanse of panoramic

Plate 9. Kensett

Adirondack Scenery

1854

oil on canvas, 40 x 59⅞ in. (101.6 x 152.1 cm.)

Hirschl and Adler Galleries, Inc., New York

Plate 10. Kensett

Bash Bish Falls

1855

oil on canvas, 36 x 29 in. (73.6 x 91.5 cm.)

National Academy of Design, New York

FIGURE 44.
*Asher B. Durand, (1796–1886), Study from Nature:
Rocks and Trees, c. 1855, oil
on canvas, 17 x 21½ in. (43.2
x 54 cm.), The New-York
Historical Society, New York.*

views implies the harmony of the universe—a harmony emphasized in Kensett's painting by the deer at streamside and the birds soaring in the sky—and a "palpable" aerial perspective that unifies light. In their rugged terrain, luminous light, and detailed accounting of arboreal domains, these paintings exemplify each artist's desire to be true to nature and affirm his fundamental confidence in Creation's power to evoke its unseen cause.

The experimentation Kensett conducted in the early 1850s is revealed in the variety of formats he used, from the topographical panorama of *North Conway*, to the composite *White Mountain Scene*, to the intimate woodland interior of *Bash Bish Falls*. These paintings vary as much stylistically as they do compositionally. The smooth, controlled brushwork of the North Conway picture, for example, contrasts to some of Kensett's most animated and vigorous painting in *Bash Bish Falls* or its counterpart, *A Woodland Waterfall* (c. 1855; Plate 11). The close viewpoint of these two works instills an intimacy that draws the viewer directly into the shallow space to experience the artist's excitement with a scene charged with the vitality of the wilderness.

The depiction of literal forms and details in these two pictures, as well as the sympathetic evocation of nature in the combination of atmosphere, light, and color, bring to mind Durand's woodland interiors, such as *Study from Nature: Rocks and Trees* (c. 1855; Fig. 44). But Kensett's brushwork in *Bash Bish Falls* or *A Woodland Waterfall* is much more crisp, angular, and incisive, while his color is more transparent and the atmosphere clearer than Durand's. Kensett's tiny highlighting in *Bash Bish Falls* sharpens details and conveys the impression of a transparent, silvery, jewel-encrusted surface, a technique akin to Constable's. Although the plein-air immediacy of these paintings establishes a connection with Durand, who advocated sketching from nature in oils, the large size of Kensett's paintings suggest that they are studio pieces. *A Woodland Waterfall* conveys a sense of animation in the rapid brushwork, spots of individual brush strokes, varied impasto, scumbled surfaces, and pentimenti, which

FIGURE 45.
Jasper F. Cropsey (1823–1900), Niagara Falls from the Foot of Goat Island, 1857, oil on canvas, 15¼ x 24 in. (38.7 x 61 cm.), Museum of Fine Arts, Boston, M. and M. Karolik Collection.

FIGURE 46.
Frederic E. Church (1826–1900), Niagara Falls, 1857, oil on canvas, 42½ x 90½ in. (108 x 228.6 cm.), Corcoran Gallery of Art, Washington, D.C., Museum Purchase, 1876.

lend an on-the-scene immediacy. Kensett, like Durand, made oil sketches from nature, but this painting, by virtue of its size and sense of resolution, is much more than a study. If in fact it was done *sur la motif*, it would be something of an innovation in 1855, as few artists, either in America or Europe, were painting large, finished works directly from nature.

The light in these paintings has a chiaroscuro not seen in the panoramic scenes. Because of Kensett's proximity to the scene and the relatively shallow perspective, contrasts between light and dark passages are more intense. The depths of the ravine, where little or no light penetrates, are dark and quiet, while exposed areas—tree trunks, rocks, and water—are enlivened by flickering touches of white which intensify the immediacy of the bright daylight. Here Kensett's textural surfaces are more animated than those usually encountered in Durand's work. Kensett's color often tends to be more heavily tinted than his mentor's and the result is a more luminous and transparent palette.

Plate 11. Kensett
A Woodland Waterfall
c. 1855
oil on canvas, 40 x 34 in. (101.6 x 86.3 cm.)
James Maroney, New York

Plate 12. Kensett
Along the Hudson
1852
oil on canvas, 18⅛ x 24 in. (46 x 61 cm.)
National Museum of American Art,
Smithsonian Institution, Washington, D.C.,
Bequest of Helen Huntington Hull

FIGURE 47.
Kensett, Niagara Falls, 1853–
54, *oil on canvas, 33 x 48 in.*
(83.8 x 121.9 cm.), The
White House Collection,
Washington, D.C.

Kensett was rarely drawn to dramatic subjects. Nature's challenging side, its awesome or threatening aspects, were alien to his sense of harmony and the sublime. Even when he painted Niagara Falls, the natural wonder that had fascinated countless Victorian visitors with its terrifying size, irresistible force, and deafening roar, he portrayed the powerful cataract as an integral part of the larger universe.

Niagara Falls became virtually a required subject for nineteenth-century American painters. Vanderlyn had painted a close-in view of the falls, full of mist, foam, and rainbow, before 1830. Cropsey painted it from many angles and during various seasons, always with a sense of wonder (Fig. 45). Church's masterpiece gave viewers vertigo by suspending the vantage point out over the precipice of the falls (Fig. 46). Artists and writers continually tried to evoke the sensual disorientation Niagara induced.

Kensett, as might be guessed, chose to view the waterfall from a different perspective. He was not at ease with the emotional excitement it caused and moved his viewpoint back to place the cataract in the comforting context of the surrounding landscape. The effect is to diminish its magnitude. In *Niagara Falls* (1853–54; Fig. 47) we see the subject at such a distance that we can neither calculate its awesome size nor sense the motion or sound of the water.

Kensett consistently employed this vantage point in his Niagara paintings. In an oil sketch, *Niagara Falls and the Rapids* (c. 1851–52; Plate 13), he worked from a high perspective and isolated the tumultuous activity of the cataract in the left foreground. The rapids occupy the central portion of the composition, tapering off into the smooth and reflective waters of the upper river. The scene presents a

broad, flat, and tranquil plane, reaching from the viewer to the horizon without interruption. The straight horizon line emphasizes the scene's stability. By separating the viewer from the falls by a rocky ridge overgrown with trees, Kensett once again reassures us of the small place this spectacle occupies in the broader context of all Creation. In another view (Plate 14), the falls are seen from downstream, from a low vantage point behind some shoreline rocks. This view distorts size relationships and again minimizes the immensity of the falls. Kensett used a similar approach in his drawings of Niagara. Typical of these are two distant views (Figs. 48 and 49). In the former, Kensett tried to establish the compositional symmetry of his panoramic vista by balancing groups of trees on either side of a central setting encompassing the falls, with a flat plain spreading into the distance. In the latter sketch, he employed a compositional design that divides the foreground and middle ground space between an area of water

Plate 13. Kensett

Niagara Falls and the Rapids

c. 1851–52

oil on canvas, 16 x 24 in. (40.6 x 61 cm.)

Museum of Fine Arts, Boston,

M. and M. Karolik Collection

Plate 14. Kensett

Niagara Falls

c. 1851–52

oil on canvas, 17 x 24½ in. (43.1 x 62.2 cm.)

Mead Art Museum, Amherst College, Amherst, Mass.

FIGURE 50.
Kensett, Birch Tree, Niagara, *1850, pencil on paper,* $16^{5}/_{8}$ x $10^{5}/_{8}$ *in. (42.2 x 27 cm.), The Metropolitan Museum of Art, New York, Morris K. Jesup Fund, 1976.*

and another of earth. The background motifs terminate the progression of space in a way that would eventually be more fully developed in the paintings *View from Cozzens' Hotel* and *The Langdale Pike* (1858; plate 29). In both drawings, the great cataract is delineated by faint contours, which contrast with the darker, thicker, and more animated lines that articulate its surroundings. The technique enhances the diminishing effect of the viewpoint and compositional design.

Though Kensett's records indicate that he did several paintings of Niagara, those which have been located, along with the drawings, suggest that it was not a congenial subject for him. After visiting the falls on several occasions in the early 1850s, he apparently did not return or even paint the subject later. Compositionally, his Niagara paintings seem to stem more from a Claudian landscape tradition than from any vision of landscape painting Kensett was trying to develop. It is not surprising, therefore, that the best of them (Fig. 47) appealed to European taste and was purchased by the Earl of Ellesmere, who took it back to England.[56]

The finest image to come out of Kensett's Niagara experience was not a view of the falls at all. It was a drawing of a tree: *Birch Tree, Niagara* (1850; Fig. 50).[57] Of all Kensett's Niagara works, this is the most animated. The arching and twisting of the tree, the quickness with which the shading was filled in, and the dark striated lines of the trunk set against the staccato notations of leaves and bark forcefully assert Kensett's fine skills as a draftsman and excitement with his subject. That Kensett singled out this extraordinary motif and drew it with such vigor says much about his character. Confronted with Niagara Falls, Kensett retreated to a safe distance, or into the woods, making certain his feet were on solid ground, well away from the drama, noise, and compulsion of the cataract.

Like his contemporaries, Kensett traveled extensively during the summer and autumn months in search of subjects to record in on-the-spot sketches and studies done in pencil, watercolor, and oil. Great camaraderie attended these sketching expeditions. Artists frequently traveled together and enjoyed the benefits of companionship, shared enthusiasms, and criticisms of the day's work. "Flake White," a pseudonymous artist-correspondent for *The Crayon*, wrote from North Conway in 1855 that "the artists here are in the habit of calling on each other, and discussing the merits of various studies."[58] At times artists would book entire hotels, or most of the accommodations of a picturesque neighborhood, and spend weeks exploring and sketching together, sometimes in good-natured competition. Rossiter wrote to Kensett from Niagara Falls in 1852 to say that Cropsey was there. "Here then is a chance for comparison. Come back then and go to work."[59] For all the conviviality of these summer rambles, the artists also faced the hardships and privations of wilderness life. Kensett is known to have fallen in a river, traveled in hostile Indian territory, and been overcome by fatigue while in search of subjects.

Kensett sketched at various times and places with Durand, Casilear, Hicks, Champney, Cropsey, Church, Rossiter, Gifford, Regis Gignoux, and Worthington Whittredge, among others. He usually left New York City early in July and returned late in October. His favorite sites were the White Mountains of New Hampshire and along the sea coast of Massachusetts, Rhode Island, and Connecticut. His summer travels extended from the Roman *campagna* to the Rocky Mountains, from Lake Como to Lake Erie, and from the Rhine to the headwaters of the Missouri. The challenges Kensett and his companions met in order to secure on-the-scene studies, and the fact that they often used these studies as references for paintings done in the winter studio and preserved them in large numbers, indicate the importance they attached to these works.

Kensett made sketching tours every summer between 1841 and 1872, sometimes visiting several and distant locales within one season.[60] He made his first American summer-long sketching expedition in 1848, soon after his return from Europe. With his friends Casilear and Durand, he traveled up the Hudson River to Albany, then on to Saratoga, Whitehall, and the shores of Lake Champlain. They sketched in the areas of Port Kent, Keeseville, Essex, and Elizabethtown before crossing the lake to Burlington, Vermont, in mid-July. During August Kensett made several sketches of Mount Mansfield before turning south to Westport, New York, where on 25 August he caught sight of a vista that made a long-lasting impression on him: the grand profile of Camel's Hump Mountain rising four thousand feet above the flat plane of the Huntington River.

Sketching was considered central to the landscape experience. In a sketch the artist could record his perception of a scene quickly and authoritatively. *Raven Hill, Elizabethtown, Essex County, N.Y.: A Study From Nature* (1848; Fig. 51), one of his earliest American plein-air oil sketches,[61] conveys through the close view of the setting and vigorous brushwork a spontaneity that connects the spectator directly with the scene. The precise titles of his sketches seem to challenge the viewer to test the artist's fidelity to the exact locale. The purpose of the imitative exercise, however, was to allow the artist to move beyond a merely visual acquaintance with the scene to a more spiritual understanding. "It shall be your endeavor to attain as minute portraiture as possible of [your] objects," wrote Durand, "for al-

FIGURE 51.
Kensett, Raven Hill, Elizabethtown, Essex County,
N.Y.: A Study from Nature,
1848, *oil on canvas, 18 x 24
in. (45.7 x 61 cm.), Private
Collection.*

FIGURE 52.
Kensett, Camel's Hump,
Lake Champlain, 1848,
pencil on buff paper, 10½
16½ *in. (26.7 x 41.9 cm.
Dan Flavin, N.Y.*

FIGURE 53.
Asher B. Durand (1796–
1886), Kindred Spirits, 1849,
oil on canvas, 44 x 36 in. (111.7
x 91.5 *cm.*), *The New York
Public Library, Astor, Lenox
and Tilden Foundations.*

though it may be impossible to produce an absolute imitation of them, the determined effort to do so will lead you to a knowledge of their subtlest truths and characteristics." The "knowledge and facility" such studies provided would allow the artist to move toward "representation"—the "highest attainment" in art—representation being equivalent to "essential characteristic."[62]

Camel's Hump, Lake Champlain (1848; Fig. 52), a pencil study, demonstrates the same concern with locale, topography, weather, atmosphere, and light Kensett expressed in his Raven Hill oil study. The variation in line unobtrusively emphasizes contours and suggests varying qualities of light and distance. In 1852 Kensett referred to this drawing for the compositional basis of the major oil painting *Camel's Hump from the Western Shore of Lake Champlain*. In both Camel's Hump images, Kensett focuses attention on the peninsula. In the drawing he achieves this through the darkened contour and more detailed rendering. In the painting, the promontory's color and reflection in the water draw the viewer's eye. While the peninsula's primary purpose in the Camel's Hump views is the definition of spatial relationships, it also augurs the elevation of such motifs to an iconic status in Kensett's later coastal scenes.

In the summer of 1849, Kensett, Durand, and Casilear made another sketching tour together, this time to the Catskill Mountains. It, too, was a pilgrimage, for they traveled up the Hudson River to the village of Catskill, home of Thomas Cole. Cole had been their spiritual, if not artistic, leader. But his

FIGURE 54.
Kensett, Tree Study, Catskill, 1849, *pencil on buff
paper,* 17½ x 12⅛ *in.* (44.5 x
30.8 cm.), *Private Collection.*

FIGURE 55.
Kensett, Tree Study, Franconia Notch, 1850, *pencil on
paper,* 13½ x 9⅞ *in.* (34.3 x
25.1 cm.), *Babcock Galleries,
New York.*

sudden and unexpected death the year before had transferred the leadership of American landscape painters to Durand. The three friends settled in nearby Tannersville and from July through October made their studies in the midst of the scenery Cole had celebrated in the allegorical context of his own work. The presence of Kensett, Durand, and Casilear, perhaps the best-known landscape painters in America at that time, sketching in Cole's neighborhood the year after his death was both poignant and symbolic. Durand, who had known Cole for more than twenty years, was then at work on what would be the most famous painting to memorialize his colleague: *Kindred Spirits* (1849; Fig. 53). Although Kensett and Casilear had known Cole less well, this pilgrimage into the master's domain must have had personal significance for their own ideas and aspirations as well.

While the Camel's Hump drawing served as the foundation for a finished oil, Kensett also made innumerable pencil sketches of isolated elements in nature—often a single tree—which he undoubtedly referred to for details in subsequent paintings. *Tree Study, Catskill* (1849; Fig. 54) was done on this tour and is representative of the detailed drawings made on all of his summer excursions. *Tree Study, Franconia Notch* (1850; Fig. 55), *Franconia Notch* (1850; Fig. 56), *Elm* (1862; Fig. 57), and *Chicago Lake* (1870; Fig. 58) are further examples of this kind of drawing, and they illustrate Durand's distinction between the needs and advantages of "imitation" in art and the higher calling of "representation." In the case of a tree, Durand asserted, the artist cannot reasonably imitate the leaves as he would the trunk or a rock beside the tree. Imitation failing, "you are to represent this foliage in every essential characteristic without defining the forms of individual leaves." Thus, as with atmosphere and light, some analysis and some conceptualization must take place. Fidelity to nature must thereby be calculated in

Durand:
Conceptualization
in the drawing
of trees.

94

FIGURE 56.
Kensett, Franconia Notch,
1850, *pencil on buff paper,*
10 x 13⅞ *in. (25.4 x 35.2*
cm.), Dia Art Foundation,
N.Y., Courtesy the Dan Flavin
Art Institute, Bridgehampton

FIGURE 57.
Kensett, Elm, 1862, *pencil*
on buff paper, 11³⁄₁₆ x 8⅛ *in.*
(28.6 x 20.6 cm.), Museum of
Art, Carnegie Institute,
Pittsburgh, Gibbons Fund,
1984.

FIGURE 58.
Kensett, Chicago Lake, 1870,
pencil on gray paper, 10 x
13¾ *in. (25.4 x 35.9 cm.),*
Babcock Galleries, New York.

essences. The evocative quality of American landscape painting, and in this instance Kensett's painting, can thus be seen to originate in the conceptual basis of drawings. Kensett's drawings are an indication that he adhered to Durand's idea of a representation as providing "such resemblance as shall satisfy the mind that the entire meaning of the scene represented is given."[63]

This conceptual aspect of Kensett's drawings is visible in the superb *Birch Tree, Niagara*, described above, and *Lake George* (1853; Fig. 59). Rather than imitating his subject, Kensett used energized staccato marks in both drawings to convey an idea of the actual substances. Instead of trying to delineate the multiplicity of leaves, he invented a notational system to indicate where the leaves were, using thick, dark, short parallel strokes. The artist would continue to use this shorthand system throughout his career to convey the scene's "essential characteristics," translating the hard facts of nature into an evocative and poetic vision. For Kensett, drawings were both tangible records of his fidelity to nature and fluid interpolations of nature's infinite variety. The ideas they embodied served as the springboard to finished compositions painted in the studio.

Kensett's experimentation in the first half of the decade of the 1850s centered on panoramic views typified by *The White Mountains—From North Conway* and woodland interiors like *Bash Bish Falls*. These subjects became less common in Kensett's work after 1855 as he devoted increasing attention to coastal scenes. He was, however, to paint one final work in acknowledgment of the landscape mode and his predecessors Cole and Durand. *Mount Chocorua* (Plate 15), painted between 1864 and 1866, was the

Plate 15. Kensett
Mount Chocorua
1864–66
oil on canvas, 48 x 84 in. (122 x 213.4 cm.)
The Century Association, New York

result of a commission from a committee of nineteen members of the Century Association, headed by transcendentalist-historian George Bancroft. At 48 by 84 inches, it was the largest painting he ever made. The agreement for the project, signed by the original members of the "body corporate" of the Century, stipulates that "a picture is to be engaged of Mr. Jno. F. Kensett" and that the picture was to be "on the part of the subscribers donated to the Century Association."[64] Each subscriber to the commission posted a sum of $250, totaling $5000—the most Kensett had ever been offered for a painting. In May 1864 Kensett received a letter from Bancroft: "Several of your fellow members of the Century have commissioned me to write you to invite you to paint a picture which, when finished, shall be presented by them to the association. For this end they have subscribed the sum of five thousand dollars."[65]

The terms of the commission were liberal. Kensett could choose any subject he wished, and he was "to complete the work if possible within two years." On 11 June 1866 Louis Lang, writing on behalf of his good friend Kensett, contacted Bancroft: "Mr. J. F. Kensett has now finished the picture ordered by 19 gentlemen of which I believe you are the chairman," and continued, "The picture is a great success and will do the artist infinite credit and honor, reflect magnificently on the kind donors and will be a central attraction in the new Century Building."[66] On 15 June Bancroft wrote to Kensett: "I am overjoyed to hear that your picture destined for the Century is finished. . . . It will stand as a monument of your own superior merit as an artist, and of the affection borne you by your friends."[67]

Considering that the country was in the midst of the Civil War when the picture was made, the tranquility of the scene Kensett depicts in *Mount Chocorua* may seem unrealistic. Yet precisely because of the war, Kensett may have felt compelled to reaffirm his confidence in the American people by once again integrating human figures into the landscape in the manner of his earlier works. The fact that the commissioning committee was headed by Bancroft may also have affected Kensett's choice of subject. Bancroft was a major and influential exponent of "man's power to guide himself in matters pertaining to art, government and religion" and believed that "humanity was to make for itself a new existence" in America.[68] In retrospect *Mount Chocorua* seems more a nostalgic rejoinder than an assertion of Kensett's then-current beliefs about painting. If the picture were undated and the circumstances of its origin unknown, its stylistic, thematic, and technical aspects—the splintered tree in the foreground, the moss-encrusted trees, strolling figures, and the tactile atmosphere—would suggest that it had been painted a decade earlier than its actual date. *Mount Chocorua* also represents a shift in subject for Kensett at the time, for in the mid-1860s he was concentrating chiefly on coastal scenes. Whatever Kensett's reasons for choosing this subject, it pays tribute to a generation of landscape painters and paintings in America, and it reveals Kensett's steadfast confidence in Creation's holiness and in human nature.

By the mid-1850s the landscape mode Kensett had explored under the influence of the Old Masters and of Cole and Durand no longer served his expressive needs. The landscape paintings that had established his reputation became a testing ground from which he developed his interests in the technical aspects of painting and realized his need for a different kind of subject matter. In a group of paintings that followed *October Day in the White Mountains* Kensett adopted coastal-scene subjects and refined his applications of compositional design, color, light, and line to produce a personal style in the last seventeen years of his life.

III. A Painter of Color and Light

From the simplicity of indigence and ignorance to the simplicity of strength and knowledge

—KENSETT, JOURNAL, 1840–41[69]

FROM 1848, WHEN KENSETT EXHIBITED *The Shrine—A Scene in Italy* at the National Academy of Design, and throughout the early 1850s, when he established a reputation as a landscape painter, he became well known for his ability to endow a scene with his own tranquil, poetic feeling. The individuality of that poetism was to be ever-present and increasingly important to his work throughout his life. Its expression, however, underwent a change in the mid 1850s, when a new style emerged from his easel. During the middle years of this decade, Kensett shifted from the more conventional anecdotal picturesque mode derived from the tradition of Cole and Durand, to the quiet openness, light, and simplification of form, color, and composition that is now recognized as his mature style and associated with the phenomenon of "luminism."[70] This new vision—for which Kensett is best remembered today—dominated the remainder of his career and is represented by such evocative masterpieces as *Shrewsbury River* of 1858, *Marine off Big Rock* of 1864, and *Lake George* of 1869.

Kensett's new stylistic concerns were intimately tied to his decided preference for a new subject: American coastal scenery. The shores and headlands of New England naturally lent themselves to his heightened preoccupation with light, color, and reflective surfaces. Such scenery also met his compelling desire to reduce compositions to nature's basic components—earth, water, and sky—which in their inherent emotional and philosophical content expressed the artist's convictions concerning nature's tranquil sublimity.

Many of the elements of Kensett's new style were deeply rooted in his artistic background. His early grounding in the graphic arts had attuned him to the importance of line and contour. Similarly, engraving taught him to manipulate subtle tonal variations, which enabled him to achieve remarkable effects within a limited palette. Even as a young artist studying the Old Masters in Europe, Kensett felt an affinity for the atmospheric effects of Claude's warm light, the precision of Canaletto's realism, and the fine color and smooth surfaces of the Dutch genre painters, much of which he later adapted to his own vision of American scenes.[71] Kensett may well also have been influenced by instruction books and drawing manuals published during the nineteenth century that provided basic guidance for both the amateur and aspiring artist. These manuals included instruction for both figure and landscape drawing, emphasizing a linear style with particular attention to fidelity of outline and contour of primary shapes and masses.[72] Kensett's drawings and paintings of landscape and marine subjects suggest that, like many of his contemporaries, he adopted the approach these manuals instilled. Unfortunately, Kensett wrote less and less about his art as his career progressed, so that his works themselves must serve as the primary documents of his aesthetic principles.

Although Kensett's new direction did not fully develop in his paintings until the mid-1850s, the drawing *Capri* of 1847 (Fig. 24) illustrates the essence of his vision and serves as a talisman of his mature style. Executed in the last months of Kensett's European sojourn, this drawing captures both the quality of a windless Mediterranean day and the character of the site with an extraordinary economy of means.

Plate 16. Kensett
Upper Mississippi
1855
oil on canvas, 18½ x 30½ in. (47 x 77.5 cm.)
The Saint Louis Art Museum,
Purchase, Eliza McMillan Fund, 22, 1950

Plate 17. Kensett
View of the Shrewsbury River
c. 1853–60
oil on canvas, 12 x 20 in. (30.5 x 50.8 cm.)
Jane Voorhees Zimmerli Art Gallery, Rutgers,
The State University, New Brunswick, N.J.,
Gift of the Interfraternity Alumni, 1952

FIGURE 60.
Kensett, Lake Pepin, 1854,
pencil on paper, 8¼ x 11 in.
(21 x 28 cm.), *Private
Collection.*

Using the horizontal format to full advantage, Kensett depicted only a few forms, setting them in a planar arrangement within a shallow space and delineating the masses with thin contours. The spare stylistic elements of the drawing presage his marine subjects of almost a decade later. Back in America, Kensett continued to refine the composition and style of his drawings in order to evoke the emotive qualities of nature. *Lake Pepin* (1854; Fig. 60), which documents Kensett's first trip up the Mississippi River and demonstrates a continued interest in refining his composition, seems to be a template for the composition of several later paintings, such as *Shrewsbury River*, *Marine off Big Rock*, and *Newport Rocks*. More immediately, the aesthetic sensibility of the drawing found expression in an 1855 painting, *Upper Mississippi* (Plate 16).

Upper Mississippi is the first major studio oil in which Kensett articulated the basic stylistic, compositional, and thematic components of his mature luminist style. Certain vestiges of the picturesque still recall the tradition of Cole, particularly the invented details of the Indians in the canoes and the rough peaks above them. But the palpable, unifying light and atmosphere and the marked degree of simplification of composition, texture, form, and palette demonstrate the departure to a new style. In comparison to the various techniques used to indicate perspective in *The White Mountains—From North Conway*, spatial depth is now indicated solely by the diminishing, overlapping forms of the mountains and enhanced by the controlled modulation of closely related hues and values, which fade as they recede to the horizon. The rhythmic pattern of the peaks reflected in the placid water gives a measured, abstract order to the composition. Smooth paint surfaces enhance the reflective quality of the glassy water. The overall effect is of a specific moment isolated on the canvas in haunting stillness. Kensett would refine many of these elements in the series of paintings that followed this work during the years from about 1853 to 1860.

In September 1853, Kensett's old friend George Curtis invited him to visit the Navesink Highlands in New Jersey, near Red Bank, where the Shrewsbury River empties into the Atlantic.[73] Kensett's

FIGURE 61.
Kensett, Shrewsbury River, 1856, *oil on academy board, 6 x 12 in. (15.2 x 30.5 cm.), Private Collection, Vermont.*

response to his visit was a series of five Shrewsbury River oils which are pivotal in the development of his style. Although the earliest dated painting in this group is 1856, another unsigned and undated version has pentimenti, which suggests that it may have been painted at the site, possibly in the fall of 1853 (Plate 17). In all five pictures, the basic compositional design and motifs remain unchanged, with only relatively minor alterations in the foreground grass and disposition of sailboats (frontispiece, Plates 18 and 19, Fig. 61).[74]

These works epitomize Kensett's early luminist aesthetic and are remarkable for their evocative mood and abstract design. In contrast to the rugged peaks in *Upper Mississippi*, the headland of Red Bank and the island marshes are regular in form. The boats and tufts of grasses which appear randomly placed are, in fact, carefully positioned to lead the viewer's eye toward the horizon. The emphasis on contour tends to flatten forms into abstract shapes that extend laterally beyond the confines of the canvas, enhancing the sense of lateral space. This, coupled with the balance between the masses and voids in the asymmetrical composition, which is organized around a strong horizontal line, promotes a feeling of calm, harmony, and measured order in nature unmatched in any of Kensett's earlier paintings. Despite the formal role these physical elements play in the composition, the real subject of these paintings seems to be the color, light, and atmosphere, which envelop and crystallize the scene. This effect is a result of Kensett's silvery palette as well as the juxtaposition of compact masses of land with great horizontal expanses of sky and water, which creates a sense of spatial infinity. Kensett's attention to smooth surfaces, heightened by the shimmering reflections on the water, removes any sense of the artist's hand, thereby diminishing the gauges by which the viewer apprehends time, sound, and motion.

During the course of painting the Shrewsbury River pictures, Kensett also began a second series in about 1855, focusing on Beacon Rock at the entrance to Newport Harbor, which culminated with *Marine off Big Rock* in 1864 (Plate 21). His methodical approach to his subject in this kind of series allowed him to explore fully the pictorial possibilities of a specific site. Like the Shrewsbury River

Plate 18. Kensett

Shrewsbury River, New Jersey

1859

oil on canvas, 18½ x 30½ in. (47 x 77.5 cm.)

The New-York Historical Society, New York

Plate 19. Kensett
Shrewsbury River
1860
oil on canvas, 15 x 24 in. (38.1 x 61 cm.)
Private Collection

Plate 20. Kensett

Beacon Rock, Newport Harbor

1857

oil on canvas, 22½ x 36 in. (57.1 x 91.5 cm.)

National Gallery of Art, Washington, D.C.,

Gift of Frederick Sturges, Jr., 1953

Plate 21. Kensett
Marine off Big Rock
1864
oil on canvas, 27½ x 44½ in. (69.8 x 113 cm.)
Cummer Gallery of Art, Jacksonville, Fla.

FIGURE 62.
Kensett, Entrance to New-port Harbor, 1855, *oil on canvas, 14 x 24 in. (35.6 x 61 cm.), Arthur and Nancy Manella.*

group, each succeeding image in the Beacon Rock series—which numbers at least four paintings—reveals Kensett's subtle refinements of compositional elements toward an increasingly abstract end. In the early versions (Fig. 62 and Plate 20), Kensett's treatment of texture is more painterly, and he instills the scene with a sense of quiet motion, especially in the rippling waves and the activity of the fishermen. His bolder palette, especially dominant in the ultramarine sea, conveys the intensity of the hot, summer light. As the series developed, however, Kensett increasingly applied a measured balance between open spaces and masses and simplified the primary compositional motifs. In *Marine off Big Rock* he brought the scene into sharp focus through the subtle manipulation of seemingly ancillary details. By substituting a solitary rock in the foreground for the waves lapping against the curved shoreline that appeared in his earlier versions, he eliminated all sense of movement and immediacy so that an aloof stillness and arresting silence prevail.

This kind of simple manipulation of a subject demonstrates Kensett's gift for eliciting a specific mood from a particular scene. The artist's fidelity to nature is asserted not so much in the details as in the clarity of the light, which heightens the sense of realism. In the Beacon Rock and Shrewsbury River paintings, the features of the site succumb to the demands of Kensett's vision.[75] Light takes on not only substantiality but also an almost iconographic significance as it isolates a particular time and setting and suggests the eternity and universality of nature.

Kensett's fascination with the eloquence of silence is perhaps the most distinctive and innovative aspect of his coastal scenes. The mood of *Marine off Big Rock* was to be reiterated later in the decade in such breathtaking images as *Newport Coast* (c. 1865–70; Plate 22) and *On the Beverly Coast, Massachusetts* (1863; Plate 23), in which the divine omnipresence of nature corresponds to the tenets of the transcendental sublime. These scenes are virtually devoid of human figures; but in such coastal scenes as

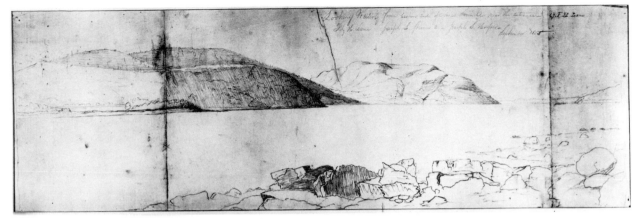

View of the Beach at Beverly, Massachusetts (1860; Plate 24), *Forty Steps, Newport, Rhode Island* (1860; Plate 25), or *Coast at Newport* (1869; Plate 26), Kensett continued to celebrate the harmonious coexistence of man and nature as he had in earlier landscapes. In place of farmers and shepherds in placid fields, fishermen and tourists here leisurely enjoy the sun-filled inlets and beaches of Massachusetts and Rhode Island. Unexpected in this context is the perfectly arranged cross of driftwood in *View of the Beach at Beverly*, tossed upon the shore by the random wisdom of the tide—a symbol of nature's divinity unusually obvious for Kensett.

Coast Scene with Figures (1869; Plate 27) provides a less passive interpretation of man's relationship to nature. Here, on the Beverly shore, the figures appear to discuss the infinity of the sky and the powerful constancy of the sea. Humankind and nature face each other in awe-inspiring sublimity. The compositional simplicity and subtle color in this painting produce an abstract combination of shapes, an effect which underlies all of Kensett's luminist compositions. With these paintings, Kensett established his leadership in the mainstream of a group of artists who derived inspiration from the vast expanses of sea and sky off the New England coastline.

Plate 22. Kensett

Newport Coast

c. 1865–70

oil on canvas, 18¹⁄₁₆ x 30¼ in. (46.1 x 76.9 cm.)

Private Collection

FIGURE 67.
Sanford Robinson Gifford (1823–1880), Hook Mountain near Nyack on the Hudson, 1866, oil on canvas, 8⅛ x 19 in. (20.7 x 48.2 cm.), Yale University Art Gallery, New Haven, Conn., Gift of Miss Annette I. Young in memory of Professor D. Cady Eaton and Mr. Innis Young.

Kensett's awe in the midst of nature's most quiet moments bears a kinship to the vision of Fitz Hugh Lane (1804–1865).[76] Though twelve years Kensett's senior, Lane's career as a painter also began in the 1840s following training in the graphic arts. Both his drawings (Fig. 63) and paintings (Fig. 64) are similar to Kensett's in the demarcation of space through carefully placed abstracted forms and the use of a uniform light to clarify the subject. These characteristics, in fact, emerge as an integral part of Lane's and Kensett's styles at about the same time in the mid-1840s, but Lane preceded Kensett by several years in applying them to paintings. Kensett, on the other hand, reduced his compositions to many fewer elements and often eliminated the anecdotal figures and accessories that Lane usually retained.

Closer to Kensett's age is Martin Johnson Heade (1819–1904) whose familiar coastal scenes are generally composed of stylistic devices similar to Kensett's. But the obvious design parallels that Heade's *Lake George* (1862; Fig. 65) or *Rocky Shore* (1868; Fig. 66) bear to Kensett's work do not carry over to the sense of mood. Where Kensett presented his subjects suspended in inviting tranquility, Heade, captivated by impending shifts in weather conditions, imbued his work with the ominous sublime of nature's changeable and often forbidding temperament.

Kensett's friend Sanford R. Gifford (1823–1880) also painted images of nature suffused with serene equanimity. Both artists retain an acute sense of fidelity to nature while at the same time idealizing their subjects to achieve a characteristic mood. For example, Gifford's *Hook Mountain near Nyack on the Hudson* (1866; Fig. 67), in its smooth brushwork, subtle color, and overall design, brings to mind Kensett's *View of the Beach at Beverly*. But the atmosphere in Gifford's pictures is typically dense and moisture-laden, in contrast to the intense crystalline light of Kensett's views, and projects a softer, more veiled tenor.

Kensett's heritage as a painter of coastal scenes descended most directly, perhaps, to a younger generation of artists including William Trost Richards (1833–1905), William S. Haseltine (1835–1900), and Alfred T. Bricher (1837–1908), as well as a host of lesser talents, such as Frederick Debourg Richards (d. 1903) and Francis Silva (1835–1886). William Trost Richards' *Santy Lighthouse on Nan-*

Plate 24. Kensett
View of the Beach at Beverly, Massachusetts
1860
oil on canvas, 14¼ x 24¼ in. (48.8 x 61.6 cm.)
Santa Barbara Museum of Art,
Gift of Mrs. Sterling Morton to the Preston Morton Collection

Plate 25. Kensett

Forty Steps, Newport, Rhode Island

1860

oil on canvas, 20⅛ x 36 in. (51.1 x 91.4 cm.)

Jo Ann and Julian Ganz, Jr.

Plate 26. Kensett
Coast at Newport
1869
oil on canvas, 11⅝ x 24¼ in. (29.5 x 61.6 cm.)
The Art Institute of Chicago,
Friends of American Art Collections

Plate 27. Kensett

Coast Scene with Figures

1869

oil on canvas, 36¼ x 60¼ in. (92 x 153 cm.)

Wadsworth Atheneum, Hartford, Conn.,

The Ella Gallup Sumner and Mary Catlin Sumner Collection

FIGURE 68.
*William Trost Richards
(1833–1905), Santy Light-
house on Nantucket, 1865,
oil on canvas, 9 x 16 in.
(22.9 x 40.7 cm.), Mr.
James H. Dempsey.*

FIGURE 69.
*William Trost Richards
(1833–1905), On the Coast
of New Jersey, 1883, oil on
canvas, 40¼ x 72¼ in.
(102.2 x 183.5 cm.), Cor-
coran Gallery of Art,
Washington, D.C., Museum
Purchase.*

tucket (1865; Fig. 68), noteworthy for its articulate draftsmanship and sparkling atmosphere, recalls Kensett's luminous serenity. Though Richards frequently painted pounding waves in his scenes to evoke greater animation, he reduced some of his later subjects to broad, shimmering expanses of sky and sea (Fig. 69), enlivened only by a few gulls or a schooner on the horizon. Kensett, in the final years of his career, abstracted his compositions to an even greater degree than any of his contemporaries. While Kensett's late works such as *Sunset on the Sea* (1872; Plate 44) are more expressive in the manner

FIGURE 70.
*William Stanley Haseltine
(1835–1900), Rocks at
Nahant, 1864, oil on canvas,
22⅛ x 40 in. (56.2 x 101.5
cm.), The Brooklyn Museum,
Dick S. Ramsay Fund,
A. Augustus Healy Fund and
A. Augustus Healy Fund B.*

FIGURE 71.
*Alfred T. Bricher (1837–
1908), Time and Tide, c.
1873, oil on canvas, 25½ x
50 in. (64.7 x 127 cm.),
Dallas Museum of Art,
Foundation for the Arts
Collection, Gift of Mr. and
Mrs. Frederick M. Mayer.*

of such painters as Courbet, Whistler, and Blakelock or Vedder, Richards' precise articulation of waves and glassy surfaces are indicative of his strong graphic training and Ruskinian bias.[77]

Haseltine was Richards' fellow pupil in Philadelphia under the German-born marine painter Paul Weber. In comparison to Kensett's work, Haseltine's coastal scenes place greater emphasis on the junction of the sea and shore by defining it with rugged, craggy rocks. These are rendered in sharp contrasts of light and dark, giving them a strong geometric appearance (Fig. 70). Like Kensett, Hasel-

tine generally preferred asymmetrical arrangements to emphasize the vastness of the sea and sky. How-ever, many of his compositions project a greater sense of drama than Kensett's do, often by showing crashing waves on rocks near the foreground.

Like Kensett before him, Bricher found the coasts along Massachusetts and Rhode Island com-pelling for their pictorial effects of light and air, and his views of them mark him as one of Kensett's closest inheritors. Bricher's *Time and Tide* (1873; Fig. 71) demonstrates the impact of Kensett's legacy in the use of projecting rocks at the union of sky and sea, the translucent atmosphere, and the modulated coloration, refined brushwork, and quiet mood.

FIGURE 74.
Kensett, Killarney, 1856,
*pencil on buff paper, 9½ x 14
in. (24.2 x 35.5 cm.), Dia
Art Foundation, N.Y.,
courtesy The Dan
Flavin Art Institute,
Bridgehampton*

Just as Kensett was beginning his Shrewsbury River and Beacon Rock pictures, he made a second trip abroad, this time with the express purpose of making "the lake scenery of England, Ireland and Scotland the special object of my visit."[78] He departed from Jersey City on 9 July 1856 in the company of his friend Bayard Taylor, a travel writer, novelist, and poet.[79] Following a brief stopover in London, where he renewed his acquaintance with Thackeray, and a tour in Warwickshire with Taylor, Kensett left for Killarney, where he established himself at Lake House. In Ireland and in the English Lake District, which he visited in early September, he was plagued by bad weather: "Rain! Rain! Rain! Having exhausted prayer and supplication for fine weather I am convinced the elements are against me. . . . I shall have little else to show but outlines."[80] The weather offered little relief on subsequent visits to Lake Windermere and Loch Lomond and at Fort William during his tour of Scotland.

Despite his apprehensions for his work, Kensett's Killarney drawings are exquisite, both technically in their subtle variation and economy of line, and compositionally in the balance of forms, which captures the essence of the subject (Figs. 72, 73, and 74). The vigorous activity in the foreground foliage of *From Rose Island, Killarney* (1856; Fig. 73) recalls some of his earlier Niagara views or even *Mount Lafayette* of 1850 (Fig. 75). The compelling reductive vision of Kensett's Killarney drawings is revealed in his selection of a few prominent natural forms executed with a subtle variation and economy of line. These drawings reassert the aesthetic preferences that had so strongly marked the 1847 *Capri* drawing, and they summarize the stylistic traits—transparent light, tranquil weather conditions, and compositional balance—prevalent in his paintings done after 1855. It is significant that these verdant landscape scenes carry no hint of the inclement weather Kensett had encountered: the arrested moment is captured in clear and sunny stillness, a stylistic preference well suited to the artist's temperament.

When Kensett returned to the United States, *The Crayon* reported that he brought with him "a number of memorandum sketches of scenery about the lovely lakes of Westmorland and Cumberland. We hope to see them embodied in pictures before long."[81] Kensett composed two easel paintings from

FIGURE 75.
Kensett, Mount Lafayette, 1850, *pencil on buff paper, 9⅞ x 13¾ in. (25.1 x 34.9 cm.), Babcock Galleries, New York.*

these drawings over the next two years, *Lakes of Killarney* (1857; Plate 28) and *The Langdale Pike* (1858; Plate 29). Thematically, stylistically, and structurally, these paintings recall Kensett's view of Camel's Hump (Plate 7) completed almost a decade earlier. Their compositions, however, have become more obviously asymmetrical, with the reflective surface of the glassy water stretching into the foreground and thereby assuming greater presence. The view of the water is unimpeded by foreground foliage and consequently is more crucial to the evocation of mood. A reviewer for *The Crayon* recorded an appreciative response:

> *Kensett's pictures are to our mind, remarkable in many points—for refinement of taste, treatment of distances, rendering of atmospheric effect, and a happy expression of the broad light of day and of a specific time of day. His perception of the poetry and harmony of nature in these respects, is remarkably subtle and delicate. . . . no one can gaze upon the Lakes of Killarney . . . without recognizing the great qualities named, and finding in them in a marked degree the highest expression of landscape art.*[82]

While *Lakes of Killarney* and *The Langdale Pike* are in part retrospective, they also presage some of Kensett's major landscapes of the next decade, including his acknowledged masterpiece *Lake George* of 1869 (Plate 33). Perhaps closest to the two Killarney paintings is *View on the Hudson* (1865; Plate 30) in which the composition has essentially been reversed. Even the more intimate glimpse of *Paradise Rocks, Newport* (c. 1865; Plate 31) draws upon a similar format. *View from Cozzens' Hotel near West Point* of 1863 (Plate 32) exaggerates the asymmetry of design even further in a more horizontal panorama of the Hudson. This particular landscape's strong underlying geometric divisions reflect the influence of the artist's concurrent preoccupation with his Beacon Rock series. As in the coastal scenes, in *View from Cozzens' Hotel* the masses of terrain are sharply divided from the great expanses of space, which simultaneously suggests a sense of equilibrium and projects a feeling of spatial release.

FIGURE 76.
Kensett, Lake George, 1853,
*pencil on buff paper, 9⅞ x
13⅝ in. (25.1 x 34.6 cm.),
Mrs. Alice M. Kaplan.*

Lake George is the culmination of Kensett's exploration of color, light, compositional design, and mood. He had visited the lake in 1853 and sketched the wildness of the Adirondack foothills (Figs. 59 and 76), and this region continued to be a subject for him for almost two decades. He exhibited at least three paintings of the site at the National Academy of Design before completing this famous version of 1869, which was one of his largest canvases. The three thousand dollars that Morris K. Jesup paid for it was the second highest sum Kensett ever received for a picture.[83] Its large size, high price, and status as the synthesis of his years of studying the scenery and conditions of the famous lake are indicative of the importance this work held for the artist.

Lake George fulfills the promise of Kensett's 1847 *Capri* drawing in achieving an expressive synthesis of composition and emotion. The scene's refined, orderly grandeur is emphasized by the rounded, idealized islands and the elegant contours of the mountains. The suffusive atmosphere, which compresses the space, is rendered through a carefully modulated palette. Kensett was able to distill the most evocative basic elements of the setting and depict them in a manner that conveys the serenity and silence of the scene and the awe it inspired in the artist.

Kensett employed a narrow palette in *Lake George*, composed primarily of greens and gray. Subtle modulations in values rather than a variety of hues account for nuances in the motifs. Variations in tonal gradations were often achieved by lightly scumbling one hue over another to produce greater depth and intensity of color as well as slight surface texture. It was probably this advanced application of color

scumbling *

Plate 28. Kensett
Lakes of Killarney
1857
oil on canvas, 24$^{1}/_{16}$ x 34$^{1}/_{4}$ in. (61.1 x 87 cm.)
Milwaukee Art Museum

Plate 29. Kensett

The Langdale Pike

1858

oil on canvas, 22¼ x 36 in. (56.5 x 91.4 cm.)

Cornell Fine Arts Center, Rollins College, Winter Park, Fla.

principles in Kensett's work that led S. G. W. Benjamin to observe in 1880 that "before the great modern question of the values began to arouse much attention in the ateliers of Paris, Kensett had already grasped the perception of a theory of art practice which has since become so prominent in foreign art."[84] Kensett's talent as a colorist had been widely acknowledged throughout his career. As early as 1845 Alexandre Calamé commented on his fine use of color, and in 1872 Daniel Huntington wrote that "perhaps the faculty which most distinguished him was coloring."[85]

Kensett's examination and distillation of color, exemplified by such works as the Shrewsbury River series, *Marine off Big Rock,* and in particular *Lake George,* anticipated and was complemented by some of the scientific explorations of color that were conducted during the 1860s by researchers like Lewis Rutherfurd, Oliver Wolcott Gibbs, and Ogden Rood, all of whose work made New York an international center for chromatic studies.[86] Kensett knew Rutherfurd and Gibbs, who both attended the 1861 Century Association testimonial dinner in his honor. All three scientists were prominent in the summer society of Newport, and they conducted research together. Rutherfurd and Gibbs were very close friends with Rood, who dedicated his 1879 book *Modern Chromatics* to Gibbs.[87]

Kensett believed that there were universal laws of color implicit in nature, and that "bright colors are sparingly distributed throughout the natural world . . . even in [the] season of bloom; while the main masses [of a scene] are made of cool greens, greys, drabs and browns intermingled, and are always harmonious and agreeable."[88] The restricted palette Kensett employed in his major works from *Shrews-*

[handwritten margin note:] Ogden Rood "Modern Chromatics

[handwritten margin note:] Bright Colors are sparingly distributed in nature.

126

FIGURE 78.
Kensett, Rowayton, Connecticut, 1868, *pencil on buff paper, 9⅞ x 14 in. (25.1 x 35.5 cm.), Babcock Galleries, New York.*

bury River to *Lake George* was developed according to this idea. Kensett's hypothesis anticipates Rood's observation in *Modern Chromatics* that "the colors of nature are usually pale and low in intensity, even when they make upon the beholder just the reverse impression."[89] "The aim of the true artist," wrote Rood, "is the production of a broad general effect by the use of a few masses of colour, properly interchanged and contrasted, variety being gained not so much by the introduction of new colours as by the repetition of main chords."[90] Kensett's consistent use of a limited palette, so forcefully demonstrated in *Lake George*, focused attention on tonal gradations and on values of hues. Rood again echoed Kensett when he asserted that "gradation of colour is almost universal in nature, and . . . skill in the use of gradation gives the artist great power to manage large masses of nearly uniform colour."[91]

Today *Modern Chromatics* is best remembered as an important influence on Georges Seurat, and it was widely read by the circle of Impressionists including Claude Monet and Camille Pissarro. Rood's discussions of the optical mixture of colors, contours, contrasts, and gradations were the direct source for Seurat's neo-Impressionist theories. But Rood disavowed the legitimacy of Seurat's and the Impressionist's interpretation of his writings. "If that is all I have done for art," he proclaimed, "I wish I had never written that book."[92] Kensett's approach to color and composition was closer to what Rood had in mind. Passages throughout *Modern Chromatics* parallel elements in Kensett's work, such as limited palette, tonal modulations, emphasis on contours, and distillation to expressive essentials.[93]

Just as Kensett's use of forms and colors matured through a process of distillation, so too did his

General Effect.

repetition of color

gradation of color
universal in nature

Distillation of
expressive essentials

Plate 30. Kensett
View on the Hudson
1865
oil on canvas, 27½ x 44½ in. (69.2 x 112.4 cm.)
The Baltimore Museum of Art,
Gift of Mrs. Paul H. Miller

Plate 31. Kensett

Paradise Rocks, Newport

c. 1865

oil on canvas, 18⅛ x 29⅞ in. (46 x 75.9 cm.)

The Newark Museum, N.J.,

Gift of Dr. J. Ackerman Coles, 1920

Plate 32. Kensett
View from Cozzens' Hotel near West Point
1863
oil on canvas, 20 x 34 in. (50.8 x 86.4 cm.)
The New-York Historical Society, New York

Plate 33. Kensett

Lake George

1869

oil on canvas, 44⅛ x 66⅜ in. (112.1 x 168.6 cm.)

The Metropolitan Museum of Art, New York,

Bequest of Maria DeWitt Jesup, 1915 *see various references to this plate:*

Plate 34. Kensett

Lake George

1870

oil on canvas, 14 x 24⅛ in. (35.5 x 61.2 cm.)

The Brooklyn Museum,

Gift of Mrs. W. W. Phelps in memory of her mother and father,

Ella M. and John C. Southwick, 1933

Plate 35. Kensett

Beach at Newport

c. 1869–72

oil on canvas, 22 x 34 in. (55.8 x 86.4 cm.)

National Gallery of Art, Washington, D.C.,

Gift of Frederick Sturges, Jr., 1978

Plate 36. Kensett

Storm, Western Colorado

1870

oil on canvas, 18⁵⁄₁₆ x 28⅛ in. (46.5 x 71.7 cm.)

The Toledo Museum of Art, Ohio,

Gift of Florence Scott Libbey

evocation of mood. The intimate tranquility of his paintings, a function of the artist's transcendental faith in the perfection of Creation, found its ultimate expression in *Lake George*. In this painting, the compressed space, smooth sheet of reflective water, narrow palette, and suffusive atmosphere convey an iconic spirituality. A forceful quality of abstraction resulted from this reductive treatment of subjects and introspective mood. The abstracting tendency of Kensett's style, indeed, of luminist painting in general, would be reinterpreted by modern artists, for example in the measured and controlled compositions of Seurat and the compelling design and refined color of Charles Sheeler's works.

In the years 1855 and 1856, when he was at work on *Upper Mississippi* and the Shrewsbury River series, Kensett reached an artistic plateau from which his mature style would emerge. In about 1870 Kensett seems to have achieved another plateau. *Lake George*, *Coast Scene with Figures*, and *Beach at Newport* (c. 1869–72, Plate 35) were ambitious compositions that seem to summarize and lock in place all the ideas he had been developing for more than a decade. In the last two or three years of his life he introduced more technical variety into his approach, which may have signaled a new development or refinement coming into his work.

Unlike Kensett's coastal scenes of the 1850s and 1860s, with their clear atmosphere and quiet presence, his work of the 1870s is more variable in mood, sometimes suggesting an impending change in the weather. In his 1870 view of Lake George (Plate 34), for example, a low ceiling of dark clouds stretches across the full width of the painting, and ripples in the water indicate a gust of wind. This animation of natural forces is, however, counterbalanced by the clearer and brighter skies and sharp contour of the mountain in the distance, lending an emotional tension to the image that is only occasionally hinted at in earlier work of the 1860s, such as *View on the Hudson* and *View from Cozzens' Hotel*. Perhaps the most dramatic sky Kensett ever painted is in *Storm, Western Colorado* (1870; Plate 36) in which the unusually colorful palette and rugged Western scenery also indicate experimentation. Similarly, the painting *Long Neck Point from Contentment Island, Darien, Connecticut* (c. 1870–72; Plate 41) has a rich, tactile paint surface that may be a further exploration of the use of slight texture found in some areas of the 1869 *Lake George* painting.

These diverse approaches suggest that as Kensett moved into the decade of the 1870s he was searching and experimenting, looking forward to further artistic growth. It would seem that just as it had taken a period of years for him to develop his theories through the Shrewsbury River and the Beacon Rock pictures, he was, in 1870, entering a new period of work. That period ended suddenly, however, with his death in December 1872, and it is therefore possible only to surmise the direction in which his stylistic development was headed. The richness of his inquiring mind is, however, amply demonstrated in a group of major paintings done during the summer of 1872, paintings that Kensett's brother called the "Last Summer's Work."

Plate 37. Kensett

Eaton's Neck, Long Island

1872

oil on canvas, 18 x 36 in. (45.7 x 91.4 cm.)

The Metropolitan Museum of Art, New York,

Gift of Thomas Kensett, 1874

THE LAST SUMMER'S WORK

Oswaldo Rodriguez Roque

I.

SINCE ITS PRESENTATION TO THE METROPOLITAN MUSEUM OF ART IN 1874, the group of pictures known as Kensett's Last Summer's Work has occupied a curious place in the history of American landscape painting. First viewed as works of genius, and by many as the purest distillation of Kensett's sensibility, these landscapes quickly fell victim to the easy disregard that cheerfully relegated the works of most American mid-nineteenth-century landscape masters to the dusty storage rooms of museums throughout the country. More recently, the rehabilitation of American landscape painting of this period led a number of scholars to inquire about these somewhat mysterious works by Kensett, but their eager curiosity, piqued by the glowing accounts printed when the pictures first came to public attention in 1873, met inevitable disappointment in canvases that had not been conserved in over one hundred years.

Happily, all this is now changed. All of the Last Summer's Work in the Metropolitan's collection has been restored to its former glory, and the pictures are now nothing less than a striking revelation. They form a chapter in the career of an important artist, and in the history of a painting tradition, which demands interpretation and analysis. From the vantage point of the late twentieth century, works such as *Eaton's Neck, Long Island* (Plate 37), *Sunset on the Sea* (Plate 44), *A Foggy Sky* (Plate 43), and *Newport Rocks* (Plate 42) foreshadow the styles of Mark Rothko, Milton Avery, and Barnett Newman. They thus forge a link with our more recent artistic past that is all the more suggestive for being a purely visual, rather than a strictly historical one.[1]

II.

A certain degree of confusion surrounded the Last Summer's Work at the time of Kensett's death. Reporters writing in New York journals, and even the executors of Kensett's estate, could not agree on the exact number of paintings in the group, or on whether they were studies or finished paintings or both. The author of "Art Matters" in the *New York Herald* of 15 March 1873 offered the following typically vague account:

Meanwhile we think the public have hardly appreciated how wonderfully industrious Mr. Kensett was during the last three months of his life, passed at Darien, Conn. Between thirty and forty studies, sketches and pictures left his brush during that incredibly short space of time.

The author goes on to supply "a complete list of them" but names only twenty-nine works.[2] Two months previously the *Evening Post*, in a general account of the extraordinarily large number of paintings left by Kensett in his New York City studio and destined for eventual sale, noted:

Every picture belonging to Mr. Kensett's estate is to be put into this sale, with the exception of thirty studies, more or less, which comprise the last works from his easel. These studies—or more properly pictures, for they bear the character of finished works—were painted from nature, in the neighborhood of Darien, on the Long Island shore [sic], during the past summer. This vacation work is considered by the executors and others so remarkable in its character that a proposition has been made to purchase the group entire, and present it to some picture gallery or institution of New York. This collection of studies is estimated to be worth $30,000, but the executors, with the consent of the heirs, offer the series for $20,000, and that sum, it is understood, will be raised by subscription and applied to the purchase. No public institution has yet been named in connection with the proposed gift.[3]

The *Brooklyn Eagle*, in an article which exhorted Brooklyn businessmen to put up the money to purchase the Last Summer's Work for their city, was quite definite as to how many works were involved:

Mr. Kensett's last work, done during the past summer, consists of thirty-four studies or sketches, and nearly all of the canvases bear the appearance of finished pictures. Thirty-four pictures painted in three months, for that was the length of Mr. Kensett's last vacation, show remarkable industry, and we know of no other artist who possesses such facility of execution, unless it is Mr. Frederic E. Church, who is reported to have made upward of one thousand studies during his last year in the Orient.[4]

Another surviving document, a private invitation card signed by the wealthy New York entrepreneur Robert M. Olyphant, who was one of the executors of Kensett's estate, announces:

The series of 34 pictures and studies painted by the late John F. Kensett at his studio on "Contentment Island", Darien, Conn., and known as his "Last Summer's Work" may be seen on Private View in the Lecture Room on the 3rd floor of the Y.M.C.A., 52 East 23rd Street.[5]

This invitation attests to the special regard in which the Last Summer's Work was held, as no other paintings from Kensett's estate were put on view before the exhibition at the National Academy of Design immediately previous to the auction sale. In the end, however, a total of thirty-eight canvases were deeded to the Metropolitan Museum in March 1874 by Kensett's brother, Thomas, a Baltimore businessman and pioneer in the marketing of canned foods. In a letter to John Taylor Johnston, president of the museum, Thomas wrote:

having a wish shared by my mother, members of the family, Robert M. Olyphant and other friends of my late brother John F. Kensett that his works thirty eight in number and known as his "last summer's work" should not be scattered. I have purchased the same and beg to present them through your good self to the Met Museum of Art. In so donating them I have in view the great interest my late brother had in the success of your institution as one of its founders and the very pleasant personal relations he held to the members of your Council.[6]

The original group of works found in Kensett's Contentment Island studio may nevertheless have numbered thirty-nine. A document entitled "Memo of Pictures belonging to the Estate of John F. Kensett" lists the paintings by contemporary artists that Kensett owned and kept in his New York studio but also itemizes thirty-nine works by the artist himself—undoubtedly an inventory, for estate appraisal purposes, of the Last Summer's Work (see Appendix).[7] The brief titles given the pictures in this list are short descriptions of their subject matter which correspond fairly well to the longer titles already attached to the Last Summer's Work by the time it was shown together with the works intended for sale. But they also suggest that the longer titles were devised by Olyphant and the painter Vincent Colyer, the executors who catalogued all the works in Kensett's estate. Many of these titles were written in pencil on the wooden stretchers in what looks to be Colyer's handwriting and are still clearly visible today. The fact that these thirty-nine items appear together with the list of pictures Kensett owned by other artists supports the conclusion that they indeed constitute the Last Summer's Work. Not long after the idea of depositing the Last Summer's Work in a public institution was publicized, Thomas Kensett offered the group of paintings by contemporary artists to the Metropolitan Museum provided it purchased the Last Summer's Work for twenty thousand dollars.[8] Since the rest of Kensett's estate was put up for sale at auction, only the Last Summer's Work and the "works by contemporaneous artists" were in need of appraisal, as the dollar value assigned to the diverse items in the "Memo" indicates.

Thus the available evidence suggests, first, that there was considerable confusion following Kensett's death as to what he had or had not painted during his last summer on Contentment Island and, second, that it was not always readily apparent, even to those who knew him best, whether these works were actually finished. To realize that the available records and documents do not provide a clear-cut description of Kensett's last painting campaign is to realize that the question of what is the Last Summer's Work remains to some extent open and that an actual examination of the works themselves is the court of last resort to which judgments regarding the state of completion of individual works must be submitted.

III.

On 6 March 1873 a group of gentlemen met at the house of Henry G. Marquand, who was a longtime friend and financial adviser of Kensett's, a businessman and philanthropist of note, and the treasurer of the Metropolitan Museum, to consider the acquisition of the Last Summer's Work as well as Kensett's own collection of paintings by other contemporary artists. Both of these groups of pictures had by this time apparently been assigned to Thomas Kensett as part of his share in his brother's estate. The resolution adopted at that time explains the circumstances of the meeting:

> WHEREAS, *Mr. Thomas Kensett, of Baltimore, Md. has consented to present the Collection of Works by Contemporaneous Artists, owned by the late* J. F. KENSETT, *and valued at $14,000, to be placed in the Metropolitan Museum of Art, on condition that the sum of $20,000 be raised to purchase a selection of his brother's works, the whole to be known as* THE KENSETT MEMORIAL. *On motion, it was*
>
> Resolved, *to obtain subscription to the amount of $20,000 to accomplish the desired effect.*[9]

The committee appointed to receive subscriptions for the "Kensett Memorial" included museum president Johnston, the painters Thomas Hicks, Daniel Huntington, and Worthington Whittredge, Olyphant and Colyer, and several distinguished New York businessmen. It is incredible that they were unable to raise the funds required by Thomas Kensett's offer, but it seems that this must have been the case. In the end Thomas offered the Last Summer's Work directly to the museum in March of 1874, though a note from Olyphant to Kensett's mother Elizabeth suggests that Thomas did not bear the full financial brunt of making the gift:

> *I have your note requesting me to dispose of the pictures remaining in my hands as Executor of the Estate of your son, the late J. F. Kensett, to your son Thomas Kensett and to receive in pay for the same his note at 12 mos—I have carried out this wish, recd the note, and sent the same to you, endorsed to your order, by your son—the amount being twenty five thousand dollars—a sum which as you say is not equal to the value of the pictures, but which you, your daughters concurring, desire to be so disposed of in view of the works being donated by your son to the Metropolitan Museum of Art.*[10]

Originally Thomas Kensett placed three conditions on his gift to the Metropolitan. He stipulated that the Last Summer's Work be called "The Kensett Collection," that the paintings be kept and exhibited together, and that the works deemed unfinished be preserved as they were. This final condition may, today, seem strange, but at the time it was not at all unusual for one artist to finish another's work. At least one painting by Kensett, the legendary *Beverly Coast*, which sold for an astonishing sixteen thousand dollars on the first day of the Kensett sale, was finished by his friend John Casilear.[11]

Ultimately only the last-named condition was honored by the museum, more as a matter of professional integrity than of legal obligation, as Thomas Kensett in subsequent communications with the museum made his gift an entirely unrestricted one.[12] In 1956, five pictures from the Kensett Collection were sold at auction and in 1957 another thirteen. One was exchanged for other works of art in 1969. Old photographs reveal that many of these works suffered considerable paint-film loss due to crackling, flaking, and blistering, doubtless the result of the artist's painting with oil over oil before the first layer had fully dried. With perhaps only one or two exceptions, which certainly must include *Fish Island* (Plate 38), now owned by the Montclair Art Museum, the Metropolitan kept the best of the Last Summer's Work, including most of the pictures that appeared unfinished (see Appendix).

FIGURE 79.
Kensett, Lake George, A Reminiscence, 1872, *oil on canvas*, 11 x 17½ *in.* (27.9 x 44.5 *cm.*), *The Metropolitan Museum of Art, New York, Gift of Thomas Kensett*, 1874.

IV.

The pictures in the Last Summer's Work were painted in three different locations: Lake George, Newport, and the area in and around Contentment Island, Darien, Connecticut, where Kensett had a studio. Since they were all found in his studio after the artist's death, it is assumed that they must have been painted in the summer of 1872. Whether this means that the artist went on sketching trips to both Lake George and Newport this same summer when he is known to have been resident on Contentment Island is an unresolved question. The title of one of the works, *Lake George, A Reminiscence* (Fig. 79) might suggest that Kensett painted from memory or from other works, and that perhaps all the Lake George works included in the Last Summer's Work are "reminiscences" and not the result of firsthand observation. However, the sketchlike quality and small size of most of these pictures makes this improbable. More likely, Kensett did travel to both Lake George and Newport. Since only two works can be associated with Newport with certainty, his stay there must have been brief.[13]

Stylistically, the Last Summer's Work does not form a cohesive whole. The Lake George pictures, mostly sketches, are not especially innovative in composition, color, or technique. The pictures painted in Newport and in the neighborhood of Darien, predominantly seascapes, are another matter. Since all of them seem to have been worked on out-of-doors, they are all in a sense sketches. They are thinly painted, always with careful, if at times obviously speedy, brushwork, and have highly varied and delicate colors. Among them are those paintings of large size and artistic ambition which, in a historical

Plate 38. Kensett
Fish Island from Kensett's Studio on Contentment Island
1872
oil on canvas, 18 x 36 in. (45.7 x 91.4 cm.)
Montclair Art Museum, N.J.,
Lang Acquisition Fund, 1960

Plate 39. Kensett
An Inlet of Long Island Sound
c. 1865
oil on canvas, 14¼ x 24 in. (36.2 x 61 cm.)
Los Angeles County Museum of Art,
Gift of Colonel and Mrs. William Keighley

sense, have overwhelmed the others and established the paradigm for the style of the Last Summer's Work. In the context of Kensett's career, these works are anomalous and somewhat difficult to understand. They are inextricably intertwined with Kensett's experience at Contentment Island and with the special scenic qualities of Long Island Sound.

Despite its proximity to New York City and its great natural beauty, the area around Darien, Connecticut, and of Long Island Sound in general, was not a part of the country widely recognized for its picturesqueness.[14] Compared to the Catskills or Lake George, or even to the coastline of Massachusetts, this territory had been left relatively unexplored by American landscape painters. For example, Nathaniel Parker Willis and William Henry Bartlett's well-known picture book of 1840, *American Scenery*, mentions the quaint old towns punctuating the Connecticut shore of the Sound but overlooks the remarkable and varied effects of natural light, especially sunrises and sunsets, so strikingly observable there.[15] Much later, the enormously popular *Picturesque America*, published in two profusely illustrated volumes in 1874, devoted a full chapter to "the Connecticut shore of the Long Island Sound" but concentrated more on the towns and cities than on the natural beauty of the region, though a number of engraved plates hint at its special qualities.[16] Altogether left out in both books, the most influential of their type, were the equally picture-worthy locations on the Long Island side of the Sound, just a few miles across the water from Connecticut. Why this should have been so is especially puzzling since from the time of the first settlements both shores had been in frequent commercial and social contact with each other, forming a common cultural area.

Kensett, born near New Haven, must have been aware of the scenic virtues of Long Island Sound since infancy, but he was specifically attracted to the Darien area (see Plate 40) immediately upon hearing about it from his friend Colyer. In 1866 Colyer, who had served throughout the Civil War as a member of both the Christian and the Indian Commissions, made a yachting trip from New York to New Haven in search of a site for a house and studio.[17] He found a suitable spot on a small island, separated from the mainland only by a small stream, within the jurisdiction of the town of Darien, and quickly purchased thirty-five acres of it. The following year Kensett bought a parcel from Colyer, probably with the intention of building a studio, on what was by then known as Contentment Island.[18] Just when Colyer built his house on the property, or Kensett his studio, is not known, but both must have spent some time there after becoming proprietors. No records confirm that Kensett lived on the island for any significant length of time before the summer of 1872, by which time his studio had certainly been built; yet the number of finished paintings included in the sale of the contents of his New York studio that by their titles indicate that they were painted or first sketched in or around Contentment Island, clearly establish that he had already begun to work there before 1872.[19] One of these pictures, *Long Neck Point from Contentment Island, Darien, Connecticut* (Plate 41), further indicates that the special beauty of the place had already begun to exercise its magic on him before 1872.

It is clear that the territory in and around their island had great meaning for Kensett and Colyer. Colyer's name for his property, "Contentment Island," clearly conveys his feelings for the spot. Unoccupied before his arrival there, the island had been generally known as Ox Pound Island because it provided a safe enclosure for grazing cattle. In the local lore, however, it was also called Contention Island because of the numerous quarrels that had arisen from time immemorial over the use of its pastureland.[20] The change from Contention to Contentment in the name of the island in 1866 echoed

FIGURE 80.
Kensett, Shore of Darien, Connecticut, 1872, *oil on canvas*, 12⅛ x 20¼ *in.* (30.8 x 51.4 cm.), *location unknown, archival photograph courtesy of The Metropolitan Museum of Art, New York.*

Colyer's own transition from the strife and pain of the Civil War, which he had ample occasion to observe firsthand, to the promise of the recently achieved peace. His exploratory voyage to New Haven in search of not only a new family domicile but also a new artistic beginning in the oldest part of the country was especially significant at a time when the nation as a whole was undergoing a similar process of self-examination and peacetime growth. This journey in "the inland sea" was also, in a way, the counterpart of those ambitious scientific-artistic expeditions to exotic foreign lands, or to our own West which became popular in the middle of the nineteenth century.[21] The personal and unpretentious character of Colyer's voyage stands in relation to the public and grandiose character of these expeditions exactly as the paintings of Kensett stand in contrast to those of Frederic Church, something that was surely not lost on either Colyer or Kensett, whose paintings were repeatedly praised for their simplicity, emotional honesty, and avoidance of sensationalistic effects. Both Colyer and Kensett surely sensed that "looking inward" geographically to find "contentment" had a parallel in their own inner lives.

The descriptive comments that appeared in the *New York Herald* when the list of Kensett's Last Summer's Work was first published hint at the profound personal significance this locale held for the artist. A number of works are identified as "seen from the window of Kensett's bedroom," "seen from the door of the artist's studio," and "seen off the studio." The picture now known as *Fish Island*, depicting two small rocky outcroppings in the waters off Contentment Island (Plate 38), was listed as "Kensett's Island," further identifying the artist with the locale.[22] In another of the paintings sold by the Metropolitan, *Shore of Darien, Connecticut* (now unlocated; Fig. 80), Kensett portrayed himself sketching outdoors under an umbrella, the only such self-portrait known.

Plate 40. Kensett

The Old Pine, Darien, Connecticut

1872

oil on canvas, 34⅜ x 27¼ in. (87.3 x 69.2 cm.)

The Metropolitan Museum of Art, New York,

Gift of Thomas Kensett, 1874

Plate 41. Kensett

Long Neck Point from Contentment Island, Darien, Connecticut

c. 1870–72

oil on canvas, 15⅜ x 24⅜ in. (39 x 61.9 cm.)

Museum of Art, Carnegie Institute, Pittsburgh,

Gift of the Women's Committee of the Museum of Art, 1980

Nothing in Kensett's output from any other time or place compares with this exhaustive and systematic pictorial survey of the territory surrounding him at Contentment Island. His enthusiasm translated itself into a frenzied activity. He produced a new work every three or four days—the probable reason why small passages in certain of the paintings were left unfinished. Challenged by a new composition or visual experience, the artist set to work on it and abandoned the picture whose problems had already been mostly resolved. Such enthusiasm, the result of a deeply felt personal communion with nature, also goes a long way toward explaining why the Contentment Island paintings have a special emotional appeal and why in so many of them the artist endeavored to find new formal means to give expression to his feelings.[23] That endeavor probably had begun before the summer of 1872, yet it was in his last painting campaign during those summer months, which probably extended into the early autumn, that Kensett made the imaginative leap that produced the masterpieces of the Last Summer's Work: *Eaton's Neck, Long Island*; *A Foggy Sky*; *Newport Rocks*; *Twilight in the Cedars at Darien, Connecticut*; *Sunset on the Sea*; *The Old Pine, Darien, Connecticut*; and *Gathering Storm on Long Island Sound*. *Newport Rocks* and *A Foggy Sky* were either painted or begun in Newport, but they conform to the aesthetic of the Contentment Island/Long Island Sound pictures and are better understood as part of that group. So close are they in feeling to the Connecticut shore paintings, in fact, that Reverend Samuel Osgood, who singled out the finest of the Last Summer's Work in remarks delivered at a meeting held in Kensett's memory at the Century Club, thought that they had been painted in the neighborhood of Darien.[24]

Clearly, the effect that his finding of and settling on Contentment Island had on Kensett must be counted as one of the chief catalysts of his Last Summer's Work style. The chief features of that style— a pronounced simplification in compositional massing, an increased sophistication and abstract quality of the scumbling used to depict sea and sky, an observable flattening of pictorial space and the use of color to complement the mood of a scene—cannot be separated from the work he did in that particular locale and seems as much a response to its physical qualities as to any abstract ideas of style Kensett might have been contemplating at the time. To be sure, the stylistic breakthrough achieved in the major paintings of the Last Summer's Work is not a complete surprise in the context of Kensett's oeuvre. In a sense, one strain of Kensett's work, the seascape, had been tending to this direction from the mid-1850s on. This is readily comprehended if we compare his *Beacon Rock, Newport Harbor* of 1857 (Plate 20) with his rendition of the same location in the painting titled *Marine off Big Rock* of 1864 (Plate 21). Yet the stylistic progression toward abstract composition and reduction of parts takes a quantum leap in the treatment of almost the same scene in *Newport Rocks* (Plate 42). This is a work of iconic boldness which, like *A Foggy Sky* (Plate 43), isolates in contrasting simplicity the three physical realms of the planet—land, sea, and air. The imaginative power of these works moved Reverend Osgood to perceive in the rock formations depicted in them natural sphinxes full of mystery and sublime beauty. His elevated reactions, however, are not really appropriate to describe either of the earlier paintings.

Under his touch we see the marvel of the Egyptian sands reappearing in the shore of our great Sound, and that stone looks upon you with the face of the Sphinx. That rock whispers to you the secret of earth, and sea, and sky. Its surface speaks out the mysterious life of nature, which glows in that rich color like blood in the cheek, and those stains, and seams, and mosses, are the impressions which ages have left

FIGURE 81
Kensett, The Sea (Long Island Sound from Fisher's Island), 1872, *oil on canvas, 15½ x 30½ in. (39.4 x 77.5 cm.), The Metropolitan Museum of Art, New York, Gift of Thomas Kensett, 1874.*

upon that stony face under the changes of the air, and water and light. This Sphinx means more than we can understand, and her features and look so faithfully report her colloquy for thousands of years with the sea and the winds.[25]

That Kensett had a good idea that, in terms of his style and of the subject matter he was dealing with, less *was* more, is amply borne out by his repeated attempts to reduce to the simplest terms the compositions of so many of the pictures in the Last Summer's Work. In the case of one painting, *The Sea* (Fig. 81), a telling transformation has taken place: its composition repeats, down to the patterns of the foam on the breaking waves, the work titled *Shore of Darien, Connecticut*, mentioned above, which contains Kensett's self-portrait. In *The Sea*, however, not only has the self-portrait been eliminated but so has a prominent sailboat and the band of land visible in the distance on the right side of the horizon. Equally important, the overall composition has been made more panoramic by reducing the ratio of height to width and more obviously geometric by moving a highly visible sailboat to the center of the horizon line. Yet *The Sea* is not a sketch for the more detailed *Shore of Darien, Connecticut*; on the contrary, its greater size and more careful execution suggests precisely the opposite.[26]

That this sort of stylistic experimentation is related to the particular place in which Kensett found himself for most of the summer of 1872 seems clear enough. But at this point one may wonder exactly what it was about the place that so motivated the artist. Again, a probable answer lies in the intelligent remarks made by Reverend Osgood shortly after the artist's death. As Osgood saw it, it was light, the omnipresent light of Long Island Sound in the summer, that set apart Kensett's last great paintings:

I have lived for over twenty years within a short distance of KENSETT'S *summer house, and I have watched month after month the effects of earth, and sky, and water, which he treats. His rendering of them is satisfactory, suggestive and imposing. He has perpetuated upon his canvas moods of the sea*

A "Less was more"

Plate 42. Kensett

Newport Rocks

1872

oil on canvas, 31 x 48 in. (78.7 x 121.9 cm.)

The Metropolitan Museum of Art, New York,

Gift of Thomas Kensett, 1874

Plate 43. Kensett
A Foggy Sky
1872
oil on canvas, 30½ x 45¾ in. (77.5 x 116.2 cm.)
The Metropolitan Museum of Art, New York,
Gift of Thomas Kensett, 1874

*and the sky that seemed to me to have passed away with the moment that organized them; and his re-
markable studies of cloud and sky under all changing hues and combinations, from sunrise to sunset,
seem like the vision of the face of a departed friend, a restoration of the very countenance, with its light
and form, its thought and feeling. Certainly, if a man can bequeath light to those who come after him,
Kensett has left a legacy of light to us all—of light too, that is all instinct with feeling, all alive with
love, and apparently with a sense of deepening seriousness as the evening shadows drew on.*[27]

The remarkably evocative effects of light visible on the Sound were real and could be translated
into paint without incurring the charge of falseness to nature. When Kensett turned his attention away
from this special area to more traditional locations such as Lake George, he reverted to a more traditional approach, so that the sketches of this site that are part of the Last Summer's Work do not
partake of the new aesthetic. Osgood's recognition that an attempt to capture a special type of light
and to make it communicate feeling directly was essential to the Last Summer's Work led him quite
correctly to identify *Sunset on the Sea* (Plate 44) as the most adventurous picture in the group.

*Perhaps his most remarkable picture in this series is that which presents the sea under the sunlight,
with nothing else to divide the interest—no land or sail, no figure, and not even a noticeable cloud to
give peculiar effect, or a rock to provoke the dash of the waves. It is pure light and water, a bridal of the
sea and sky. Is it presumption in a poor novice in art like me, to say that this is a great picture?*[28]

Yet in spite of an almost symbolic simplicity, which appears to divorce the scene from a specific
geographical location, *Sunset on the Sea* is more a portrait of the setting sun at a definite time and place
—the light of the Sound is unmistakable—than a generalized landscape of mood, though it is that too.
In this it contrasts strongly with Ralph Albert Blakelock's *The Sun, Serene, Sinks into the Slumberous
Sea* (1880s; Fig. 82), perhaps the only other work of this type painted by an important nineteenth-
century landscape artist, where the specificity of Kensett's approach is abandoned in favor of a more

actively expressed personal interpretation of the theme. Thus, even when dealing with a work of obvious symbolic import—a work in which the inherently sublime nature of the subject matter might have led the painter to expressionistic conceits, for, after all, such a subject is only a step away from abstract painting—Kensett's style remains site specific.[29] In the words of Reverend Osgood, the work is "rendered with severe truthfulness," a characterization he extended to all the paintings in the Last Summer's Work.[30]

V.

In addition to the decisive influence of the natural environment on the development of Kensett's Last Summer's Work, a number of factors related to the artistic environment in which he moved must be taken into account in order to understand these works more fully. These factors concern Kensett's reputation among his friends and colleagues, the place of his works prior to 1870 in the spectrum of American landscape painting of the time, and the relation of his personal life to his work.

In the mid-1850s, Kensett began to turn away from what might be called an early Hudson River School pictorial mode—with contorted tree trunks, zigzagging recession into deep space, and an emphasis on wilderness subjects—toward a quieter, more atmospheric and contemplative mode. After making this change, he was consistently praised for his lyricism, his fidelity to nature, and his unpretentiousness.[31] An early assessment of this mature and distinctive style appeared in *The Crayon*, in a review of the National Academy of Design Exhibition of 1858:

> *Kensett's pictures are, to our mind, remarkable in many points,—for refinement of taste, treatment of distances, rendering of atmospheric effect, and a happy expression of the broad light of day and of a specific time of day. His perception of the poetry and harmony of nature in these respects, is remarkably subtle and delicate. There is no ostentation in his pictures, no insincerity or negligence, no affectation of color, or aim to force striking contrasts. So far as we can see in his works, he paints faithfully whatever excites his sympathy.*[32]

This review has special significance because only two years before, *The Crayon*, surely the most influential American art journal of the time, had severely criticized his painting of the Franconia Mountains for lack of detail.[33] Kensett apparently took this criticism to heart. By 1859 the detailed sharpness of his style prompted responses like the one conveyed in a touching letter from the well-known Baltimore businessman and collector William T. Walters:

> *I entirely forgot when I was in New York to ask you to take me to refresh my recollection of that Newport picture which was in the exhibition two years ago—of which I have spoken to you about before—there was a "realism"—real, well defined actual water—and equally real Rocks—no vagueness—no uncertainty—and does anybody believe it hadn't true sentiment, and fine feeling—but I don't*

Plate 44. Kensett

Sunset on the Sea
1872
oil on canvas, 28 x 41⅛ in. (71.1 x 104.5 cm.)
The Metropolitan Museum of Art, New York,
Gift of Thomas Kensett, 1874

think you ever have, or can *paint a picture without fine feeling—and therefore it is, I have been drawn more closely to those of your works which contained more of the realistic and less of the uncertainly defined—there is a poetry of* art, *as well as* letters—*and there is no art without it—and that poetry of* yours *has gone most deeply in my heart where you have spoken in the* plainest *and most clearly defined words—for certainly—trees - mountains - Rocks air &c &c are the artists poetic words.*[34]

In the following years, attention to detail became a trademark of Kensett's art, and by the mid-1860s Henry T. Tuckerman in his *Book of the Artists* could write that

in some of his pictures the dense growth of trees on a rocky ledge, with the dripping stones and mouldy lichens, are rendered with the literal minuteness of one of the old Flemish painters. It is on this account that Kensett enjoys an exceptional reputation among the extreme advocates of the Pre-Raphaelite school, who praise him while ignoring the claims of other American landscape-artists.[35]

But Tuckerman also knew that "this fidelity to detail is but a single element of his success. His best pictures exhibit a rare purity of feeling, an accuracy and delicacy, and especially a harmonious treatment, perfectly adapted to the subject."[36] A few lines later, quoting "an able critic," Tuckerman reaffirmed his perceptions:

Mr. Kensett has long been accepted as a most consummate master in the treatment of subjects full of repose and sweetness, and been honored by critics and painters for the simple and unpretending character of his works—works venerable for tenderness and refinement of feeling, exquisite quality of color, and a free and individual method of painting certain facts of nature.[37]

The astonishing consistency in published evaluations of Kensett's style even extended to James Jackson Jarves, a publicist and collector who in general did not have much use for the realism of Hudson River School painting. Jarves thought that "Kensett is more refined in sentiment, and has an exquisite delicacy of pencil. He is the Bryant of our painters,—a little sad and monotonous, but sweet, artistic, and unaffected."[38] For many, Kensett's style was not just an aspect of his chosen career, it *was* Kensett. Once again, Tuckerman ably summed up the prevalent feeling:

*a little
sad and monotonous*

Of all our artists, he has the most thoroughly amiable disposition, is wholly superior to envy, and pursues his vocation in such a spirit of love and kindliness, that a critic must be made of very hard material who can find it in his heart to say a severe, inconsiderate, or careless word about John F. Kensett. Perhaps some of our readers will think all this is quite irrelevant to the present object, which is to define Kensett's position in art, wherewith personal qualities, it may be argued, have nothing to do. But we are of a contrary opinion. The disposition or moral nature of an artist directly and absolutely influence his works. We constantly talk of a "feeling for color"—of a picture exhibiting a fine or a true "feeling," and thus instinctively recognize a transfusion of the natural sentiment and a tone of mind into and through the mechanical execution, design, and spirit of a pictorial work. . . . The calm sweetness of Kensett's best efforts, the conscientiousness with which he preserves local diversities—the evenness of manner, the patience in detail, the harmonious tone—all are traceable to the artist's feeling and innate disposition, as well as to his skill.[39]

The "calm sweetness" perceived in Kensett's style was generally acknowledged to be a reflection of the artist's character:

So balanced, harmonious, quiet, cheerful and modest was he, that his talents and character presented little to perplex or differ about. Either as to his genius as an artist, or his worth as a man, or his total characteristics in both lights, there was less variety of opinion than in respect to almost any man of equal eminence. His sweetness of disposition, ready sympathy, lively appreciation of the merits of fellow artists, humility in regard to his own works, delicacy of feeling and prudence of speech, made him a universal favorite among his brother painters, and a person always welcome, and always praised.[40]

But while most American writers and critics of the mid-nineteenth century were in agreement concerning Kensett's style and its reflection of those personality traits that made him so well-loved, some more perceptively saw it as antithetical to the grander style of Frederic Church and Albert Bierstadt, who with Kensett formed what was frequently thought of as the leading trio of American landscape painters. Jarves, who reserved some of his most venomous phrases for Church and Bierstadt, said of their works:

With [Church] color is an Arabian Nights' Entertainment, a pyrotechnic display, brilliantly enchanting on first view, but leaving no permanent satisfaction to the mind, as all things fail to do which delight more in astonishing than instructing. Church's pictures have no reserved power of suggestion, but expend their force in coup-de-main effects. Hence it is that spectators are so loud in their exclamations of delight. Felicitous and novel in composition, lively in details, experimentive, reflecting in his pictures many of the qualities of the American mind, notwithstanding a certain falseness of character, Church will long continue the favorite with a large class. . . . But a competitor for the popular favor in the same direction has appeared in Bierstadt. . . . Kensett is more refined in sentiment.[41]

The famous letter from Walters to Kensett written shortly after the collector purchased Church's now world-famous *Twilight in the Wilderness* (1860; The Cleveland Museum of Art) also reveals an awareness of the fundamental opposition of Kensett's style to Church's. Walters' tone is slightly apologetic—doubtless because Church's prices were astronomical compared to Kensett's—and he seems to confide to Kensett that he believes Church's style is not really in good taste but that *Twilight* is as close as that artist can come to it:

I was in New York 10 days ago and took Church's Twilight—a little "Fire worksey" perhaps but a good specimen of him—in "unity of design" far more satisfactory than the Andes—and in some other respects I think you will like it better than anything you have seen of his. . . . When I saw it a month ago I had no intention of having it but before its completion it became better.[42]

How widespread the dissatisfaction with the style of Church and Bierstadt was in the 1850s and 1860s is difficult to ascertain, but their blockbuster approach apparently was held deeply suspect in some quarters. It is also equally difficult to ascertain whether the opposition of Kensett's style to that of these artists can be construed as a vote of preference in favor of the type of picture we would today call luminist.[43] At least one commentary on Kensett's mature style, however, seems to do so. It appeared in the *New York Daily Tribune* for 15 March 1873:

> *Kensett's work had the same charm for the English and for Americans as Longfellow's poetry; it was like Bryant and like Wordsworth in some of his moods. A gentle sweetness, a calm content, a happiness to be with nature in calm and sunny hours, those are the traits of Kensett's artistic character. And yet he was not weak, though the dislike he had for exhibitions of skill for their own sake, for startling subjects, for scenes where Nature seems to have worked with her high-heeled shoes on, may have led many to think him weak. . . . His pictures are still springs of refreshment in the heat and turmoil of the world, fair glimpses of the cool, pure sky caught between the dust clouds of this weary fighting-ground. The happy stood before them and recalled other happy days; hearts touched with sadness were soothed in their simplicity; the artist admired the facile hand, and the unlearned recognized the truth to nature's every-day aspect. . . . Kensett is the flower of the school of landscape we call American, a school that boasts of several chosen names; they all belong to this pastoral band, and their hold on the public is by this note in them of gentle meditation. So long as that note is loved Kensett must also be loved.[44]*

The writer's answer to the charge of "weakness" in Kensett's style is one of the more interesting elements of this panegyric. He asserts, in effect, that even if Kensett did not emulate the pictorial showmanship for which Church and Bierstadt were renowned, his approach was nonetheless worthy. This concern with the artist's standing among the painters of his time was well warranted, for amidst the chorus of praise for Kensett's poetic, unpretentious style and for his equally appealing personality, a sour note was frequently heard: the suggestion that he was not really first-rate. This note was sounded early on in an article, first published in *The Century* and reprinted in *The Crayon*, dealing with the qualifications of the artists selected to serve on the newly formed presidential commission that was to take charge of the decoration of the nation's Capitol: "Mr. Kensett enjoys a popularity well earned and fully deserved. He stands very nearly, if not quite, at the head of our landscape art."[45] Even Tuckerman betrayed some misgivings: "Other artists may have produced single pictures of more genius; may be in certain instances superior; but, on the whole, for average success, Kensett's pictures are—we do not say always the most brilliant, effective, or original—but often the most satisfactory."[46] Reverend Osgood also thought that Kensett had his limitations: "He was not as romantic as Cole, nor had he the transfiguring imagination and the grand historical vision of Turner."[47] Reverend Henry Whitney Bellows, speaking at the Kensett memorial proceedings held at the Century Club, neatly summarized the nature of the artist's limitations:

> *He had none of that "vaulting ambition that o'erleaps itself," nothing of that impetuous passion for great achievements, which is often unaccompanied by the power of successful performance. Far be it from me to dispraise or undervalue a bold and daring temperament in art. Probably no man can attain*

the first rank without it. First-class genius is always courageous and soaring; nay, it is versatile and various. It attempts many things, fails in many things, but at last succeeds greatly, and sometimes in many ways. But below the very first-class (and how few can belong there?) there is nothing more fortunate in an artist, than a just and modest appreciation of his own powers—an exact measurement of the limits of his faculties, and a cultivated instinct for the legitimate sphere within which his executive faculties lie. . . . Mr. KENSETT was specially happy in a just estimate of his own faculties. His genius, pure, delicate, poetic, was limited within a moderate range.[48]

Nothing in Kensett's letters or in relevant documents conclusively establishes that he was aware of a lack of ambitiousness in his work, but it seems unlikely that he could have been ignorant of the remarks published in *The Crayon* and by Tuckerman. Further, the energy and enthusiasm with which he approached the boldly reductive style of his Last Summer's Work suggests that the great final pictures were indeed an attempt to reach for a higher level of achievement.

In terms of his personal welfare, Kensett could not have picked a more opportune moment for making his move. By 1870 he was an established and respected figure, both artistically and socially; he was also by all reckonings a rich man. His investments, made under the guidance of Marquand, among others, had been highly lucrative, and his family—his mother and unmarried sisters—were financially secure. He had, in a sense, little to worry about other than his art. But by this time, the Hudson River School tradition from which he had sprung was under serious assault from the school of landscape painters Jarves characterized as depicting "the ideal," as opposed to "the real." This group included not only George Inness, who was influenced by the French Barbizon painters, but also Elihu Vedder and John La Farge.[49] In this siegelike context, it is not surprising that Kensett felt compelled to experiment and to surpass his previous successes, or that he tried to do so within the parameters of the detailed realism, site specificity, and lyrical repose that had been the distinguishable and praiseworthy features of his style. In his mind also was probably the example of the by-now universally admired Turner. Kensett was familiar with Turner's work and had undoubtedly read at least part of Ruskin's *Modern Painters*.[50] Turner's complex style, his freedom of execution and sheer ambitiousness, and his attempt to forge a modern landscape style set an example for all landscape painters to follow. Kensett, of course, could not adopt a style like Turner's without abandoning his long-held principles, but he could, like Turner, attempt to achieve a landscape sublime through the interpretation of light. His Last Summer's Work in its finest aspects accomplished this and held great promise, not only for the artist's own artistic development, but for the revitalization of Hudson River School painting in general.[51]

Unfortunately, Kensett died shortly after his season of artistic experimentation and adventure. The promise of his Last Summer's Work remained unfulfilled even as many of the works remained unresolved, posing more questions than they answer.

VI.

Since a good deal of recent critical thought in the field of American art has been devoted to the examination of the luminist style, or mode, in nineteenth-century landscape painting, it would be inappropriate to close this essay without some assessment of the relationship of the Last Summer's Work to current notions and ideas about luminism. Something of a charged term, "luminism" has done long and able service as a conceptual vehicle that groups together those paintings of quiet stillness, executed on a small scale and with painstaking attention to detail, which were so frequently produced in this country in the years between 1850 and 1875. At first employed in a fairly descriptive way, luminism has now come to be used to define the most innovative of nineteenth-century American landscape styles, the most reflective of native sensibility, and the visual counterpart of important philosophical ideas popularized during roughly the same years.[52] Yet the words "movement" or "school"

cannot be easily attached to the term: the lines of influence linking one artist to another are unclear; practically all luminist painters produced important works not readily defined by the concept; and, more important, precious little has come down to us in the way of documentation establishing any contemporary awareness of the style as either a separate mode of landscape painting or one particularly endowed with special meaning. Still, the evidence presented by the works themselves is suggestive and inescapable, and there can be little doubt that, despite its problems, the idea of luminism as a distinct American landscape type has enormous critical, if perhaps not truly historical, validity.

Probably because the concept of a luminist style has not identified the kinds of historical processes which form the basis of much traditional art history, investigation of it almost of necessity has taken place at the more general level of cultural history. But here many interesting relationships have emerged, though not necessarily cause-and-effect ones. The idea that luminism and Emersonian transcendentalism are manifestations of the same cultural spirit has gained wide acceptance, as has the view that the all-pervasive national tragedy of the Civil War exerted considerable influence on the underlying mood, if not the purely formal aspects, of the works.[53]

Without a doubt, Kensett's Last Summer's Work stands as one of the lasting monuments of the American luminist style. The paintings' concern with formal simplicity, with the poetry of light as reflected in sky and water, with silence, intimacy, and a contemplative quietism, are all well within the canon of luminism. Less so is the palpably visible brushwork employed in some areas of some of the major works, as in, for example, the sea in *Sunset on the Sea*, the sky in *Gathering Storm on Long Island*

Sound (Fig. 83), and the red band of light on the horizon of *Twilight in the Cedars at Darien, Connecticut* (Fig. 84). In these works, as in the actively scumbled sky of *Long Neck Point from Contentment Island*, Kensett seems to be moving away from the perfectly smooth brushwork of his earlier, but still mature, luminist works, and toward a more dramatic approach to painting. To be sure, the drama of Kensett's late brushwork is a small one, and quite safely distanced from Turner's, but its somewhat surprising presence in the Last Summer's Work further attests to the enormous personal involvement he had with these pictures. In them, the artist's "labor trail" never disappears altogether, and in some it is very much present.[54]

If Kensett's emotional involvement with his Last Summer's Work made him something less than the perfectly "transparent eyeball" called for by Emerson, neither does the mood of his last great paintings accord perfectly well with Emerson's energetic optimism.[55] As we have seen, a good deal of the special quality of these works has to do with a location that was meant to function as an artistic refuge for a man, Colyer, who was surely attempting to recover the personal and domestic tranquility he had lost as a result of the Civil War. Kensett too had been touched by the war, not as deeply as Colyer perhaps, but he had been an ardent pro-Union sympathizer and a tireless organizer of the Metropolitan Fair held in New York in 1864. In a sense, their retreat to Contentment Island was symptomatic of the national mood in the years following the war. An immense sense of relief mingled with lost innocence, a desire to escape the political and social complexities of Reconstruction, a feeling that a renewed concentration on work and individual enterprise was a key part of the national agenda—all these were elements of this mood. Also very important, especially in relation to the written word, was the perception that the inflated rhetoric and intellectual posturings characteristic of the years leading up to the war had been at least partially responsible for its occurrence. The war, it seems, invalidated this embellished prose style and ushered in, chiefly in the speeches and writings of Abraham Lincoln, a spare, taut, direct, simple, and highly analytic approach to writing, which was to have enormous influence on the subsequent course of American letters. According to Edmund Wilson, who first perceived this shift in our national culture, this was not the only manifestation of the war's influence on the psychology of thinkers and writers. Another, and opposite, result seems to have been effected on writers who took no part in the war at all but who were nevertheless intensely aware of it. In them, the development of a style marked by "ambiguity, prolixity, [and] irony" reflected "a kind of lack of self-confidence, a diffidence and a mechanism of self-defense."[56]

If these major stylistic changes in the world of American letters can be directly linked with the experience of the Civil War, there is ample reason to suppose that at least somewhat similar processes took place in the world of American painting, even if painting had not been a politically charged medium, like prose writing. If this is so, then Kensett's concern with simplicity, clarity, and an almost abstract reductionism parallels that "chastening" which Wilson accurately diagnosed in American prose style. In both cases, simplicity comes as the result of disillusion but also as a saving grace. The old Hudson River School precepts of truth to nature and artistic self-effacement had never precluded the magniloquence of Church, the detailed clutter of Durand, or the wooden incidentals painted by other luminists such as Fitz Hugh Lane and Martin Johnson Heade. In the Last Summer's Work these old values are largely retained, but to these is added the peculiarly postwar perception that the less said the better, that truth lies in the way of restraint and not in the way of artifice.

Plate 45. Kensett

Twilight on the Sound, Darien, Connecticut

1872

oil on canvas, 11½ x 24½ in. (29.2 x 62.2 cm.)

The Metropolitan Museum of Art, New York,

Gift of Thomas Kensett, 1874

JOHN F. KENSETT'S PAINTING TECHNIQUE

Dianne Dwyer

I. Working Methods

THE COLLECTION OF TWENTY-TWO PAINTINGS AND STUDIES BY KENSETT at the Metropolitan Museum of Art affords a unique opportunity to study the artist's materials and working method. Of these twenty-two canvases, all but three, *Hudson River Scene* (1857), *Lake George* (1869), and *Summer Day on Conesus Lake* (1870), date from the final months of his career and are part of the group of paintings and sketches known as the Last Summer's Work of 1872. Originally thirty-eight in number, they were exhibited under that title at the National Academy of Design in 1873, together with other pictures from Kensett's estate. Thomas Kensett, the artist's brother, eventually purchased the Last Summer's Work, which had been excluded from the estate sale and was "on exhibition only" at the National Academy, and presented it in 1874 to the recently founded Metropolitan Museum of Art as a memorial to the painter. Most of the information about Kensett's technique contained in the present study was obtained by visual examination, aided by a microscope; however, cross sections of paint samples and, to some degree, infrared reflectography also provided useful information.[1] Because the research focuses on the Metropolitan's holdings, the findings pertain chiefly to Kensett's later paintings.

The physical evidence of Kensett's work reflects a methodical mind and working method and suggests that he was able to visualize the completed composition from the moment he began his pencil sketch on the blank canvas. There are, for example, almost no pentimenti, or traces of changes, in his pictures. The extensive underdrawing found in Kensett's landscapes indicates that before beginning a painting or a painted sketch, the artist made a drawing, usually in graphite pencil, directly on the chalk ground that established all the major outlines of the composition and frequently even the minor details.

Hudson River Scene (Plate 6) shows two types of underdrawing, both of which are unusual in American painting of this period: brush drawing, which has pearled slightly on the ground as if it were in an aqueous medium, and some crayon or charcoal drawing. The contours of the landmasses are defined in crayon (Fig. 85a); the boats in the water as well as a very freely drawn tree were done with a brush and altered in the final composition (Fig. 85b).

Extremely detailed drawing is found throughout the 1863 *View from Cozzens' Hotel near West Point* (Plate 32). Kensett recorded every detail of the landscape on the right in graphite pencil, still visible under the thinly painted surface. Similar underdrawing, in pencil or brush, sometimes quite elaborate, has been noted in works by Sanford Gifford, Jasper Cropsey, and Francis Silva.

Where no underdrawing is visible, it cannot be assumed that none was made. Abundant evidence suggests that much of Kensett's underdrawing is concealed by opaque paint containing white lead,

which is not easily penetrated by infrared rays. The lines of the drawing are, in any case, gray and rather faint, so that they are not readily perceived using reflectography. In the 1869 *Lake George* (Plate 33), for example, underdrawing is visible along the profile of the landmasses but only in those areas where the artist deviated slightly from his design; the thinly painted sky does not conceal the

FIGURE 86
Kensett, Lake George, 1869
*(detail of plate 33), taken
under infrared light. Pencil
underdrawing appears at the
top of the central peak, along
the left ridge, and above the
lower peak at the left.*

drawing at these points, as do the more thickly painted mountains (Fig. 86). The horizon line has an extremely mechanical quality and was almost certainly drawn with a ruler.

The technique Kensett used to build up even a large and ambitious painting like *Lake George* is, due to his extraordinary economy of means, easily ascertained upon close examination. The artist first made a pencil sketch that defined at least the major outlines of the composition, for example, the horizon, the profile of mountains or of a landmass, and occasionally other details. In this case, he thinly washed a reddish priming over the white ground so that the rather schematic underdrawing remained visible. He then blocked in the sky and the water, leaving areas of priming exposed to represent the shadows and the reflections of islands in the water. Thin scumbles of paint over the warm priming give substance to these reflections. The mountains were the last major element to be painted, followed by such details as trees, birds, the boat, and the distant shoreline. *Lake George* contains one of the rare pentimenti in Kensett's oeuvre: at some stage after the picture had been completed, the artist rather clumsily altered the rocks in the foreground with badly matched paint.

In the smaller paintings and sketches, Kensett used a similarly direct procedure, which he did not vary from the decade of the fifties until his last paintings in 1872. *Nahant Rock and Seashore* of 1859 (Fig. 87), unlike *Lake George*, is painted on a white ground. Kensett painted the shapes of the rocks first, followed by the sky and finally the water. The figures and the boats again were added last. Each of the major elements of the composition—the sky, landmasses, and water—were painted separately and, like pieces of a jigsaw puzzle, do not intrude on one another except at the boundaries. The order in which Kensett fitted these separate pieces together varies from one picture to another. In *Sea Shore* (Fig. 88), dated 1861, the sky appears to have been painted first, following the guidelines of the pencil drawing, some of which are still visible, while in *The Old Pine, Darien, Connecticut* of 1872 (Plate 40) the rocks and bit of land at the horizon were laid in before the sky and water.

reddish Priming [handwritten marginal note]

white ground. [handwritten marginal note]

Since few preparatory drawings are known for Kensett's major paintings, the elaborate under-drawing found in a work like *View from Cozzens' Hotel near West Point* suggests that the artist began his composition by sketching on the canvas at the site. Kensett undoubtedly painted frequently *en plein air*, following the usual practice of landscape painters in this period. In a letter dated 1854 to his uncle John R. Kensett the artist describes a summer expedition to Lake George, traveling to the islands for the day "with my basket of provisions & my painting materials." A month later "having filled a moder-ate sized folio of pencil & oil sketches & studies I packed and started on an excursion of a week simply with a sketch book and pencil to Scroon Lake and the Adirondack mountains."[2]

For painting out-of-doors, artists frequently brought along unstretched canvases for convenience sake. These were pinned to a board, as shown in Thomas Cole's *Study for Dream of Arcadia* (Fig. 89). Tack holes in the corners of a canvas therefore suggest that Kensett painted it not in the studio but in the field. The same conclusion can be drawn from the presence of irregularly painted tacking margins where the painted area is not confined within the borders of the stretcher but spills over the folded edges. At least one of these indications of plein-air origin can be found in eight of the Kensetts in the Metropolitan's collection.[3] However, it should be noted that the absence of such indications does not prove that a painting was done in the studio: tack holes can be concealed in the folded corners of the tacking margins, the edges of the canvas may be lost or damaged, and the artist might well have painted outdoors on a stretched canvas.

Judging by its irregularly painted and cropped tacking edges, *Twilight on the Sound, Darien, Connecticut* (Plate 45), part of the Last Summer's Work and therefore dated 1872, is a plein-air sketch. Here Kensett painted the single boat directly on the ground, not over already completed water, as he

FIGURE 88.
Kensett, Sea Shore, 1861,
*oil on canvas, 18 x 30 in.
(45.7 x 76.2 cm.), The New-
York Historical Society,
New York.*

FIGURE 89.
Thomas Cole (1801–1848),
Study for Dream of Arcadia,
1830, *oil on panel, 8¾ x 14½
in. (22.2 x 36.8 cm.), The
New-York Historical Society,
New York.*

usually did with such small elements in earlier pictures. The landmass on the right, together with its reflection and the boat, were underpainted in warm earth brown on the blank canvas. The cool values of the water and sky were washed in, scumbling over the shadowed reflections, to incorporate them into the plane of the still water. Finally Kensett added the deep rose color of the sunset. The small scale of this sketch allowed the artist to capture the specific quality of a particularly transient moment on the

FIGURE 90.
Jan van Goyen (1596–1656),
View of Haarlem on the
Haarlemer Meer, 1646, *oil on
panel, 13⅝ x 19⅞ in. (34.6 x
50.5 cm.), The Metropolitan
Museum of Art, New York.*

Sound. Nowhere in the picture does one feel the somewhat abstract and schematic character necessarily imposed by the studio.

Some works begun as plein-air sketches may have been finished in the studio. *Newport Rocks* (Plate 42) has tack holes in some corners indicating that it was painted at the site. The bottom of the canvas has been let out approximately one-half inch (there is a second set of paint-covered tack holes). The paint that covers the tack holes and unprimed canvas along the lower edge is continuous with the rest of the water, suggesting that Kensett added this section in the studio after he had stretched the canvas for the second time. It is more difficult to conjecture why the canvas was let out along the bottom: this is a minor adjustment to a composition of this size and can only be explained by assuming that the frame had been mismeasured and was slightly too large. It is worth noting here that the sight size of Kensett's frames is frequently nearly identical to the size of the painted image. In order that the picture sit securely in the rebate, Kensett usually nailed strips of wood to the stretcher on all four sides. Since these strips never carry traces of paint or varnish, he probably added them when the work was very near completion so that he could work on the picture in its frame.[4]

In his late work, Kensett further explored the uses of a warm red or red-brown priming over the commercially prepared white ground, an experiment he appears to have started with *Lake George*. Cole, Kensett's mentor, occasionally used this technique, common in seventeenth-century landscape painting. The warm color of the priming subtly unifies disparate color relationships while deepening and giving tonal variation to the shadows. Areas painted with ultramarine blue, such as the passages of sky and water that dominate Kensett's late compositions, are intensified by the orange hue of the priming, an effect similar to that produced by the terra-cotta body underlying a ceramic glaze. The resulting brilliant hue plays against its orange complement, simulating the shimmering haze of sunlight scattered by a moist atmosphere.

This bold use of a warm ground, while having many art historical precedents, most clearly recalls the silvery atmospheric effects achieved by the seventeenth-century Dutch painter Jan van Goyen, who

168

Plate 46. Kensett

Summer Day on Conesus Lake

1870

oil on canvas, 24⅛ x 36⅜ in. (61.3 x 92.4 cm.)

The Metropolitan Museum of Art, New York,

Bequest of Collis P. Huntington

FIGURE 91.
Kensett, October in the
Marshes, 1872, *oil on canvas,*
18½ x 30½ in. (47 x 77.5
cm.), *The Metropolitan
Museum of Art, New York,
Gift of Thomas Kensett, 1874.*

used a similar warm underlayer over which thinly painted passages of sky and water play (Fig. 90).[5]
The similarities in handling, the shared compositional preference for horizontal bands and a low horizon, and the poetic sensitivity to light indicate the influence on Kensett of seventeenth-century Dutch
landscape paintings.

yellow priming

To achieve a slightly different effect, Kensett applied a yellow priming over the chalk ground in
Summer Day on Conesus Lake (Plate 46). He seems to have used this underlayer to impart warmth to
the exceptionally thinly painted sky. The lakeside park in the left half of the composition is filled with
dappled sunlight, and the warm tone of the sky intensifies the pervasive sense of a hot summer day.

opaque scumbles

Like other luminist painters, Kensett made extensive use of a sophisticated scumbling technique.
Lake George is executed entirely in thin, opaque scumbles over the warm priming. Mountains, sky, and
water are rendered with the same mix of colors; the variations in tone are created by the handling of the
paint. In *On the Coast* of 1870 (Private Collection), he stippled a textureless pale-blue layer over opaque
pink washes in the sky and a darker blue underpaint in the water. The effect approximates a scene

gossamer veil

viewed through a gossamer veil and immediately conveys that singular stillness so characteristic of
luminist painting.

Kensett executed most of his sketches and paintings, even his later work, much more directly,
with a versatile, stiff, pastelike paint, which handles easily. A variety of effects are possible with this
material: it can be smoothly stippled to produce a subtly gradated field of sky from horizon to zenith,
as in *Passing Off of the Storm* (Plate 47), or dramatically to juxtapose brush strokes of different colors,
as in *A Foggy Sky* (Plate 43). The stiffness of the paint, due to the high ratio of pigment to medium,
also relates to its opacity. This excellent characteristic is very desirable for sketching out-of-doors, as

FIGURE 92.
Kensett, Study of Beeches,
oil on canvas, 14¾ x 10⅜ in.
(37.5 x 26.4 cm.), The
Metropolitan Museum of
Art, New York, Gift of
Thomas Kensett, 1874.

it allows for rapid coverage of the white ground using only one layer. This is clearly the technique Kensett used in *Eaton's Neck, Long Island* (Plate 37): the brushwork in the sky attests to his quick and vigorous manner of painting. There are other advantages to this stiff paint: it does not run, and because it is so opaque, the ground can be used to maximum effect. In *Passing Off of the Storm*, the lower bands of sky and water, although visually distinct from each other, are of the same paint, manipulated so as to let more ground show through in one area than in another, resulting in a grayer, lighter color at the horizon, and a bluer, darker color in the upper sky and water.

passing of the Storm Plate 47

Kensett used various techniques to add textural relief. In *October in the Marshes* (Plate 48 and Fig. 91), he used the end of the brush extensively to define and emphasize the marsh grass and to expose additional white ground, which reads as flashes of light reflected from the water's surface. This sgraffito work functions both as highlight and calligraphy. The clump of yellow grass on the left is also stippled and textured, here with the tip of the brush, less to mimic the form of the grass than to convey the sense of pleasure the artist took in the brushwork.

In *Study of Beeches* (Fig. 92), Kensett manipulated details of the impasto, seen under magnification, in a sculptural way to imitate the texture and form of the rocks and foliage in low relief. His technique reveals unexpected beauty in an almost abstract way. The tiny peaks of paint are composed of as many as five different colors. Although these retain their separate identities, at normal viewing distance they blend into a single color and recognizable shape.

The simplified compositions of the Last Summer's Work, some of which were reduced to just the

Plate 47. Kensett

Passing Off of the Storm

1872

oil on canvas, 11⅜ x 24½ in. (28.9 x 62.2 cm.)

The Metropolitan Museum of Art, New York,

Gift of Thomas Kensett, 1874

Plate 48. Kensett
October in the Marshes (detail)
1872
oil on canvas, 18½ x 30½ in. (47 x 77.5 cm.)
The Metropolitan Museum of Art, New York, Gift of Thomas Kensett, 1874
This detail shows the techniques of sgraffito and stippling that
Kensett used to add textural relief to the paint surface.

basic elements of sea and sky, coupled with the suddenness of Kensett's death in the midst of an active career, has led to some discussion as to which paintings in this group were left unfinished. In the letter accompanying the gift of his late brother's work to the Metropolitan, Thomas Kensett requested that "such of the pictures as are unfinished shall remain in the condition in which my brother left them."[6] It is interesting to note that in the 1873 catalogue of the Last Summer's Work, only *Newport Rocks* is referred to as unfinished.[7] Although the lower part of *Sunset Sky* (Fig. 93) is blank, the catalogue did not qualify it in this way, perhaps because it so clearly was an unfinished picture. Judging from their exposed ground, an additional dozen or so paintings visible in the photographs of the National Academy of Design sale are also unfinished but were not characterized as such.[8] Perhaps because *Newport Rocks* is completely covered with paint the National Academy felt it was necessary to caution the viewer that the work was not completed.

Since *Newport Rocks* was either known or considered by Kensett's contemporaries to be unfinished, and in light of the confusion surrounding the status of other pictures in this group, an analysis of the buildup of the paint layers in relation to what is already known about the artist's working method would seem to be in order. Kensett painted this work on a white ground with a salmon-colored priming and, as described above, began it as an outdoor sketch. The addition of clouds, painted in opaque pink over a freely applied blue field, is characteristic of Kensett's usual treatment of sky, as are such typical finishing touches as the small pink strokes of impasto that delineate the reflection of the clouds on the slightly ruffled surface of the water. The rocks, however, are clearly unfinished. Areas of shadow and light as well as the general shapes of the rocks were blocked in but were not fully resolved and lack final modeling. A dark area of shadow above the angled line of the rocks' reflection is just

[handwritten annotations in left margin:]
Newport Rocks
plate 42

Salmon-colored ground

opaque pinks over freely applied Blue field

174

FIGURE 94.
Kensett, Sunset, 1872, *oil on canvas, 18 x 20 in. (45.7 x 76.2 cm.), The Metropolitan Museum of Art, New York, Gift of Thomas Kensett, 1874.*

barely indicated. As a result of the visual confusion in this area, the rocks do not convincingly emerge out of the water.

A Foggy Sky, which is nearly the same size as *Newport Rocks* and reverses the basic composition, was brought to the same stage of completion. The sky is very well developed, as is the water, which has a rather pebbly texture achieved by stippling with a brush. Kensett here deviated from his usual working method by painting the rocks over both water and sky, although, judging from the early drying cracks in the area of water covered by the rocks, the water was not completely dry when he added them. Again, the rocks appear to be unfinished: the underpainted shadows at their bases disturbingly fail to connect to the water.

The close visual correlation between *Newport Rocks* and *A Foggy Sky* and the fact that they seem to possess the same degree of finish, or incompletion, suggest that they may have been painted in tandem. There are two other possible pairs in this group of late pictures: *The Old Pine, Darien, Connecticut* (Plate 40) and *Gathering Storm on Long Island Sound* (Fig. 83), both of which are painted on a somewhat unusual twill weave, and *Twilight on the Sound, Darien, Connecticut* and *Passing Off of the Storm* (Plates 45 and 47). In all three pairs, the paintings have identical frames, and each painting of the pair depicts opposite mood or light.

It has been suggested that the stunning emptiness of the *Sunset on the Sea* (Plate 44) would eventually have been filled by the land masses familiar throughout Kensett's work, such as those that appear in *Sunset* (Fig. 94). Considering Kensett's methodical approach, it seems unlikely that he would have made such an extensive alteration at this point in the picture's development. None of the earlier pictures examined underwent such a major change. With the single exception of *A Foggy Sky*, which, as mentioned, was altered at an early stage in its development, Kensett painted sky, landmasses, and water as separate elements that do not overlap one another. The only variation is an occasional deviation from the contours of the pencil drawing or the alteration of the small brush strokes of impasto that define a wave. Details such as the tiny boats and figures used to establish the scale of the space and the distance to the horizon were added after the basic compositional elements of sky, land, and water had been completed. One can imagine, then, that the artist might have added to *Sunset on the Sea* a few sailboats in the middle and far distance but little else. The rather fussy treatment of the sun's reflection on the sea, represented by flicks of white, pink ,and yellow impasto, suggests that the artist had done all that he intended with this sketch.

Apart from *Sunset Sky*, *Newport Rocks*, and *A Foggy Sky*, no other paintings belonging to the Last Summer's Work have internal evidence that they are unfinished except, perhaps, for minor details. A comparison of *Salt Meadow in October* (Fig. 96b) with other works by the artist does not point to unresolved passages. The landmasses are fully developed, and the junction of the marsh grass with its reflection works convincingly. The blending of the thinly scumbled water over the warm underpaint of the marsh grass' reflection is entirely consonant with the treatment of similar passages in other paintings.

In *Eaton's Neck, Long Island*, the sailboats, a detail Kensett always added as the final touch, are already present. The vegetation on the sandy strip of beach is more summarily described, perhaps, than is usual in his earlier work. However, it is composed according to the artist's accustomed working method: in two layers, a darker underpaint and a lighter scumble. The freer brushwork is not out of keeping with Kensett's development in this period. One could postulate the ultimate addition of some small figures on the beach, as in *Beach at Newport* (Plate 35). To this degree *Eaton's Neck* may be unfinished.

Some information about the Last Summer's Work is recorded on the stretchers of the paintings. Attached to most of the stretchers are brittle fragments of paper labels bearing the title of the painting written in graphite pencil and a stamped number in the upper right corner. *Lake George, A Reminiscence* (Fig. 79) has an exceptionally intact paper label on which is inscribed "Lake George 1872" and the printed number "239" in the upper right. Since the number for this work in the 1873 catalogue of the Last Summer's Work is 709, the labels may represent an estate inventory. In the few cases where that part of the label containing the number has survived, it does not correspond with the number assigned to the same picture by the 1873 exhibition catalogue.[9]

Nearly every picture's title appears on its stretcher, written by the same hand in red pencil. When the title differs from that used in the National Academy exhibition, it is the one given in the *Descriptive Catalogue of the Last Summer's Work* published by the Metropolitan Museum in 1874 on the occasion of the gift. The handwriting does not resemble that of John Kensett or his brother, Thomas. Several stretchers have been boldly marked "Metropolitan Museum of Art, New York City" in black flowing script. The letters are as high as the stretcher bar is wide, and the legend continues on three sides. On the back of both *Old Pine, Darien, Connecticut* and *Gathering Storm on Long Island Sound* is the stamp of the looking-glass maker and artist's colorman Williams, Stevens, Williams, and Company of New York.

II. Problems of Conservation and State

KENSETT IS A SOUND AND STRAIGHTFORWARD PAINTER, and his artistic intentions are not easily misunderstood. His materials have withstood the changes due to time and are not particularly susceptible to solvents normally used by restorers to remove discolored varnish. Nevertheless, a significant number of works have been damaged in the past by cleaning. In the 1869 *Lake George*, the thin scumbles over the dark priming that define the reflections on the right have been partially removed, as has some of the underpaint. The skies of *October in the Marshes*, the 1872 study *Lake George* (Fig. 95), and *Summer Day on Conesus Lake*, painted in white lead and therefore relatively resistant to the usual solvents, all have suffered from abrasion. All three paintings show remnants of a discolored, slightly gray layer caught in the interstices of the brush strokes. The possibility that these are the remains of a layer of drying oil applied by the artist is indicated by the presence of an intact layer on *Twilight on the Sound*. This somewhat yellowed but transparent and perfectly even film stained positive for oil in a microchemical test and contains particles of brown iron oxide and a coarse black similar to charcoal black. This black most likely is not common dirt since the layer does not contain any other airborne contaminants and the distribution of particles is very uniform. The brown iron oxide may be a constituent of the underlying paint layer, which migrated into the oil layer, since the sky contains iron earth, evidence that the oil layer was added very shortly after the painting was finished.

While it is extremely unlikely that Kensett resorted to pigmented final glazes, he appears occasionally to have used drying oil, rather than a natural resin, as a final varnish. The chemicals and force required to remove such a layer, which is not only insoluble but intimately bound up with the paint underneath, could easily cause the sort of abrasion observed in some of his paintings and in other nineteenth-century American landscapes.

Whether Kensett intended his sketches or studies to be varnished is uncertain. Many of the paintings that remained in his studio appear to have come to the Metropolitan unvarnished; several sketches have remained in that condition and retain a most beautiful surface. However, a version of *Shrewsbury River* (Frontispiece) which descended in the family of Thomas Kensett, was covered with what appeared to be the original varnish, since it was sufficiently discolored to have been more or less contemporary with the picture itself.

In Kensett's late pictures, including the Last Summer's Work, problems associated with faulty technique appear more frequently than in the artist's earlier works. One of the defects manifests itself as a slight discoloration occuring in patterns resembling wide brush strokes but seems to be coming from a layer under the paint. Kensett's experimentation with colored or toned primings may account for some of the problems in his late work. Another factor may be the modification of his usual paint mixture to achieve greater freedom and fluidity of brushwork. *Twilight in the Cedars at Darien, Connecticut* (Fig. 84), *Sunset on the Sea*, and *October in the Marshes* all suffer severely from drying cracks, that type of cracking that occurs as the paint begins to dry and which is not the result of mechanical stress. This disfiguring alteration is usually caused by an excessively high ratio of medium to pigment, or by painting over a medium-rich layer without allowing sufficient drying time between applications.

FIGURE 95.
Kensett, Lake George, 1872,
oil on canvas, 10⅛ x 13½ in.
(25.7 x 34.3 cm.), The
Metropolitan Museum of
Art, New York, Gift of
Thomas Kensett, 1874.

These pictures, particularly *Sunset on the Sea*, give every indication of having been executed very quickly and painted, in some areas, wet into wet.

The most disfiguring and least explicable alteration occurs in *Salt Meadow in October* (Figs. 96a and 96b). In the blue foreground and sky, large stained patches not associated with a particular form in the composition have appeared with time. When cross sections were compared, the darkening was identified as a chemical alteration of white lead: the upper particles of this pigment, which is normally quite opaque, had been transformed into transparent crystals, which have not, to date, been specifically identified. The well-known alteration of basic carbonate of lead into the black lead sulfide has, however, been ruled out. Although *Salt Meadow in October* has a warm priming composed of white lead, iron earth, red lake, and a small amount of an organic brown, it is unlikely that any of these substances are responsible for the change in the blue as it has been noted in other paintings where there is no red priming. The combination of the red ground and thinness of the blue paint layer may have made the darkening effect of the altered white lead more obvious. This type of change frequently has been called "ground staining" because it is commonly thought to originate in that layer. It has been noted in many nineteenth-century American paintings.

Ground Staining

III. A Note on Materials

KENSETT NORMALLY PAINTED on commercially primed linen canvas. The stretchers are of white pine, with mortise-and-tenon joints and oak keys. Microscopic identification of ground and paint samples taken from a variety of canvases indicates that the white ground is calcium carbonate.[10] The yellow priming layer in *A Summer Day on Conesus Lake* is composed of lead white, yellow ochre, and charcoal black. "Red" primings are of varying composition: that of *Salt Meadow in October* contains yellow or brown iron earth, small amounts of red lake, lead white, and an organic brown such as Van Dyck brown. In *Newport Rocks*, a more orange priming was identified as yellow or brown earth, white lead, an anisotropic[11] red (red earth or vermilion), and a coarse black (bone or charcoal). Blue sky samples were invariably found to contain lead white and synthetic ultramarine. A sample of pale, intense yellow from *Sunset Sky* proved to be nothing more exotic than lead white and yellow earth with a trace of synthetic ultramarine. Pink-orange samples from that same sky contained those pigments but with a higher percentage of synthetic ultramarine and an anisotropic red, while in purple samples yet more synthetic ultramarine was noted. The purple-gray passages of the sky in *A Foggy Sky* were made by combining yellow ochre, coarse black, and calcium carbonate. The several greens in the foreground of *The Sea* (*Long Island Sound from Fisher's Island*; Fig. 81) were as follows: the yellowest green is composed of Prussian blue, lead white, yellow ochre, a coarse black, and a glass drier. Another lime green consists of Prussian blue, yellow ochre, lead white, and a glass drier, as does the duller green, with the addition in this case of an anisotropic red. A significant amount of glass was also identified in a sample of underpaint from the shadow area of the water of *A Summer Day at Conesus Lake*, along with yellow earth, red lead, and a coarse black.

Red Primings contain Lead White.

glass drier

180

APPENDIX

I.

The following document is among a group of Kensett papers owned by Kennedy Galleries, Inc., New York. A microfilm copy is in the Archives of American Art.

Memo of pictures belonging to the Estate of John F. Kensett [with appraised values]

Newport (large)   1,550

Newport unfinished   1,250

Lake George   800

Sunrise   2,000

Sunset   1,800

Eight small studies (Darien) ea $325.   2,600

Pine Tree   1,000

Storm Effect   800

Sunset, Twilight   ea $800.   1,600   Pair

Twilight, thro' Trees   1,500

Fish Island, unfinished   800

Eaton's Neck - Beach   500

Studies 1. finished and one not ea. $600   1,200   Pair

Autumn Studies ea $400   800

Sky & Sea   1,000

Sunset Sky, unfinished   100

Sunset Sea, Sky & Rock   500

Two Sea Pieces   ea. $500   1,000

Two Sea Pieces   (small, ea. $225)   450

Two small studies   (fog & companion, ea $225)   450

After Sunset   Autumn   150

Five Lake George Studies   (small ea $100)   500

[The list continues with the works by contemporary artists owned by Kensett.]

II.

The following is a complete list of the items in the Last Summer's Work given to the Metropolitan Museum of Art by Thomas Kensett in 1874, taken from the museum's catalogue cards. Some of the original titles have been crossed off and changed; the crossed out portions are here noted in italics. Those marked with an asterisk are still in the museum's collection.

*74.3   Sunset on the Sea   28 x 41⅛ in.

*74.4   Twilight in the Cedars at Darien, Connecticut   28½ x 41 in.

74.5   Sunrise on [The Connecticut Shore of] Long Island Sound   31 x 48 in.

*74.6   Newport Rocks   31 x 48 in.

*74.7   Lake George, N.Y.   22½ x 36½ in.

*74.8   A Foggy Sky   30½ x 45¾ in.

74.9   Sunrise on *the Sea* Long Island Sound   13¾ x 17¾ in.

74.10   Sunrise from Contentment Island on the Sea   14 x 18 in.

*74.11   Lake George, A Reminiscence   11 x 17½ in.

*74.12   Lake George   10⅛ x 13½ in.

*74.13   Study of Beeches   14¾ x 10⅜ in.

74.14   *Landscape Study, Hillside* Near Lake George   10 x 13⅝ in.

74.15   *Long Island Sound from Fish Island*

        Shore of Darien, Connecticut   12⅛ x 20¼ in.

74.16   Evening—Cedar Grove   14 x 18 in.

74.17   Twilight Near Darien   14 x 18 in.

74.18   *Twilight—A Study*

        After Sunset (unfinished)   12¾ x 16 in.

74.19   *Autumn Sunset*   Sunset in the Woods   18 x 14 in.

*74.20   Lake George, Free Study   10 x 14⅛ in.

74.21   After Sunset   17 x 30 in.

74.22   *Rocks and Waves*

        Long Island Sound from Fish Island   12⅝ x 20⅝ in.

74.23   *Coast at Darien*

        Study—On The Long Island Shore   15⅛ x 30¼ in.

*74.24   Twilight on The Sound, Darien, Connecticut   11½ x 24½ in.

*74.25   October in The Marshes   18½ x 30½ in.

74.26   Twilight in The Cedars—A Study   18 x 14 in.

*74.27 Passing Off of The Storm   11⅜ x 24½ in.

*74.28 Salt Meadow in October   18 x 30 in.

*74.29 Eaton's Neck   18 x 36 in.

*74.30 Sunset Sky   20 x 32 in.

 74.31 Rocks at Darien   15¼ x 30¼ in.

 74.32 Twilight After a Storm   15 x 30 in.

 74.33 *Sea and Rocky Shore*

         Rocks and Waves   18½ x 30½ in.

 74.34 Evening at Contentment Island, Darien   17⅛ x 30¼ in.

*74.35 *Long Island Sound from Fish Island*

         The Sea   15½ x 30½ in.

 74.36 *Fish Island from Kensett's Studio*

         Kensett's Island from his Studio   18 x 36 in.

*74.37 Sunset   18 x 30 in.

*74.38 The Old Pine, Darien, Connecticut   34⅜ x 27¼ in.

*74.39 Gathering Storm on Long Island Sound   34½ x 27¼ in.

 74.40 Twilight on Contentment Island   28 x 42½ in.

NOTES

Kensett's World

1. Samuel Bradlee Doggett, *A History of the Doggett-Daggett Family* (Boston, 1894), p. 192. The Kensett house, a two story clapboard saltbox, no longer stands. It was located at 242 South Main Street, Cheshire. See Howard T. Oedel, ed., *Landmarks of Old Cheshire* (Cheshire, Conn., 1976), p. 107.

2. John Warner Barber, *Connecticut Historical Collections* (New Haven, Conn., 1838), pp. 193–94.

3. Jedediah Morse, *The American Universal Geography*, 7th ed., 2 vols. (Charlestown, Mass., 1819), 1: 370. In 1818 the state had 213 Congregational, 70 Baptist, and 69 Episcopal churches.

4. Doggett, *A History*, p. 148.

5. Oedel, *Landmarks*, pp. 57, 160.

6. Captured, robbed, beaten, kicked, pricked, and cut by bayonets, and finally released, Daggett died a year later at the age of fifty-three. See *Dictionary of American Biography*, s.v. "Daggett, Naphtali," and Barber, *Connecticut Historical Collections*, pp. 193–94.

7. Doggett, *A History*, p. 192. A letter dated 26 December 1807 from their mother to John, who was living on a plantation in Jamaica, says that Thomas "was doing business for Mr. La Fon . . . Engraver New Orleans North America" (Edwin D. Morgan Collection, New York State Library, Albany). La Fon is probably Barthelemy La Fon (1769–1820), an architect, surveyor, printer, and real estate entrepreneur who was active laying out new sections of New Orleans in the early years of the nineteenth century.

8. Thompson R. Harlow, "Connecticut Engravers, 1744–1820," *The Connecticut Historical Society Bulletin* 36, no. 4 (October 1971): 110.

9. Ronald Vern Jackson, Gary Ronald Teeples, and David Schaefer Meyer, eds., *Connecticut 1820 Census Index* (Bountiful, Utah, 1977), p. 58.

10. Harlow, "Connecticut Engravers," p. 110, nos. 56–62, and Carl Drepperd, *Early American Prints* (New York and London), 1930, p. 110.

11. The 1820 census listed John R. Kensett in both New Haven and Connecticut (1820 *Census Index*, p. 65). In 1822 he testily wrote his brother asking for repayment of "that capital which you have so long had in your possession and which you know very well ought to have been restored since" (John R. Kensett to Thomas Kensett, 18 June 1822 [Morgan Collection]).

12. Oedel, *Landmarks*, p. 50.

13. Harlow, "Connecticut Engravers," pp. 115–16.

14. Oedel, *Landmarks*, p. 50.

15. *Catalogue of the Officers, Teachers and Alumni of the Episcopalian Academy of Connecticut, Cheshire, Connecticut, now known as Cheshire School* (Cheshire, Conn. 1916[?]), unpaginated.

16. Morse, *American Universal Geography*, 1:368.

17. *The Crayon* 1, no. 8 (21 February 1855).

18. Quoted in Gene Hessler, "U.S. Essay Proof and Specimen Notes," *A Brief History of Paper Money Components* (Portage, Ohio, 1979), pp. 12–13.

19. George C. Groce and David H. Wallace, *The New-York Historical Society's Dictionary of Artists in America, 1564–1860* (New Haven, Conn., 1957) contains entries on Spencer, Rollinson, Durand, and Gobrecht.

20. Casilear to Kensett, 20 January 1833 (Morgan Collection).

21. Morse, *American Universal Geography*, 1:374.

22. Casilear to Kensett, 2 November 1831 (Kellogg Collection) and Casilear to Kensett, "My Worthy Companion in Arms," 19 October 1832 (Morgan Collection).

23. Casilear to Kensett, 3 January 1833 (Morgan Collection).

24. See letter of John R. Kensett to Kensett, 8 April 1835 (Morgan Collection).

25. Kensett to Sarah Kensett, 7 September 1837 (Morgan Collection).

26. Casilear to Kensett, 27 January 1838 (Morgan Collection).

27. *Daily Albany Argus*, 21 June 1838, p. 2.

28. Ibid., 14 November 1838, p. 2.

29. Stephen J. Field to Kensett, 4 February 1840; 20 July 1840 (Morgan Collection).

30. Joel Munsell, *The Annals of Albany*, vol. 10 (1859), pp. 322–23.

31. Kensett to John R. Kensett, 22 June 1840 (Morgan Collection).

32. Kensett to John R. Kensett, 25 August 1840 (Morgan Collection).

33. Galignani, *Galignani's New Paris Guide* (Paris, 1859), p. 44.

34. Ibid., p. 126.

35. A. P. Van Dam, *An Englishman in Paris (Notes and Recollections)*, 2 vols. (New York, 1892), 1:2–3, 125.

36. Ibid., 1:2–3.

37. Kensett to John R. Kensett, 6 December 1840 (Morgan Collection).

38. See letter of Casilear to Kensett, 26 November 1840 (Morgan Collection).

39. Galignani, *Paris Guide*, p. 91. The rules for public access were remarkable, and worth notice now when general public access is given first place: "All these museums are open to students, and foreigners with passports, on Tuesdays, Wednesdays, Thursdays, Fridays, and Saturdays; and to the public on Sundays, from 10 to 4."

40. Jules Janin, *The American in Paris During the Summer; or Heath's Picturesque Annual for 1844* (London, 1844), p. 132.

41. Kensett to John R. Kensett, 19 March 1842 (Morgan Collection).

42. Robert Noxon Toppan, *A Hundred Years of Bank Note Engraving in the United States* (New York, 1896), p. 8.

43. Kensett to John R. Kensett, 27 February 1841 (Morgan Collection).

44. Kensett to John R. Kensett, 3 November 1842 (Morgan Collection).

45. Benjamin Champney, *Sixty Years' Memories of Art and Artists* (Woburn, Mass., 1900), p. 20.

46. Ibid., p. 30.

47. Ibid., pp. 24–25.

48. Kensett to John R. Kensett, 3 November 1842 (Morgan Collection).

49. Kensett to John R. Kensett, 27 February 1841 (Morgan Collection).

50. Mary Bartlett Cowdrey, ed., *American Academy of Fine Arts and American Art-Union: Exhibition Record, 1818–1852* (New York, 1953), pp. 212–15.

51. Casilear to Kensett, 29 January 1844 (Morgan Collection).

52. Cowdrey, with James T. Flexner, Theodore Sizer, Charles E. Baker, and Malcolm Stearns, Jr., *American Academy of Fine Arts and American Art-Union: Introduction, 1816–1852* (New York, 1953), p. 162.

53. Champney, *Sixty Years' Memories*, p. 32.

54. Ibid., p. 54.

55. Champney to Kensett, 18 June 1843 (Morgan Collection).

56. Champney, *Sixty Years' Memories*, pp. 49–51.

57. Leigh's *New Picture of London* (London, 1834), p. 167.

58. William Howitt, *Visits to Remarkable Places* (Philadelphia, 1841), pp. 289–92.

59. Benjamin Moran, *The Footpath and Highway; or, The Wanderings of an American* (Philadelphia, 1853), p. 214.

60. Christopher Wood, *Dictionary of Victorian Painters* (Woodbridge, Suffolk, 1971), p. 27; and Clara Erskine Clement and Laurence Hutton, *Artists of the Nineteenth Century and Their Works* (Boston and New York, 1894), p. 142.

61. Kensett to Rossiter, 11 February 1844 (Morgan Collection).

62. Kensett to Thomas Kensett, March 1844 (Morgan Collection).

63. Kensett to John R. Kensett, 8 August 1844 (Morgan Collection).

64. Kensett obituary, *New York Daily Tribune*, 16 December 1872.

65. Champney to Kensett, 8 January 1845 (Morgan Collection).

66. Kensett's passport bears the endorsement "Vu au Ministre de l'Interieur Paris le 9 Juin 1845 Le Chef de bureau chargé du Visa." His movements throughout

Europe from 1840 through 1847 are recorded in detail by numerous visa endorsements (Morgan Collection).

67. Champney, *Sixty Years' Memories*, p. 60.

68. George G. Wynne, *Early Americans in Rome* (Rome, 1966), p. ii.

69. Theodore Dwight, *A Journal of a Tour in Italy in the Year 1821* (New York, 1824), p. 245.

70. Newton Arvin, ed., *The Heart of Hawthorne's Journals* (Boston and New York, 1929), p. 260.

71. George Stillman Hillard, *Six Months in Italy*, 2 vols. (Boston, 1853), 2:20, 19.

72. Ibid., p. 253.

73. Champney, *Sixty Years' Memories*, p. 72.

74. Champney to Kensett, 30 May 1846 (Morgan Collection).

75. William Wetmore Story, *Roba di Roma* (London, 1862), p. 208.

76. Leonora Cranch Scott, *The Life and Letters of Christopher Pearse Cranch* (Boston and New York, 1917), pp. 104, 107, 111, 109.

77. Karl Baedeker, *Central Italy* (Leipsic and London, 1900), p. 423.

78. Kensett to Sarah D. Kellog, 1 October 1846 (Morgan Collection).

79. Kensett to Rossiter, undated (Morgan Collection).

80. *Dictionary of American Biography*, s.v. "Curtis, George William."

81. George Curtis to Kensett in New York, 22 June 1848 (Morgan Collection).

82. Ibid.

83. Curtis in *Harper's New Monthly Magazine* 46, no. 274 (March 1873): 611.

84. Ibid, p. 612.

85. Baedeker, *The United States* (Leipsic and New York, 1893), p. 22.

86. George S. Foster, *New York in Slices, by an Experimental Carver; Being the Original Slices Published in the New York Tribune* (New York, 1850).

87. John H. Gourlie (secretary protem of the Century) to Kensett, 14 May 1849 (Morgan Collection).

88. Gourlie, *The Origin and History of the Century* (New York, 1856), p. 6.

89. Manuscript minutes of first meeting, 13 January 1847 (Century Association Archives, New York).

90. Allen Nevins, "The Century, 1847–1866," in Rodman Gilder et al., eds., *The Century, 1847–1946* (New York, 1947), p. 4.

91. Thomas Seir Cummings, *Historic Annals of the National Academy of Design* (Philadelphia, 1865), p. 198.

92. Sketch Club Minutes (Archives of the Century Association), unpaginated.

93. Nevins, "The Century, *1847–1866*," p. 13.

94. See Asher B. Durand Papers (New York Public Library).

95. Bancroft to Kensett, 4 May 1864 (Morgan Collection).

96. Eyre Crowe, *With Thackeray in America* (New York, 1893), p. 51.

97. James Grant Wilson, *Thackeray in the United States, 1852–3, 1855–6* (New York, 1904), p. 18.

98. Ibid., pp. 43–44, 47.

99. Gordon N. Ray, *The Letters and Private Papers of William Makepeace Thackeray*, 4 vols. (Cambridge, Mass., 1946), 3:498.

100. Cummings, *Annals of the NAD*, p. 199.

101. Kensett to J. H. Shegogue (acting secretary, NAD), 11 May 1849 (Archives of the National Academy of Design, New York).

102. Cummings, *Annals of the NAD*, p. 314.

103. Ibid., p. 327. Hoe's biography appears in the *Dictionary of American Biography*.

104. Eliot Clark, *History of the National Academy of Design, 1825–1953* (New York, 1954), p. 80.

105. Receipt from Eastman Johnson to Kensett, 14 April 1859 (Morgan Collection).

106. Charles E. Fairman, *Art and Artists of the Capitol of the United States of America* (Washington, D.C., 1927), p. 162.

107. Cummings, *Annals of the NAD*, p. 269.

108. Fairman, *Art and Artists of the Capitol*, p. 189.

109. Ibid.

110. *Executive Document, No. 43*, 36th Cong., 1st. sess., House of Representatives.

111. Quoted in Fairman, *Art and Artists of the Capitol*, p. 189.

112. Brown to Kensett, 16 April 1862 (Morgan Collection).

113. Will Irwin, Earl Chapin May, and Joseph Hotchkins, *A History of the Union League Club of New York City* (New York, 1952), p. 9.

114. Henry Whitney Bellows, *Historical Sketch of the Union League Club of New York* (New York, 1879), p. 37.

115. Ibid., p. 64.

116. Ibid., p. 58.

117. United States Sanitary Commission, *A Record of the Metropolitan Fair in the Aid of the United States Sanitary Commission, Held at New York, in April, 1864* (New York, 1867), p. 2.

118. The final account of the fair, documented in the *Record*, ran to 261 pages.

119. *Record*, pp. 244–45.

120. *Record*, p. 97. Not all activities supporting the fair took place in its buildings, however. For example, on 6 April there was a special exhibit at Knoedler's Gallery, New York, of Kensett's *October Afternoon on Lake George*, several lectures were given at churches, and there was "a billiard tournament, as it was somewhat fancifully called, between the best players of New York, Philadelphia, Washington, and Cincinnati" (p. 97). The fair organizers and participants obviously approached things in a serious but hearty and happy manner that had extremely fortunate results.

121. The *Record* reports that the art exhibition earned $73,638.58 (p. 103). Total received by the fair in gifts and receipts before deduction of costs was $1,340,050.37 (p. 58).

122. C. Nash (assistant secretary of the fair) to Kensett, 28 April 1864 (Morgan Collection).

123. Henry T. Tuckerman, *Book of the Artists, American Artist Life* (1867; New York, 1966), p. 11. See also Winifred E. Howe, *A History of the Metropolitan Museum of Art* (New York, 1913), pp. 90–93.

124. *A Metropolitan Art-Museum in the City of New York; Proceedings of a Meeting Held at the Theatre of the Union League Club, Tuesday Evening, November 23, 1869* (New York, 1869), p. 6.

125. Ibid., p. 7.

126. Howe, *Metropolitan Museum*, p. 117.

127. Ibid., pp. 103–23.

128. Trustee Minutes, 4 January 1873 (Archives of the Metropolitan Museum, New York).

129. *The New York Times*, 15 December and 19 December 1872; *The Evening Post*, 16 December and 18 December 1872; *The Daily Tribune*, 16, 17, 18, and 19 December 1872.

130. *The New York Times*, 15 December 1872.

131. *The Evening Post*, 18 December 1872.

From Burin to Brush: The Development of a Painter

1. Kensett to Rossiter, 31 December 1841 (Rossiter file, New-York Historical Society).

2. Kensett's passport application was not filled out until 26 May 1840, and he then waited until Thursday, the 28th, to mail it from New York to Washington. On his application, Kensett stated his intention to travel "through Germany and Switzerland on our route to Italy." Kensett was issued passport 1572, 30 May 1840, which he received by return mail before boarding the *British Queen* on the night of 1 June 1840 (Passport Letters, January 5–June 30, 1840. National Archives, Washington, D.C.).

3. Kensett, *Journal*, 2 vols. 2: 19 October 1840 (Frick Art Reference Library, New York).

4. Kensett to Rossiter, 31 December 1841 (Rossiter file, New-York Historical Society).

5. George W. Curtis, "Editor's Easy Chair," *Harper's New Monthly Magazine* 46 (March 1873): 611.

6. Kensett to John R. Kensett, 13 March 1841 (Edwin D. Morgan Collection, New York State Library, Albany).

7. Kensett to Champney, 22 October 1843 (James R. Kellogg Collection, Archives of American Art, Smithsonian Institution, Washington, D.C., roll no. N68–84).

8. Kensett to John R. Kensett, 3 November 1842 (Morgan Collection); Kensett to Elizabeth Kensett, 3 June 1842 (Kellogg Collection).

9. Kensett to John R. Kensett, 3 November 1842 (Morgan Collection).

10. Quoted from Asher B. Durand, *Journal*, 18 June 1840 (New York Public Library); also see Kensett, *Journal* 1: 18 June 1840.

11. Kensett, *Small Album*, 1841 (Private Collection).

12. Kensett, *Journal*, 1: 12 September 1840.

13. Ibid., 19 June 1840.

14. Titian's influence on landscape painters was important and widespread. Constable delivered a discourse at the Hampstead Assembly Rooms in June 1833 in which he discussed Titian's "respect for Nature" and asserted that the background of the Venetian's *St. Peter Martyr* (c. 1525–30) "may be considered as the foundation of all the styles of landscape in every school of Europe in the [seventeenth century]" (C.R. Leslie, *Memoirs of Constable* [London, 1951], pp. 293–94.

15. Kensett, *Journal*, 1: 19 June 1840.

16. Ibid.

17. Durand, *Journal*, 25 June, 1 July, and 29 July 1840.

18. Ibid., probably *Salisbury Cathedral*, 1823, Sheepshanks Collection at the Victoria and Albert Museum, London.

19. Kensett to John R. Kensett (?), 10 November 1840 (Morgan Collection).

20. Kensett to Elizabeth Kensett, 18 April 1841 (Kellogg Collection).

21. Kensett to Rossiter, undated (Morgan Collection).

22. Kensett liked the work of Henry J. Boddington, for example, noting his "truthful and admirable manner. . . . [He] is a close observer of nature." (Kensett to unknown, 10 March 1844 [Morgan Collection]). Constable was admired, according to Champney, because he was the first to "trust the inspiration nature gave him" (*Sixty Years' Memories of Art and Artists* [Woburn, Mass., 1900], p. 174).

23. The packet inscribed with a description of its contents is owned by descendants of the artist. Rousseau's fame rests in part on his theories that God, nature, and man are inherently good and can act in harmony.

24. Quoted in Henry T. Tuckerman, *Book of the Artists: American Artist Life* (1867; New York, 1966), p. 510.

25. Kensett to Elizabeth Kensett, 3 January 1844 (Kellogg Collection).

26. Curtis, "Editor's Easy Chair," p. 611.

27. George Curtis recalled that "Kensett was constantly at work. . . . He would pass a day faithfully studying and painting a mullein. His sketches were so vivid and faithful and delicate that afterward there was no wall in New York so beautiful as that of his studio . . . upon which [such studies] were hung in a solid mass" (ibid., pp. 611–12). This suggests that Kensett focused more upon nature than architectural ruins, a suggestion reinforced by the fact that few if any studies of ruins have survived.

28. Leonora Cranch Scott, *The Life and Letters of Christopher Pearse Cranch* (Boston, 1917), p. 107; Champney, *Sixty Years' Memories*, p. 74.

29. Curtis, "Editor's Easy Chair," p. 612.

30. "The Fine Arts," *The Literary World*, 6 May 1848, p. 266.

31. Kensett to J. W. Moore, 28 February 1848, in American Art-Union Letters from Artists, 1 (American Art-Union Papers, New-York Historical Society).

32. Kensett, "Record of Sales, 1848–1871" (Kellogg Collection; typescript at the Metropolitan Museum of Art, New York), and Kensett to Thomas K. Kensett, 26 January 1849 (Kellogg Collection).

33. Kensett to Elizabeth Kensett, 16 December 1844 (Kellogg Collection).

34. Arthur Bestor, "Patent-Office Models of the Good Society: Some Relationships between Social Reform and Westward Expansion," *The American Historical Review* 58 (April 1953): 505–26, rpt. in *American History, Recent Interpretations*, ed. Abraham S. Eisenstadt (New York, 1969), pp. 412–31.

35. Frederick Jackson Turner's ideas are contained in his *Frontier in American History* (New York, 1921). George W. Pierson has provided the best critique of Turner's ideas in "The Frontier and Frontiersmen of Turner's Essays," *Pennsylvania Magazine of History and Biography* 64 (October 1940): 449–78; and "The Frontier and Our Institutions," *New England Quarterly* 15 (June 1942): 224–55.

36. Peter C. Marzio, "The Art Crusade: An Analysis of American Drawing Manuals, 1820–1860," *Smithsonian Studies in History and Technology* 34 (1976): 70.

37. Washington Irving, *The Sketchbook of Geoffrey Crayon, Gent*, ed. Haskell Springer (Boston, 1978), pp. 8–9; John Ruskin, *Modern Painters*, 5 vols. (New York, 1868), 1:90.

38. "Description of the Engraving, *A Poet's Grave*, Engraved by Adams," *New York Mirror*, 4 May 1837, quoted in Barbara Novak, "On Diverse Themes from Nature," in *The Natural Paradise*, ed. Kynaston McShine et al. (Museum of Modern Art, New York, 1976), p. 79.

39. Kensett to Elizabeth Kensett, 3 January 1844 (Kellogg Collection).

40. Kensett to unknown, 16 February 1847 (Kellogg Collection).

41. Quoted in Novak, *American Painting of the Nineteenth Century* (New York, 1969), p. 66. From an original

Robert Gilmore, Jr., manuscript, 13 December 1826 (New-York Historical Society).

42. Champney, "The White Hills in 1850: The Advance Guard of the Grand Army of Painters," *White Mountain Echo and Tourist Register*, 12 August 1893, p. 6. *The White Mountains—From North Conway* is the title given for this painting on two old labels attached to the back of the frame. The painting was first owned by shipbuilder William H. Webb from 1852 to 1876. Listed in the 1876 sale of works of art from Webb's estate with the present title, this painting has also had other titles associated with it. Kensett's own handwritten record of paintings sold for 1851 lists it as "Mt. Washington." However that record contains several abbreviated titles, and it is unlikely that this notation made in a private account book is the formal one Kensett wished the painting to be known by. The 1851 American Art-Union engraving of the painting bears the earliest published title for the painting, *Mount Washington from the Valley of Conway*. But it is slightly inaccurate, as the scene is taken from Sunset Hill, just above the village of North Conway. Recently the painting has been referred to as *The White Mountains, Mount Washington* in Donald Keyes et al., *The White Mountains: Place and Perceptions* (University Art Galleries, Durham, N.H., 1980). The labels attached to the frame, and the listing in the Webb catalogue indicate that the painting was known by the title *The White Mountains—From North Conway* early in its existence, and therefore that title has been employed here.

43. Champney to "Chère Amie," 14 July 1850 (Private Collection).

44. Benjamin Willey, *Incidents in White Mountain History* (Boston, 1856), p. 174.

45. Quoted in Novak, *American Painting*, p. 87, from an original Durand manuscript, 25 July 1855 (New-York Historical Society).

46. Alexis de Tocqueville, *Journey to America*, trans. George Laurence, ed. J.P. Mayer (London, 1959), p. 333. A fine discussion of the relationship between the land and the people, with consideration of Tocqueville's remarks and the ideas of historian Frederick Jackson Turner, is contained in Carl N. Degler, *Out of Our Past* (New York, 1962) pp. 123–34.

47. *The Literary World*, 8 May 1852, p. 331.

48. Champney, "The White Hills in 1893," p. 6.

49. David C. Huntington, *The Landscapes of Frederic Edwin Church* (New York, 1966), p. 35.

50. James Jackson Jarvis, *The Art-Idea* (New York, 1864), p. 193.

51. Howard S. Merritt, "Correspondence between Thomas Cole and Robert Gilmore, Jr.," *Studies on*

Thomas Cole, An American Romanticist, Baltimore Museum of Art Annual, no. 2 (1967), p. 19.

52. Durand, "Letters on Landscape Painting, III," *The Crayon* 1, no. 5 (31 January 1855): 66.

53. Durand, "Letters on Landscape Painting, VIII," *The Crayon* 1, no. 23 (6 June 1855): 354.

54. Kensett to Elizabeth Kensett, 16 December 1844 (Kellogg Collection).

55. Durand, "Letters on Landscape Painting, II," *The Crayon* 1, no. 2 (17 January 1855): 34.

56. Kensett's "Record of Sales" for 1854 lists a *Niagara Falls* sold to the Earl of Ellesmere for five hundred dollars, the second highest sum Kensett had, to that point, received for a painting.

57. Although this drawing is signed and dated 1850, Kensett apparently was not at Niagara Falls in that year. Drawings Kensett made during August 1850 in the vicinity of Conway Valley, New Hampshire, as well as a newspaper account of his itinerary and his correspondence, seem to preclude even a hasty trip to Niagara Falls that summer. This is supported by Champney's account of their itinerary that summer in *Sixty Years' Memories* (p. 100). A letter written by Kensett on 24 August 1851 from Cataract House indicates his visit to the falls the following year. Because the inscription on the drawing appears to be contemporary with the image, Kensett may simply have erred in setting down the date. Further discussion of this question is in Driscoll, *John F. Kensett Drawings* (Museum of Art, Pennsylvania State University, State College, Pa., 1978), pp. 64–66.

58. Flake White [pseud.], "Letter from North Conway," *The Crayon* 2, no. 14 (3 October 1855): 217, and Poppy Oil [pseud.], "Letter from West Campton," *The Crayon* 3, "part" 10 (October 1856): 317–18. See also Linda Ferber, "Luminist Drawings," in John Wilmerding, et al., *American Light* (National Gallery of Art, Washington, D.C., 1980), p. 240.

59. Rossiter to Kensett, 11 August 1852 (Morgan Collection).

60. The summer of 1860 may be an exception to this, as no sketching tour of that time has been documented. Instead, Kensett seems to have spent that summer working in Washington, D.C.

61. Kensett to J. W. Moore, 7 December 1848 (American Art-Union Papers). Kensett sent this sketch and another yet unlocated to the American Art-Union for "disposal" at seventy-five dollars, taking deliberate care to point out that they were both "studies from nature."

62. Durand, "Letters on Landscape Painting, V," *The Crayon* 1, no. 10 (7 March 1855): 146.

63. Ibid.

64. George Bancroft et al., "Agreement," c. 1864 (Bancroft Papers, Massachusetts Historical Society, Boston).

65. Bancroft to Kensett, 4 May 1864 (Morgan Collection).

66. Louis Lang to Bancroft, 11 June 1866 (Bancroft Papers).

67. Bancroft to Kensett, 15 June 1866 (Bancroft Papers).

68. Quoted in Russell B. Nye, *George Bancroft, Brahmin Rebel* (New York, 1972), pp. 195–96.

69. Kensett, *Journal*, 2: inside cover.

70. See John I. H. Baur, "Early Studies in Light and Air by American Landscape Painters," *Brooklyn Museum Bulletin* 9 (Winter 1948): 1–9; and Wilmerding et al., *American Light*.

71. See Kensett, *Journal*, 1: esp. entries for 19 and 22 June, 7 and 13 July, 5 and 12 September; and 2: esp. entry for 10 November.

72. For discussions of the influence of drawing books, see Huntington, "Church and Luminism: Light for America's Elect," and Ferber, "Luminist Drawings," in Wilmerding et al., *American Light*.

73. Curtis to Kensett, September 1853 (Kellogg Collection).

74. In 1858 Kensett recorded the sale of *Red Bank from Shrewsbury River* to F. S. Cozzens for $125. The next year his record of paintings sold lists two works of identical title: *Red Bank, Shrewsbury River*. One went to his brother Thomas Kensett for $150 and the other went to "S.G." (S. Gandy) for $300. Another entitled *Shrewsbury Inlet, N.J.* was lot number 163 in Kensett's estate sale. See Kensett, "Record of Sales, 1848–1871" (Kellogg Collection); and Robert Somerville, *The Collection of over Five Hundred Paintings and Studies by the Late John F. Kensett* (Association Hall, New York, 1873).

75. See S. G. W. Benjamin, "Fifty Years of American Art," *Harper's New Monthly Magazine* 59 (July 1879): 256. Benjamin was among the first writers to note that "It is not so much things as feeling that (Kensett) tries to render or suggest."

76. Whether or not Kensett and Lane ever actually met, or discussed art theory or paintings, is uncertain. They each had a background in the graphic arts, and they shared a close mutual friend in Champney. The north shore of Massachusetts, where Lane lived, was an area where Kensett often sketched and painted before Lane's death in 1865. Some of Kensett's favorite spots were Nahant, Beverly, Manchester, and Cape Ann. He painted a view called *Beverly Shore* which he sold to someone named Mellen in 1868 for $400. This could have been Mary B. Mellen, Lane's pupil. It would seem unlikely that Kensett and Lane would have been ignorant of each other's work. For additional information on Lane and Kensett, see Wilmerding, *Fitz Hugh Lane* (New York, 1971), pp. 53–54, 49.

77. With regard to *Sunset on the Sea*, reference is made to Courbet's *L'Immensité* (1869; Victoria and Albert Museum), Whistler's Trouville paintings of the mid- to late 1860s such as *The Sea* (c. 1865; Montclair Art Museum, N.J.), Blakelock's *The Sun, Serene, Sinks into the Slumberous Sea* (1880s; Museum of Fine Arts, Springfield, Mass.), and Vedder's *Memory* (1870; Los Angeles County Museum of Art).

78. Kensett to James R. Lambdin, 2 July 1856 (Kensett Papers, Archives of American Art, roll P–22, frame 263).

79. Taylor was a well-known and much-admired writer who was a member of the Century Association, an amateur painter, and a poet who dedicated his verses entitled "The Picture of St. John" to his artist friends Kensett, Gifford, Church, Whittredge, Jervis McEntee, Samuel Coleman, and Eastman Johnson. See Albert H. Smyth, *Bayard Taylor* (Boston and New York, 1896), p. 227.

80. Kensett to unknown, 28 September 1856, and Kensett to Thomas Gold Appleton, 28 September 1856 (Morgan Collection).

81. *The Crayon* 4, "part" 2 (February 1856): 56.

82. *The Crayon* 5, "part" 5 (May 1858): 146.

83. Kensett, "Record of Sales, 1848–1871," 1869 entries (Kellogg Collection).

84. Benjamin, "Fifty Years of American Art," p. 256.

85. Calamé's statement "c'est très jolie de couleur" is recorded in Champney *Sixty Years' Memories*, p. 66, and Huntington's in Sommerville, *Collection*, p. 3.

86. See Edward L. Nichols, "Ogden N. Rood," National Academy of Sciences Biographical Memoirs, no. 6 (1909), pp. 442–72; F. W. Clark, "Biographical Memoir of Wolcott Gibbs, 1822–1908"; National Academy of Sciences Biographical Memoirs, no. 7 (1910), pp. 1–22; and D. J. Warner, "Lewis M. Rutherfurd, Pioneer Astronomical Photographer and Spectroscopist," *Technology and Culture* 12 (1971): 180–216.

87. Rood was interested in art from an early age and, while studying to become a physicist in Germany, took lessons in drawing and painting from Joseph Wilhelm Melchoir, a Munich genre and animal painter. Later Rood

gave lectures at the National Academy of Design, was an honorary member of the American Watercolor Society, and a life member of the Metropolitan Museum of Art. He was also a member of the Century Club. When *Modern Chromatics* was published in 1879, he personally delivered copies to Gifford, Johnson, Smillie, and several other artists and collectors, all of whom had been friends of Kensett's.

88. *The Crayon* 7, "part" 4 (April 1860): 107.

89. Ogden Rood, *Modern Chromatics, with Applications to Art and Industry* (1879; New York, 1973), p. 319.

90. Ibid.

91. Ibid, p. 321.

92. Ibid, p. 28.

93. The best study of the relationship between Rood and Seurat is William Innes Homer's landmark book, *Seurat and the Science of Painting* (Cambridge, Mass., 1964).

The Last Summer's Work

1. For a more thorough explanation of the relation between American Abstract Expressionism and landscape painting, see Robert Rosenblum, "The Primal American Scene," in *The Natural Paradise*, ed. Kynaston McShine (New York, Museum of Modern Art, 1976), pp. 13–38.

2. "Art Matters," *New York Herald*, 15 March 1873.

3. "The Late Mr. Kensett's Pictures," *New York Evening Post*, 10 January 1873.

4. *Brooklyn Eagle*, 16 January 1873.

5. James R. Kellogg Collection, microfilm in Archives of American Art, Smithsonian Institution, Washington, D.C., roll no. N68–84.

6. Thomas Kensett to John Taylor Johnston, 19 March 1874 (Archives of the Metropolitan Museum of Art, New York).

7. "Memo of Pictures Belonging to the Estate of John F. Kensett" (microfilm copy in Archives of American Art, roll no. N737).

8. "Art Matters," *New York Herald*, 15 March 1873.

9. Reprinted in Robert Somerville, *The Collection of over Five Hundred Paintings and Studies by the Late John F. Kensett* (Association Hall, New York, 1873), n.p.

10. Robert M. Olyphant to Elizabeth Kensett, 26 March 1874 (Kellogg Collection).

11. The present whereabouts of this *Beverly Coast* is unknown to the author. *Fourth Annual Report of the Trustees . . .* (New York: Metropolitan Museum of Art, 1874), p. 51; "The Kensett Art Sale," *New York Daily Tribune*, 25 March 1873.

12. Note (Archives of the Metropolitan Museum of Art, New York).

13. These are *Newport Rocks* (plate 42) and *A Foggy Sky* (plate 43).

14. One of the few paintings of Long Island Sound painted before Kensett's is William Sidney Mount's *Crane Neck across the Marsh* (c. 1851; the Museums at Stony Brook, New York).

15. W. H. Bartlett and N. P. Willis, *American Scenery* (London and Paris: 1840), pp. 217–20.

16. William Cullen Bryant, ed., *Picturesque America*, 2 vols. (New York: 1874), 2: 436–50.

17. *Appleton's Cyclopaedia of American Biography*, vol. 1 (New York: 1888), p. 700.

18. *Land Records, Town of Darien*, vol 6 (1866–67), cited in Darien Historical Society, *John Frederick Kensett, 1816–1872: Centennial Exhibition* (Darien, Conn.: 1972), p. 14.

19. See Somerville, *The Collection.*

20. Arthur H. Hughes and Morse S. Allen, *Connecticut Place Names* (Hartford, Conn.: 1976), pp. 108–10.

21. On exotic expeditions and art, see Barbara Novak, *Nature and Culture* (New York: 1980), pp. 137–56.

22. "Art Matters," 15 March 1873. In this account *Eaton's Neck* is described as "with the lighthouse not yet introduced."

23. Their special quality was fully recognized at the time they first came to light as established in the newspaper accounts quoted above: the finest ones were hung in prominent locations at the National Academy of Design Exhibition that preceded the Kensett sale.

24. See Daniel Huntington et al., *Proceedings at a Meeting of the Century Association Held in Memory of John F. Kensett, December, 1872* (New York, 1872), p. 22.

25. Ibid.

26. This was not the first time Kensett had simplified a composition by removing incidental details. See, e.g., his *Beach at Newport* (plate 35) and *Newport Coast* (plate 22), in which the same scene is repeated without the distracting foreground elements of a boat and a man. This change, however, is not as drastic as the one noted here, since it replaces the foreground elements with rocks, as opposed to eliminating them altogether. It may

well be that in some paintings Kensett included foreground elements like those in *Beach at Newport* in order to please his patrons. A letter to Kensett from the Reverend A. D. Gridley of Clinton, in Oneida County, New York, is interesting in this respect: "It is now two years since I saw that 'Narragansett,' but I cannot forget the wreck of a boat in foreground, the water, the far-reaching shore, the fine aerial perspective, and the few clouds near the horizon. While I would not attempt to criticize or find any fault with that picture, it has seemed to me that for a landscape to cheer my home, I should like, if consistent with your views, to have the *foreground* contain some hint of home-life like that of your 'Noon on the Sea Shore,' engraved in colors by S. V. Hunt, and published by Goupil" (letter undated, but probably 1866; Kellogg Collection).

27. Century Association *Proceedings*, p. 22.

28. Ibid., p. 23.

29. On sunsets in landscape painting, see Rosenblum, "Primal American Scene." A frequent association was that of the setting sun with human death. See *The Crayon* 2 (January 1855): 56, for a long explanation of this theme in the context of a discussion of Newport's scenic beauty.

30. See Century Association *Proceedings*, p. 21. Tuckerman also noted this: "It is rarely that, to use a common phrase, we can *locate* a landscape so confidently as Kensett's; the vein of rock, perhaps, identifies the scene as in New Jersey,—the kind of cedar or grass assures us that it was taken on the Hudson,—and the tint of water or form of mountains suggests Lake George" (*Book of the Artists, American Artist Life* [New York, 1867], p. 514).

31. On Kensett's change of style in the mid-1850s, see Theodore E. Stebbins, Jr., "Luminism in Context: A New View," in John Wilmerding et al., *American Light* (National Gallery of Art, Washington, D.C., 1980), pp. 211–12.

32. *The Crayon* 5 (May 1858): 146–47.

33. *The Crayon* 3 (May 1856): 145.

34. Walters to Kensett, 20 July 1859 (Kellogg Collection).

35. Tuckerman, *Book of the Artists*, p. 511.

36. Ibid.

37. Tuckerman, *Book of the Artists*, p. 512.

38. James Jackson Jarves, *The Art-Idea*, ed. Benjamin Rowland (1864; Cambridge, Mass., 1960), p. 192.

39. Tuckerman, *Book of the Artists*, p. 514.

40. Remarks made by Reverend Henry Whitney Bellows. Century Association *Proceedings*, p. 16.

41. Jarves, *Art-Idea*, p. 191.

42. Walters to Kensett, n.d. probably 1860 (Kellogg Collection).

43. For the clearest and most concise attempt at defining this term, see Barbara Novak, "On Defining Luminism," in Wilmerding et al., *American Light*, pp. 23–29.

44. *New York Daily Tribune*, 15 March 1873.

45. *The Crayon* 6 (July 1859): 220.

46. Tuckerman, *Book of the Artists*, p. 514.

47. Remarks made by Reverend Samuel Osgood. Century Association *Proceedings*, p. 20. The quoted passage again demonstrates what is now generally perceived, that Turner had become a household word in American art circles, certainly by the 1860s, if not well before.

48. See Century Association *Proceedings*, p. 17.

49. Jarves, *Art-Idea*, pp. 195–208.

50. Kensett probably became aware of Turner during his first trip to England and, since that time, kept up a keen interest in his works and reputation as is evidenced by a number of letters. In 1852 he corresponded with his uncle John R. Kensett in London, about the Turner sale. On 10 November of that year his uncle wrote that he had purchased a Turner drawing—*The Gulf of Genoa*—which he would present to his nephew when the latter next went to London. In an undated letter, probably of 1856 or 1857, the dealer S. P. Avery brought to Kensett's attention the fourth volume of Ruskin's *Modern Painters*, which he sent over, noting that it had "some fine plates —if you have not seen it—I know you will be pleased." On 4 June 1858, Robert Olyphant, then in London, sent Kensett a letter which included his impressions of Turner's works: ". . . I have had several spare hours, some of which I have occupied in studying Turner's paintings. How awfully I have been humbugged by Ruskin; with what delight have I hung over those beautifully turned periods and drank in his Miltonic prose— spending hour after hour with the 'Modern Painter,' and here I now am, to look at the works which seemed to inspire the writer, and I find them for the most part what could only be the ravings of an insane colorist on canvass —and in the milder and more subdued pictures while there may be a pleasing effect, or a spirited passage, no where is anything satisfactory. I suppose that you will think that I am the crazy one, but my dear fellow you have taught me better, and in studying nature and what is next to it, *your rendering of her*—I have got a *long way* ahead of Turner." Olyphant's compliment to Kensett notwithstanding, the implication here is that Kensett recognized the importance of Turner's achievement. (All these documents are in the Kellogg Collection.)

51. There is little doubt that Kensett's death was a contributing factor to the decline of the school. See Wilmerding, "The Luminist Movement: Some Reflections," in *American Light*, p. 146.

52. These ideas were first formulated by Novak in "Luminism: An Alternative Tradition," *American Painting of the Nineteenth Century* (New York, 1969), pp. 92–109.

53. The chief expounder of the link between luminism and Emersonian transcendentalism has been Novak. Her most recent thinking on this relationship may be conveniently found in numerous passages in her well-indexed *Nature and Culture*. The association of luminism and mid-nineteenth-century political developments, including the Civil War, has been made by Wilmerding: see, e.g., his comments in "Luminist Movement," pp. 108–10.

54. The term was first used by James Jackson Jarves but has been frequently employed by Novak in defining what is, in her view, one of the key aspects of the luminist style: "only in luminist quietism does the presence of the artist, his 'labor trial,' disappear. Such paintings, in eliminating any reminders of the artist's intermediary presence, remove him even from his role of interpreter. In their quiet tranquility, they reach to a mystical oneness above time and outside of space. In this new concept of sublimity, oneness with the Godhead is complete" (*Nature and Culture*, p. 44).

55. Ibid., p. 198.

56. Edmund Wilson, *Patriotic Gore: Studies in the Literature of the American Civil War* (1962; New York, 1977), pp. 635–69. The quoted passage is on page 654.

John F. Kensett's Painting Technique

1. Since, as will be shown, Kensett made very few changes in his paintings and, in addition, painted very thinly, x-radiographs yield little if any information that is not already obvious. Infrared reflectography has helped to confirm the presence of pencil drawing where already somewhat visible. Infrared rays do not penetrate white lead very easily, making the technique's utility for the examination of this group of pictures somewhat limited.

2. Kensett to John R. Kensett, 30 March 1854. James R. Kellogg Collection, microfilm in Archives of American Art, Smithsonian Institution, Washington, D.C., roll no. N68–84.

3. *Study of Beeches*; *Salt Meadow in October*; *Newport Rocks*; *Sunset Sky*; *Gathering Storm on Long Island Sound*; *Lake George, A Reminiscence*; *Lake George*; *Twilight on the Sound, Darien, Connecticut*.

4. A photograph of Kensett working on framed pictures in his studio appears in John Howat's *John Frederick Kensett* (American Federation of the Arts, New York, 1968).

5. Van Goyen did not, however, add a priming but worked on a semitransparent ground that allows the warm color of the oak panel to dominate.

6. Letter of gift, Thomas Kensett (Archives of the Metropolitan Museum of Art, New York).

7. *On Exhibition Only, Mr. Kensett's Last Summer's Work*, National Academy of Design, 1873.

8. Photographs of National Academy exhibition.

9. *On Exhibition Only*.

10. Microscopic identification of paint samples was made by Laura Juszczak, Fellow, Paintings Conservation, The Metropolitan Museum of Art, New York.

11. In regard to crystalline materials, a crystal is said to be anisotropic if it allows light to pass through with different speeds in different crystal directions. Both vermilion and earth reds exhibit this characteristic.

BIBLIOGRAPHY

Manuscripts

American Art-Union Papers. New-York Historical Society, New York.

George Bancroft Papers. Massachusetts Historical Society, Boston.

Asher B. Durand Papers and John Durand Papers. New York Public Library, New York.

Edward Everett Papers. Massachusetts Historical Society, Boston.

James R. Kellogg Collection, microfilm in Archives of American Art, Smithsonian Institution, Washington, D.C.

Kensett Correspondence in Edwin D. Morgan Collection. New York State Library, Albany.

John F. Kensett File. Archives of the Metropolitan Museum of Art, New York.

John F. Kensett File. National Academy of Design, New York.

John F. Kensett *Journal*, 1840–41. 2 vols. Frick Art Reference Library, New York.

John F. Kensett Papers. Archives of American Art, Smithsonian Institution, Washington, D.C.

John F. Kensett Papers: Metropolitan Fair in Aid of the United States Sanitary Commission, 1864. Museum of the City of New York.

John F. Kensett Photograph File. Witt Art Reference Library, London.

Ogden Rood Papers. The Rare Book and Manuscript Library, Columbia University Library, New York.

Passport Application Letters, 1840–1870. National Archives, Washington, D.C.

Rossiter File, Manuscript Collection. New-York Historical Society.

Royal Academy File. Witt Art Reference Library, London.

Catalogues

Bermingham, Peter. *Jasper F. Cropsey, 1823–1900: A Retrospective View of America's Painter of Autumn.* University of Maryland Art Gallery, College Park, Md., 1968.

Brown, Jeffrey. *Alfred Thompson Bricher, 1837–1908.* Indianapolis Museum of Art, Indianapolis, Ind., 1973.

Cikovsky, Nikolai, Jr. *Sanford Robinson Gifford.* The University of Texas Art Gallery, Austin, Tex., 1970.

Davidson, Gail, Phyllis Hattis, and Theodore E. Stebbins, Jr. *Luminous Landscape: The American Study of Light, 1860–1875.* Fogg Art Museum, Harvard University, Cambridge, Mass., 1966.

Driscoll, John Paul. *John F. Kensett Drawings.* Museum of Art, The Pennsylvania State University, State College, Pa., 1978.

Eldredge, Charles. *The Arcadian Landscape: Nineteenth-Century American Painters in Italy.* University of Kansas Museum of Art, Lawrence, Kans., 1972.

Ferber, Linda. *William Trost Richards: American Landscape and Marine Painter, 1833–1905.* Brooklyn Museum, New York, 1973.

Hills, Patricia. *The Painter's America: Rural and Urban Life, 1810–1910.* Whitney Museum of American Art, New York, 1974.

———. *Turn-of-the-Century America.* Whitney Museum of American Art, New York, 1977.

Howat, John K. *John Frederick Kensett.* American Federation of the Arts, New York, 1968.

"The Last Summer's Work." Descriptive Catalogue of Thirty-eight Paintings Given to the Metropolitan Museum of Art by Thomas Kensett. The Metropolitan Museum of Art, New York, 1874.

Lawall, David B. *A. B. Durand, 1796–1886.* Montclair Art Museum, Montclair, N.J., 1971.

Maddox, Kenneth W. *An Unprejudiced Eye: The Drawings of Jasper F. Cropsey.* The Hudson River Museum, Yonkers, N.Y., 1979.

McShine, Kynaston, et al. *The Natural Paradise: Painting in America, 1800–1950.* Museum of Modern Art, New York, 1976.

Merritt, Howard S. *Thomas Cole.* Memorial Art Gallery of the University of Rochester, Rochester, N.Y., 1969.

Mead, Katherine H. *The Preston Morton Collection of American Art.* Santa Barbara Museum of Art, Santa Barbara, Calif., 1981.

Prokopoff, Stephen S., James K. Kettlewell, and Joan C. Siegfried. *John Frederick Kensett: A Retrospective Exhibition.* Hathorn Gallery, Skidmore College, Saratoga Springs, N.Y., 1967.

Richardson, Edgar P., and Otto Wittman, Jr. *Travelers in Arcadia: American Artists in Italy.* Detroit Institute of Arts, Detroit, Mich., 1951.

Somerville, Robert. *The Collection of Over Five Hundred Paintings and Studies by the Late John F. Kensett.* Association Hall, New York, 1873.

Stebbins, Theodore E., Jr. *Close Observations: Selected Oil Sketches by Frederic E. Church.* Cooper-Hewitt Museum, Smithsonian Institution, Washington, D.C., 1978.

Stein, Roger B. *Seascape and the American Imagination.* Whitney Museum of American Art, New York, 1975.

Strickler, Susan E. *Toledo Museum of Art: American Paintings.* The Toledo Museum of Art, Toledo, Ohio, 1979.

Talbot, William S. *Jasper F. Cropsey, 1823–1900.* National Collection of Fine Arts, Smithsonian Institution, Washington, D.C., 1970.

United States Sanitary Commission. *Catalogue of Arts, Relics and Curiosities on Exhibition at the Taylor House, U.S. Sanitary Fair Commission.* Brooklyn, N.Y., 1864.

United States Sanitary Commission. *Catalogue of the Art Exhibition at the Metropolitan Fair in Aid of the U.S. Sanitary Commission.* New York, 1864.

United States Sanitary Commission. *Catalogue of Paintings and Other Works of Art Presented to the Metropolitan Fair in Aid of the U.S. Sanitary Commission.* New York, 1864.

Wilmerding, John, et al. *American Light: The Luminist Movement, 1850–1875.* National Gallery of Art, Washington, D.C., 1980.

Articles and Books

"The Academy of Design: The Forty-fourth Exhibition —A Run through the Galleries." *Evening Post*, 27 April 1869, p. 1.

"The Academy of Design: The Opening of the Season." *New York Daily Tribune*, 15 April 1870, p. 4.

"American Art-Union." *New York Daily Tribune*, 18 December 1852, p. 6.

"An Artist's Funeral: Closing Tribute to John F. Kensett." *New York Daily Tribune*, 19 December 1872, p. 2.

"Art Items." *New York Daily Tribune*, 21 July 1860, p. 7.

"Art Items." *New York Daily Tribune*, 7 November 1860, p. 7.

"Art Items." *New York Daily Tribune*, 26 May 1861, p. 3.

Benjamin, S. G. W. *Art in America: A Critical and Historical Sketch.* New York, 1880.

———. "Fifty Years of American Art." *Harper's New Monthly Magazine* 59 (July 1879): 254–56.

Blaugrund, Annette. "*Up through the Snow* to Kensett's Studio." *Archives of American Art Journal* 23, no. 3 (1983): 31–32.

Baur, John I. H. *American Painting in the Nineteenth Century: Main Trends and Movements.* New York, 1953.

Baur, John I. H., ed. "The Autobiography of Worthington Whittredge, 1820–1910." *Brooklyn Museum Journal* (1942): 5–66.

Bellows, Henry Whitney. *Historical Sketch of the Union League Club of New York City.* New York, 1879.

Born, Wolfgang. "Sentiment of Nature." *Gazette des Beaux-Arts* n.s. 6, 36, no. 974 (April 1948): 219–38.

Breuning, Margaret. "Kensett Revalued in Light of Today." *Art Digest* 1 (February 1945): 10.

Brooklyn Art Association. *A History of the Brooklyn Art Association with An Index of Exhibitions.* New York, 1970.

Brumbaugh, Thomas B. "A Venice Letter from Thomas P. Rossiter to John F. Kensett, 1843." *American Art Journal* 5 (May 1973): 74–78.

Bryant, William Cullen, ed. *Picturesque America.* New York, 1874.

Callow, James T. *Kindred Spirits: Knickerbocker Writers and American Artists, 1807–1855.* Chapel Hill, N.C., 1967.

Champney, Benjamin. "The White Hills in 1850: The Advance Guard of the Grand Army of Painters." *White Mountain Echo and Tourist Register*, 12 August 1893, p. 6.

——— *Sixty Years' Memories of Art and Artists* (Woburn, Mass., 1900).

Clement, Clara Erskine and Laurence Hutton. *Artists of the Nineteenth Century and Their Works*. 1879, 1884; reprint: Saint Louis, 1969.

Cowdrey, Mary Bartlett, ed. *American Academy of Fine Arts and American Art Union: Exhibition Record, 1816–1852*. 2 vols. New York, 1953.

———. *National Academy of Design Exhibition Record, 1826–1860*. 2 vols. New York, 1943.

———. "The Return of John F. Kensett, 1816–1872, Painter of Pure Landscape." *Old Print Shop Portfolio* (February 1945): 123–26.

The Crayon: A Journal Devoted to the Graphic Arts and the Literature Related to Them. 8 vols. New York, 1855–61.

Cummings, Thomas Seir. *Historic Annals of the National Academy of Design*. Philadelphia, 1865.

Curtis, George W. "Editor's Easy Chair." *Harper's New Monthly Magazine* 46 (March 1873): 610–12.

———. *Lotus Eating: A Summer Book*. New York, 1852.

Degler, Carl N. *Out of Our Past*. New York, 1962.

Doggett, Samuel Bradlee. *A History of the Doggett-Daggett Family*. Boston, 1894.

Degler, Carl N. *Out of Our Past*. New York, 1962.

"Domestic Art Items and Gossip." *Cosmopolitan Art Journal* (September 1858): 207.

Dunlap, William. *A History of the Rise and Progress of the Arts of Design in the United States*. 3 vols. 1834; reprint: New York, 1965.

Durand, Asher B. "Letters on Landscape Painting." *The Crayon*, vols. 1–2 (January–July 1855). Vol. 1: 3 January 1855, pp. 1–2; 17 January 1855, pp. 34–35; 31 January 1855, pp. 66–67; 14 February 1855, pp. 97–98; 7 March 1855, pp. 145–46; 4 April 1855, pp. 209–11; 2 May 1855, pp. 273–75; 6 June 1855, pp. 254–55; Vol. 2: 11 July 1855, pp. 16–17.

Durand, John. *The Life and Times of Asher B. Durand*. New York, 1894.

Eisenstadt, Abraham S., ed. *American History: Recent Interpretations*. New York, 1969.

"Exhibition of the National Academy of Design." *Knickerbocker* 45 (May 1855): 529–33.

Fairman, Charles E. *Art and Artists of the Capitol of the United States of America*. Washington, D.C., 1927.

Fielding, Mantle. *Dictionary of American Painters, Sculptors, and Engravers*. Addendum by James F. Carr. Reprint: New York, 1965.

"Fine Arts." *New York Daily Tribune*, 16 March 1864, p. 4.

"Fine Arts: Mr. Avery's Collection." *New York Daily Tribune*, 5 May 1870, p. 4.

"Fine Arts: The Goupil Gallery." *New York Daily Tribune*, 16 February 1874, p. 2.

"Fine Arts: The Paintings at the Somerville Gallery." *New York Daily Tribune*, 2 April 1870, p. 2.

Freeman, James E. *Gatherings from an Artist's Portfolio, Rome*. Boston, 1883.

French, Henry. *Art and Artists in Connecticut*. Boston and New York, 1879.

Graves, Algernon, F.S.A. *The British Institution, 1806–1867*. London, 1908.

———. *Dictionary of Artists Who Have Exhibited at the Principal London Exhibitions from 1760–1863*. 1901; reprint: Bath, 1969.

Groce, George, and David Wallace. *The New-York Historical Society's Dictionary of Artists in America, 1564–1860*. New Haven, Conn., 1957.

Harlow, Thompson R. "Connecticut Engravers, 1774–1820." *The Connecticut Historical Society Bulletin* 36, no. 4 (October 1971): 97–136.

Howat, John K. *The Hudson River and Its Painters*. New York, 1972.

———. "John F. Kensett, 1816–1872." *The Magazine Antiques* 96 (September 1969): 397–401.

Howe, Winifred E. *A History of the Metropolitan Museum of Art*. New York, 1913.

Huntington, Daniel, et al. *Proceedings at a Meeting of the Century Association Held in Memory of John F. Kensett*. New York, 1872.

Huntington, David C. *The Landscapes of Frederic Edwin Church: Vision of an American Era*. New York, 1966.

Jarves, James Jackson. *Art-Thoughts: The Experiences and Observations of an American Amateur in Europe*. New York, 1869.

———. *The Art-Idea*. 1864; reprint: Cambridge, Mass., 1960.

———. *Art-Hints, Architecture, Sculpture, and Painting.* New York, 1855.

Johnson, Ellen H. "Kensett Revisited." *Art Quarterly* 20 (Spring 1957): 71–92.

Kilbourne, Frederick W. "A White Mountain Artist of Long Ago." *Appalachia* 13 (December 1947): 447–55.

Lawall, David B. *A. B. Durand: A Documentary Catalogue of the Narrative and Landscape Paintings.* New York, 1978.

Leslie, C. R. *Memoirs of the Life of John Constable.* 1843; reprint, rev. ed.: London, 1951.

Lewis, R. W. B. *The American Adam.* Chicago, 1958

Lewison, Florence. "John Frederick Kensett: A Tribute to Man and Artist." *American Artist.* October 1966, p. 32–37.

"Literary Legislators, The Earl of Ellesmere." *Fraser's Magazine* 35 (June 1847): 714–22.

Lively, Jack. *The Social and Political Thought of Alexis de Tocqueville.* London and New York, 1962.

Merritt, Howard S. "Correspondence between Thomas Cole and Robert Gilmore, Jr.," *Studies on Thomas Cole, An American Romanticist.* Baltimore Museum of Art Annual, no. 2, 1967.

Miller, Perry. *The Life of the Mind in America, from the Revolution to the Civil War.* New York, 1965.

Monk, Samuel H. *The Sublime.* 1935; reprint: Ann Arbor, 1960.

Moure, Nancy Dustin Wall. "Five Eastern Artists out West." *American Art Journal* 5 (November 1973): 15–31.

"National Academy Exhibition." *New York Mirror,* 26 May 1838, p. 382.

"National Academy Exhibition," *New York Daily Tribune,* 5 April 1861, p. 7.

Nash, Roderick. *Wilderness and the American Mind.* New Haven, Conn., 1967.

Naylor, Maria. *The National Academy of Design Exhibition Record, 1861–1900.* 2 vols. New York, 1973.

Noble, Louis L. *The Life and Works of Thomas Cole.* 1853; reprint: Cambridge, Mass., 1964.

Novak, Barbara. "American Landscape: Changing Concepts of the Sublime." *American Art Journal* 4 (Spring 1972): 36–42.

———. "American Landscape and the Nationalist Garden and Holy Book." *Art in America* 60 (January–February 1972): 46–57.

———. *American Painting of the Nineteenth Century: Realism, Idealism, and the American Experience.* New York, 1969.

———. *Nature and Culture: American Landscape and Painting, 1825–1875.* New York, 1980.

———. "Thomas Cole and Robert Gilmore." *Art Quarterly* 25 (Spring 1962): 41–53.

Nye, Russell B. *George Bancroft, Brahmin Rebel.* New York, 1972.

———. *Society and Culture in America, 1830–1860.* New York, 1974.

"Obituary Mr. Kensett." *American Bibliopolist* 5 (January 1873): 13–14.

"Obituary—Kensett." *Harper's Weekly,* 4 January 1873, p. 5.

Perkins, Robert F., and William J. Gavin III, eds. *Boston Athenaeum Art Exhibition Index, 1827–1874.* Boston, 1980.

Rigney, Daria. *John William Casilear.* Graduate paper, Columbia University, 1979.

Ringe, Donald A. "James Fenimore Cooper and Thomas Cole: An Analogous Technique." *American Literature* 30 (March 1958): 26–36.

———. "Kindred Spirits: Bryant and Cole." *American Quarterly* 6 (Fall 1954): 233–44.

———. "Painting as Poem in the Hudson River Aesthetic." *American Quarterly* 12 (Spring 1960): 71–83.

———. "Bryant's Criticism of the Fine Arts." *College Art Journal* 17 (Fall 1957): 43–54.

Rood, Ogden N. "On a New Theory of Light." *American Journal of Science and Art* 30 (September 1860): 182–86.

———. *Modern Chromatics Students' Text-Book of Color with Applications to Art and Industry.* 1879; reprint: New York, 1973.

Ormsby, Waterman L. *A Description of the Present System of Banknote Engraving, Showing Its Tendency to Facilitate Counterfeiting to Which Is Added a New Method of Constructing Bank Notes to Prevent Forgery.* New York and London, 1852.

Rosenberg, John D. *The Genius of John Ruskin.* New York, 1963.

Ruskin, John. *Modern Painters.* 5 vols. New York, 1868.

Rutledge, Anna Wells. *Cumultive Record of Exhibition Catalogues: The Pennsylvania Academy of the Fine Arts, 1807–1870.* Philadelphia, 1955.

"Sale of the Blodgett Collection." *New York Daily Tribune,* 28 April 1876, p. 4.

Scott, Leonora Cranch. *The Life and Letters of Christopher Pearce Cranch.* Boston and New York, 1917.

Sheldon, George W. *American Painters.* New York, 1879.

———. *Hours with Art and Artists.* New York, 1882.

———. *Recent Ideals of American Art.* 3 vols. New York, 1888.

Smyth, Albert. *Bayard Taylor.* Boston and New York, 1896.

Stauffer, David. *American Engravers Upon Copper and Steel.* New York, 1907.

Stebbins, Theodore E., Jr. *The Life and Works of Martin Johnson Heade.* New Haven, Conn., 1975.

Stein, Roger B. *John Ruskin and Aesthetic Thought in America, 1840–1900.* Cambridge, Mass., 1967.

Stern, Madeleine B. "New England Artists in Italy, 1835–1855." *The New England Quarterly* 14 (March 1941): 243–71.

Sullivan, Mark White. "John F. Kensett, American Landscape Painter." Ph.D. diss., Bryn Mawr College, 1981.

Tocqueville, Alexis de. *Journey to America.* Edited by J. Mayer. Translated by George Lawrence. Garden City, N.J., 1971.

Toppan, Robert Noxon. *A Hundred Years of Bank Note Engraving in the United States.* New York, 1896.

Tuckerman, Henry T. *Book of the Artists: American Artist Life.* 1867; reprint: New York, 1966.

Weiss, Ila. *Sanford Robinson Gifford, 1823–1880.* New York, 1977.

Williams, Hermann Warner, Jr. "A Rare Engraving by Kensett Identified." *The Magazine Antiques* 41 (January 1942): 47.

United States Sanitary Commission. *A Record of the Metropolitan Fair in Aid of the United States Sanitary Commission, Held at New York, in April, 1864.* New York, 1867.

Wilmerding, John. *Fitz Hugh Lane.* New York, 1971.

———. *Robert Salmon, Painter of Ship and Shore.* Boston, 1971.

Werner, Deborah Jean. "Lewis M. Rutherfurd: Pioneer Astronomical Photographer and Spectroscopist." *Technology and Culture* 12 (April 1971): 190–216.

EXHIBITION CHECKLIST

Paintings

View from Richmond Hill, c. 1843–45
oil on canvas
13 x 19⅛ in. (33 x 48.6 cm.)
Private Collection

The Shrine—A Scene in Italy, 1847
oil on canvas
30⅜ x 41⅝ in. (77.1 x 105.7 cm.)
signed and dated lower right: J.F. KENSETT. ROME, 1847
Mr. and Mrs. Maurice N. Katz, Naples, Florida

The White Mountains—From North Conway, 1851
oil on canvas
40 x 60 in. (101.6 x 152.4 cm.)
Wellesley College Museum, Wellesley, Massachusetts,
Gift of Mrs. James B. Munn (Ruth C. Hanford, '09)
in the name of the class of 1909

A Holiday in the Country, 1851
oil on canvas
21 x 30 in (53.3 x 76.2 cm.)
signed and dated lower left: J.F.K. 51
On extended loan to the Columbus Museum of Art, Ohio,
from the collection of Mr. and Mrs. W. Knight Sturges

Niagara Falls and the Rapids, c. 1851–52
oil on canvas
16 x 24 in. (40.6 x 61 cm.)
Museum of Fine Arts, Boston,
M. and M. Karolik Collection

Niagara Falls, c. 1851–52
oil on canvas
17 x 24½ in. (43.1 x 62.2 cm.)
Mead Art Museum, Amherst College,
Amherst, Massachusetts

Along the Hudson, 1852
oil on canvas
18⅛ x 24 in. (46 x 61 cm.)

signed and dated lower left: J.F.K. '52
National Museum of American Art,
Smithsonian Institution, Washington, D.C.,
Bequest of Helen Huntington Hull

*Camel's Hump from the Western Shore of
Lake Champlain*, 1852
oil on canvas
31 x 45 in. (78.7 x 114.3 cm.)
signed and dated lower right: J.F.K. '52
High Museum of Art, Atlanta,
Gift of Virginia Carroll Crawford

Adirondack Scenery, 1854
oil on canvas
40 x 59⅞ in. (101.6 x 152.1 cm.)
signed and dated lower right: J.F.K. 54
Hirschl and Adler Galleries, Inc., New York

October Day in the White Mountains, 1854
oil on canvas
31⅜ x 48⅜ in. (80 x 123.5 cm.)
signed and dated lower right: J.F.K. '54
The Cleveland Museum of Art,
John L. Severance Fund and gift of various donors

Conway Valley, New Hampshire, 1854
oil on canvas
32¾ x 48 in. (81.2 x 122 cm.)
signed and dated lower left: J.F.K. 54
Worcester Art Museum, Worcester, Massachusetts

Upper Mississippi, 1855
oil on canvas
18½ x 30½ in. (47 x 77.5 cm.)
signed and dated lower right: J.F.K. 55
The Saint Louis Art Museum, Purchase,
Eliza McMillan Fund, 22, 1950

Bash Bish Falls, 1855
oil on canvas
36 x 29 in. (73.6 x 91.5 cm.)
signed and dated lower right: J.F.K. 55
National Academy of Design, New York

A Woodland Waterfall, c. 1855
oil on canvas
40 x 34 in. (101.6 x 86.3 cm.)
signed lower left: J.F.K.
James Maroney, New York

View of the Shrewsbury River, c. 1853–60
oil on canvas
12 x 20 in. (30.5 x 50.8 cm.)
Jane Voorhees Zimmerli Art Museum, Rutgers,
The State University, New Brunswick, New Jersey,
Gift of the Interfraternity Alumni, 1952

Beacon Rock, Newport Harbor, 1857
oil on canvas
22½ x 36 in. (57.1 x 91.5 cm.)
signed and dated lower right: J.F.K. 57
National Gallery of Art, Washington, D.C.,
Gift of Frederick Sturges, Jr., 1953

Lakes of Killarney, 1857
oil on canvas
24¹/₁₆ x 34¼ in. (61.1 x 87 cm.)
signed and dated lower right: J.F.K. 57
Milwaukee Art Museum, Wisconsin

Hudson River Scene, 1857
oil on canvas
32 x 48 in. (81.3 x 121.9 cm.)
signed and dated lower right: J.F.K. 57
The Metropolitan Museum of Art, New York,
Gift of H. D. Babcock, in memory of S. D. Babcock, 1907

The Langdale Pike, 1858
oil on canvas
22¼ x 36 in. (56.5 x 91.4 cm.)
signed and dated lower right: J.F.K. 58
Cornell Fine Arts Center, Rollins College,
Winterpark, Florida

*Shrewsbury River, 1858
oil on canvas
15 x 27 in. (38.1 x 68.6 cm.)
signed and dated lower left: J.F.K. '59
Erving and Joyce Wolf

Shrewsbury River, New Jersey, 1859
oil on canvas
18½ x 30½ in. (47 x 77.5 cm.)
signed and dated lower left: J.F.K. '59
The New-York Historical Society, New York

*To be exhibited in Los Angeles and New York only.

Shrewsbury River, 1860
oil on canvas
15 x 24 in. (38.1 x 61 cm.)
signed and dated lower right: J.F.K. 1860
Private Collection

View of the Beach at Beverly, Massachusetts, 1860
oil on canvas
14¼ x 24¼ in. (48.8 x 61.6 cm.)
signed and dated lower right: J.F.K. '60
Santa Barbara Museum of Art, California,
Gift of Mrs. Sterling Morton to the
Preston Morton Collection

Forty Steps, Newport, Rhode Island, 1860
oil on canvas
20⅛ x 36 in. (51.1 x 91.4 cm.)
signed and dated lower right: J.F.K. 1860
Jo Ann and Julian Ganz, Jr.

On the Beverly Coast, Massachusetts, 1863
oil on canvas
12 x 20 in. (30.4 x 50.8 cm.)
signed and dated lower right: J.F.K. '63
Erving and Joyce Wolf

View from Cozzens' Hotel near West Point, 1863
oil on canvas
20 x 34 in. (50.8 x 86.4 cm.)
signed and dated lower center: J.F.K. '63
The New-York Historical Society, New York

Marine off Big Rock, 1864
oil on canvas
27½ x 44½ in. (69.8 x 113 cm.)
signed and dated lower right: J.F.K. '64
Cummer Gallery of Art, Jacksonville, Florida

An Inlet of Long Island Sound, c. 1865
oil on canvas
14¼ x 24 in. (36.2 x 61 cm.)
signed at lower left: J.F.K.
Los Angeles County Museum of Art,
Gift of Colonel and Mrs. William Keighley

Paradise Rocks, Newport, c. 1865
oil on canvas
18⅛ x 29⅞ in. (46 x 75.9 cm.)
The Newark Museum, New Jersey,
Gift of Dr. J. Ackerman Coles, 1920

View on the Hudson, 1865
oil on canvas
27½ x 44½ in. (69.2 x 112.4 cm.)
signed and dated lower left: J.F.K. '65
The Baltimore Museum of Art,
Gift of Mrs. Paul H. Miller (BMA 1942.4)

Mount Chocorua, 1864–66
oil on canvas
48 x 84 in. (122 x 213.4 cm.)
The Century Association, New York

Newport Coast, c. 1865–70
oil on canvas
18¹/₁₆ x 30¼ in. (46.1 x 76.9 cm.)
Private Collection

Coast Scene with Figures, 1869
oil on canvas
36¼ x 60¼ in. (92 x 153 cm.)
signed and dated lower right: J.F.K. 69
Wadsworth Atheneum, Hartford, Connecticut,
The Ella Gallup Sumner and
Mary Catlin Sumner Collection

Beach at Newport, c. 1869–72
oil on canvas
22 x 34 in. (55.8 x 86.4 cm.)
National Gallery of Art, Washington, D.C.,
Gift of Frederick Sturges, Jr., 1978

Coast at Newport, 1869
oil on canvas
11⅝ x 24¼ in. (29.5 x 61.6 cm.)
signed and dated lower right: J.F.K. 1869
The Art Institute of Chicago,
Friends of American Art Collections

Lake George, 1869
oil on canvas
44⅛ x 66⅜ in. (112.1 x 168.6 cm.)
signed and dated lower right: J.F.K. 1869
The Metropolitan Museum of Art, New York,
Bequest of Maria DeWitt Jesup, 1915

Storm, Western Colorado, 1870
oil on canvas
18⁵/₁₆ x 28⅛ in. (46.5 x 71.7 cm.)
signed on reverse (now covered by lining canvas):
J.F. KENSETT
The Toledo Museum of Art, Ohio,
Gift of Florence Scott Libbey

Lake George, 1870
oil on canvas
14 x 24⅛ in. (35.5 x 61.2 cm.)
signed and dated lower right: J.F.K. '70
The Brooklyn Museum, New York,
Gift of Mrs. W. W. Phelps in memory of
her mother and father, Ella M. and John C. Southwick,
1933

*Long Neck Point from Contentment Island, Darien,
Connecticut*, c. 1870–72
oil on canvas
15⅜ x 24⅜ in. (39 x 61.9 cm.)
Museum of Art, Carnegie Institute, Pittsburgh,
Gift of the Women's Committee of the Museum of Art,
1980

Eaton's Neck, Long Island, 1872
oil on canvas
18 x 36 in. (45.7 x 91.4 cm.)
The Metropolitan Museum of Art, New York,
Gift of Thomas Kensett, 1874

Sunset on the Sea, 1872
oil on canvas
28 x 41⅛ in. (71.1 x 104.5 cm.)
The Metropolitan Museum of Art, New York,
Gift of Thomas Kensett, 1874

Newport Rocks, 1872
oil on canvas
31 x 48 in. (78.7 x 121.9 cm.)
The Metropolitan Museum of Art, New York,
Gift of Thomas Kensett, 1874

A Foggy Sky, 1872
oil on canvas
30½ x 45¾ in. (77.5 x 116.2 cm.)
The Metropolitan Museum of Art, New York,
Gift of Thomas Kensett, 1874

The Old Pine, Darien, Connecticut, 1872
oil on canvas
34⅜ x 27¼ in. (87.3 x 69.2 cm.)
The Metropolitan Museum of Art, New York,
Gift of Thomas Kensett, 1874

Fish Island from Kensett's Studio on Contentment Island,
1872
oil on canvas
18 x 36 in. (45.7 x 91.4 cm.)
Montclair Art Museum, New Jersey,
Lang Acquisition Fund, 1960

Drawings

Eton School, 1843
pencil on paper
7⅝ x 11½ in. (19.4 x 29.2 cm.)
inscribed lower right: *Eton School, July 26th, 1843*
Mr. and Mrs. Stuart P. Feld

Windsor Castle from the Park, 1843
pencil on paper
8 x 11⅜ in. (20.3 x 28.9 cm.)
inscribed lower right: *Windsor Castle from the Park,
July 26th, 1843*
Private Collection

Stolzenfels, 1845
pencil, pen, and sepia ink on gray paper
10⅛ x 14⅛ in. (25.7 x 35.9 cm.)
inscribed lower left: *Stoltzenfels* (sic) *Augt. 3, 1845*
Dia Art Foundation, N.Y., courtesy The Dan Flavin
Art Institute, Bridgehampton

Standing Monk Holding a Staff, c. 1845–47
pencil on gray paper
9⅞ x 6¾ in. (25 x 17.2 cm.)
Susan and Herbert Adler

Huntsman with Rifle, c. 1845–47
pencil and watercolor on tan paper
11½ x 8½ in. (29.2 x 21 cm.)
Babcock Galleries, New York

Standing Artist, c. 1845–47
pencil and watercolor on gray paper
11⁵⁄₁₆ x 8⅝ in. (28.6 x 21 cm.)
National Museum of American Art,
Smithsonian Institution, Washington, D.C.

Capri, 1847
pencil on paper
11¾ x 18⅜ in. (29.8 x 46.7 cm.)
inscribed lower left: *Capri May 16th 1847*
Dan Flavin, N.Y.

Camel's Hump, Lake Champlain, 1848
pencil on buff paper
10½ x 16½ in. (26.7 x 41.9 cm.)
inscribed lower left: *Camel's Hump, Westport [?]
L Champlain, Augt. 25th 48*
Dan Flavin, N.Y.

Tree Study, Catskill, 1849
pencil on buff paper
17½ x 12⅛ in. (44.5 x 30.8 cm.)
inscribed lower left: *Catskill, Oct 9[?] 49*
Private Collection

Franconia Notch, 1850
pencil on buff paper
10 x 13⅞ in. (25.4 x 35.3 cm.)
inscribed lower right: *Franconia Notch, Oct. 20th 50*
Dia Art Foundation, N.Y., courtesy The
Dan Flavin Art Institute, Bridgehampton

Tree Study, Franconia Notch, 1850
pencil on buff paper
13½ x 9⅞ in. (34.3 x 25.1 cm.)
inscribed lower right: *Franconia Notch, Oct 22d 1850*
Babcock Galleries, New York

Mount Lafayette, 1850
pencil on buff paper
9⅞ x 13¾ in. (25.1 x 34.9 cm.)
signed lower right: J.F.K.
inscribed lower left: *Mt. Lafayette, Oct. 22d 50*
Babcock Galleries, New York

Birch Tree, Niagara, 1850
pencil on paper
16⅝ x 10⅝ in. (42 x 27 cm.)
signed lower right: J.F.K.
inscribed lower right: *Birch Tree, Niagara, Aug. 26th /50*
The Metropolitan Museum of Art, New York,
Morris K. Jesup Fund, 1976

Niagara Falls, 1852
pencil on paper
12¼ x 18⅛ in. (31.2 x 46 cm.)
inscribed lower right: *Niagara Falls 52 C.W. Oct 52*
Mr. and Mrs. Stuart P. Feld

Niagara Falls, c. 1852
pencil on buff paper
11⅜ x 18 in. (28.9 x 45.7 cm.)
Babcock Galleries, New York

Lake George, 1853
pencil on buff paper
9⅞ x 13⅝ in. (25.1 x 34.6 cm.)
inscribed lower left: *Lake George, Augt. 23r. 53*
Mrs. Alice M. Kaplan

Lake George, 1853
pencil and white on buff paper
9¹⁵⁄₁₆ x 14 in. (25.2 x 35.5 cm.)
inscribed lower left: *Lake George Aug. 23 '53*
Private Collection

Lake Pepin, 1854
pencil on paper
8¼ x 11 in. (21 x 28 cm.)
inscribed lower left: *Lake Pepin Mississippi June 9th 54*
Private Collection

From Rose Island, Killarney, 1856
pencil on buff paper
9⅞ x 14 in. (25.1 x 35.5 cm.)
inscribed lower left: *From Rose Island, Killarney
Augt. 22, 1856*
Dia Art Foundation, N.Y., courtesy The
Dan Flavin Art Institute, Bridgehampton

Killarney, 1856
pencil on buff paper
9⅝ x 14 in. (24.4 x 35.5 cm.)
inscribed lower left: *Killarney, Augt. 20th, 58*
Dia Art Foundation, N.Y., courtesy The
Dan Flavin Art Institute, Bridgehampton

Killarney, 1856
pencil on buff paper
9½ x 14 in. (24.2 x 35.5 cm.)
inscribed lower left: *Killarney, Augt. 13th. 56*
Dia Art Foundation, N.Y., courtesy The
Dan Flavin Art Institute, Bridgehampton

Elm, 1862
pencil on buff paper
11³⁄₁₆ x 8⅛ in. (28.6 x 20.6 cm.)
inscribed lower left: *Elm, July 17 62* [?]
Museum of Art, Carnegie Institute, Pittsburgh;
Gibbons Fund, 1984

Rowayton, Connecticut, 1868
pencil on buff paper
9⅞ x 14 in. (25.1 x 35.5 cm.)
signed lower left: J. F. K.
inscribed lower left: *Rowaton, Aug. '68*
Babcock Galleries, New York

Chicago Lake, 1870
pencil on gray paper
10 x 13¾ in. (25.4 x 34.9 cm.)
inscribed lower left: *Chicago Lake July 30th 70*
Babcock Galleries, New York

Newport, 1871
pencil on buff paper
9⅝ x 13⅝ in. (24.5 x 34.6 cm.)
inscribed lower right: *Newport Sept. 71*
Babcock Galleries, New York

INDEX

Page numbers in italic refer to illustrations.

Adirondack Scenery (Kensett), 79, *80*
Albany—Taken from the East Side of the River (Cole), *17*, 18
Along the Hudson (Kensett), 85
American Art-Union, 26, 28, 34, 35, 61, 67
American Harvesting (Cropsey), 72, *72*
American in Paris During the Summer, or Heath's Picturesque Annual for 1844, The (Janin), 22, 23
American Scenery (Willis and Bartlett), 144
Apollo Association for the Promotion of the Fine Arts in the United States, 26
Arch of Octavius, The (Bierstadt), 28, 31
Ariadne (Vanderlyn), 25
Art Commission, 40–42
Artists' Fund Society of New York, 40
"Art Matters," 137–38
Art-Union *Bulletin*, 26
Audubon, John James, 50
Autumn Leaves, engraved frontispiece for (Kensett), 16, *16*
Avenue in Hatfield Park, the Seat of the Marquis of Salisbury, An (Kensett), 28–29

Baker, George A., 32
Bancroft, George, 36, 98
bank notes, engraving of, 15, 16, 18–19
Barber, John Warner, 13
Bartlett, William Henry, 141
Bash Bish Falls (Kensett), 52, 79, *81*, 82, 96
Beach at Newport (Kensett), *131*, 135, 176
Beacon Rock, Newport Harbor (Kensett), 57, 62, *106*, 108, 121, 148

Beacon Rock series, 108, 121
Beeches, The (Durand), *78*, 79
Bellows, Henry Whitney, 37, 40, 43, 44, 157
Benjamin, S. G. W., 126
Bierstadt, Albert, 28, 31, 42, 43, 156–58
Bingham, Robert Jefferson, 45
Birch Tree, Niagara (Kensett), 90–91, *90*, 96
Blakelock, Ralph Albert, 152
Bliss, George, 42
Bloor, Alfred J., 46
Book of the Artists (Tuckerman), 45, 155–56
Both, Jan, 52
Branson, Tillotson, 14
Bread and Cheese, The, 36
Bricher, Alfred T., 113, 119, 120
British Queen, 20, 49
Brook Farm, 34
Brooklyn Eagle, 138
Brown, Henry Kirke, 41–42
Brumidi, Constantio, 40
Bryant, William Cullen, 62
Buchanan, James, 41

Caffè Greco, 32, 50
Calamé, Alexandre, 126
Camel's Hump, Lake Champlain (Kensett), 58, *92*, 93, 94
Camel's Hump from the Western Shore of Lake Champlain (Kensett), 52, 74, *76*, 93, 122
Canaletto, Antonio, 52, 99
Canova, Antonio, 31
Capri (Kensett), 57, *57*, 99–102, 121, 123
Carpenter, Samuel, 24
Casilear, John, 16, 18, 20, 24, 49, 54, 63, 91, 93, 94, 140
Catlin, George, 29, 50
Century, 157

Century Association, 35–37, 98, 132, 148, 157
Champney, Benjamin, 24, 25, 27, 30, 42, 50, 63, 66
Cheshire Episcopal Academy, 13, 14
Chicago Lake (Kensett), 94, *95*
Chouteau, Pierre, 42
Church, Frederic E., 42, 138, 145, 156–57
   Kensett compared to, 66, 70–72, *70*, 83, 86
Coast at Newport (Kensett), 109, *116*
Coast Scene with Figures (Kensett), 52, 109, *117*, 135
Cobbett, Edward John, 29
Cole, Thomas, 17, 18, 26, 166, 167
   Kensett influenced by, 62, 70, 73–78, 93–94, 98, 99
Coleman, Samuel, 40
Colyer, Mrs. Vincent, 46
Colyer, Vincent, 43, 139, 144–45, 161
Constable, John, 52, 54, 59, 82
Contentment Island, Conn., Kensett's residence on, 139, 141–48, 149
Conway Valley, New Hampshire (Kensett), *77*, 78
Cooper, James Fenimore, 36
Cornwall, Asa, 14
Courier français, 27
Course of Empire, The (Cole), 74
Courtyard of the École des Beaux-Arts, The (Vinit), *19*, 21
Cozzens, Frederick, 37
Cranch, Christopher Pearse, 32–33
Crawford, Thomas, 31
Crayon, The, 14–15, 41, 91, 121, 153, 158
Cropsey, Jasper F., 72, 83, 86, 91, 163
Crowe, Eyre, 37
Cummings, Thomas S., 36
Currier and Ives, 70
Curtis, George William, 32, 34–35, 37, 50, 102

Curtis, James Burrill, 32, 34, 57
Cushman, Thomas H., 19–20

Daggett, Alfred, 16, 17
Daggett, Eunice Tuttle, 13
Daggett, Ezra, 13
Daggett, Naphtali, 13
Daggett and Ely, 17, 18
Daggett and Hinman and Company, 18
Daily Albany Argus, 18–19
Deposition (Titian), 52
Descriptive Catalogue of Last Summer's Work, 176
Distant View of the Mansfield Mountain, Vermont (Kensett), 61
Doolittle, Amos, 14
Dou, Gerard, 52
Driscoll, John Paul, 49–136
Durand, Asher B., 18, 20, 49, 61, 62, 63, 66, 70, 72, 161
    Kensett compared to, 78, 79–82, 83, 91–93, 94, 96, 98, 99
Durand, Cyrus, 16
Dwight, Theodore, 30
Dwyer, Diane, 163–80

Eaton's Neck, Long Island (Kensett), 136, 137, 148, 170–71, 176
École des Beaux-Arts, 19, 21
École Préparation des Beaux-Arts, 54
Edmonds, Francis William, 26, 40
Elm (Kensett), 94, 95
Emerson, Ralph Waldo, 34, 37, 62, 160
Englishman in Paris (Notes and Recollections), An (Van Dam), 21–22
engraving, history of, 13–17
En plein air painting, 166
Entrance to Newport Harbor (Kensett), 108, 108
Eton School (Kensett), 55, 56
Expulsion from the Garden of Eden (Cole), 74, 75

Falconer, John M., 40
Fellowship Fund, 39
Field, Stephen Johnson, 19
Fish Island from Kensett's Studio on Contentment Island (Kensett), 140, 142, 145
"Flake White," 91

Foggy Sky, A (Kensett), 137, 146, 148, 170, 175, 176, 180
Footpath in Burnham Forest (Kensett), 28
"*Forest Hymn, A*" (Bryant), 62
Forty Steps, Newport, Rhode Island (Kensett), 109, 115
Franconia Notch (Kensett), 94, 95
Free Academy, 43
Freeman, James., 32
Frith, William, 29
From Rose Island, Killarney (Kensett), 120, 121

Galignani's New Paris Guide, 21
"Gatherings from an Artist's Portfolio" (Freeman), 32
Gathering Storm on Long Island Sound (Kensett), 148, 160, 159, 175, 176
Gibbs, Oliver Wolcott, 132
Gibbs, Wolcott, 43
Gibson, John, 31
Gifford, Sanford Robinson, 42, 72–73, 113, 163
Gilmore, Robert, Jr., 63
Gobrecht, Christian, 15
ground staining, 178

Hall, J. H., 18
Hall, Packard and Cushman, 18
Hampton Court, England, Kensett's residence at, 26–28
Hanky, Captain, 25
Harper's Weekly, 34, 39, 43, 44
Haseltine, William S., 113, 119–20
Hawthorne, Nathaniel, 30
Heade, Martin Johnson, 112, 113, 161
Hicks, Thomas, 24, 33, 34, 37, 50, 57, 140
Hillard, George Stillman, 30–31, 32
Hillhouse, James A., 17
"History and Progress of Bank Note Engraving" (Toppan), 14–15
Hoe, Robert, 39–40
Holiday in the Country, A (Kensett), 63, 64
Hook Mountain near Nyack on the Hudson (Gifford), 113, 113
Horsford, E. N., 20
Howat, John K., 13–47
Hudson River Scene (Kensett), 69, 70, 163, 164
Hudson River School, 153, 155, 159, 161

Hunt, William Morris, 27
Huntington, Daniel, 126, 140
Huntsman with Rifle (Kensett), 58, 58

Impressionism, 127
Inlet of Long Island Sound, An (Kensett), 147
Inness, George, 72–73, 158
Intervale at North Conway (Church), 66, 66
Irving, Washington, 62

Janin, Jules, 22, 23
Jarves, Jackson, 155, 156, 158
Jarvis, James Jackson, 73
Jay, John, 45
Jesup, Morris K., 122
Jocelyn, Nathaniel, 17
Jocelyn, Simeon, 17
John F. Kensett (Staigg), 33, 38
John Frederick Kensett (Bingham), 45
Johnson, Eastman, 40
Johnston, John Taylor, 138–39, 140

Kensett, Elizabeth Daggett (mother), 13, 140
Kensett, John Frederick:
    on Art Commission, 40–42
    artistic training of, 57–58, 99
    artistic views of, 23–24, 94–96
    in Century Association, 35–37
    childhood of, 13–14
    coastal scenery painted by, 99, 113, 135
    as colorist, 83, 123–33, 156
    conservation of paintings by, 177–80
    criticism of, 37, 153–157
    death of, 46–47
    drawings by, 87, 94–96, 122, 166
    Dutch influence on, 52, 54, 59, 168–70
    effect of Civil War on, 159–60, 161
    in England, 20–21, 27–30, 49, 50–51, 55–56, 59
    as engraver, 14–20, 26, 49, 56, 57
    financial situation of, 24–25, 26, 27, 49, 57, 61, 157–58
    influence of Old Masters on, 50–52, 63, 98, 99
    in Ireland, 121–22
    in Italy, 30–35, 50, 52, 56–58
    late style of, 141, 148–49, 152, 158

Kensett, John Frederick:
 as luminist, 99, 103, 109, 118, 133,
  156, 158, 159
 in National Academy of Design, 37–
  40
 nature as important to, 55, 62–63, 66,
  71–72, 79–80, 96, 109, 122, 145–48,
  156–57
 in New York, 35–47
 as organizer of the Metropolitan Fair,
  43–45
 painting techniques of, 70, 78, 82–83,
  102, 163–80
 in Paris, 21–27, 30, 50, 52
 personality of, 16–17, 50, 90–91, 155,
  156
 reputation of, 20, 22, 26, 29, 30, 35,
  37, 42, 47, 61, 99, 156–59
 rheumatic illness of, 32
 as Romantic, 55–56, 58
 in Sketch Club, 36
 sketching tours of, 54–56, 63, 91, 93
 social life of, 16–17, 18, 19
 as trustee of Metropolitan Museum,
  45–46
 in Union League Club, 42–43
Kensett, John R. (uncle), 22, 24, 50, 166
Kensett, Thomas (brother), 29, 135,
  138, 140, 163, 174, 176
Kensett, Thomas (father), 13, 14, 16, 17
Killarney (1856, pencil on buff paper,
  9½ x 14) (Kensett), 121, 122
Killarney (1856, pencil on buff paper,
  9⅝ x 14) (Kensett), 120, 122
Kindred Spirits (Durand), 93, 94

Lackawanna Valley (Inness), 72–73, 73
La Farge, John, 158
Lake George (Heade), 112, 113
Lake George (1853, pencil and white on
  buff paper) (Kensett), 95, 96
Lake George (1853, pencil on buff
  paper) (Kensett), 123
Lake George (1869) (Kensett), 57, 99,
  122–23, 129, 126, 128, 135, 163,
  164–65, 165, 168, 170, 177
Lake George (1870) (Kensett), 130
Lake George (1872) (Kensett), 177, 178
Lake George, A Reminiscence (Kensett),
  141, 141, 176
Lake Nemi (Kensett), 61
Lake Pepin (Kensett), 102, 102
Lakes of Killarney (Kensett), 122, 124

Lambdin, James R., 41
Landing of Columbus, The (Vanderlyn),
  25, 26
Landscape with Birches (Durand), 79–
  82, 79
Landscape with Narcissus and Echo
  (Lorrain), 58–59, 59
Lane, Fitz Hugh, 109, 113, 161
Lang, Louis, 32, 35, 98
Langdale Pike, The (Kensett), 90, 122,
  125
Laroche, Benjamin, 27
"Last Summer's Work" (collection),
  135, 137–61, 170–74, 176
lathes, geometric, 16
Leslie, C. R., 52
Lincoln, Abraham, 160
London Art Union Annual, 59
Long Neck Point from Contentment
  Island, Darien, Connecticut
  (Kensett), 135, 144, 151, 159
Looking Westerly from Eastern Side of
  Somes Sound near the Entrance
  (Lane), 109, 113
Lorrain, Claude, 51–52, 58–59, 99
Louvre museum, 54
luminism, 99, 103, 109, 118, 133, 156,
  158, 159
Lyon, William, 14

Manifest Destiny, 62
Marble Fawn, The (Hawthorne), 30
Marine off Big Rock (Kensett), 99, 102,
  103, 107, 108, 126, 148
Marius Amidst the Ruins of Carthage
  (Vanderlyn), 25
Marquand, Henry G., 139–40
Marzio, Peter, 62
Maverick, Peter, 16, 18
Mayer, Francis Blackwell, 42
Mayland, Caroline, 18, 19
Meigs, Montgomery C., 41
"Memo of Pictures belonging to the
  Estate of John F. Kensett," 139
Metropolitan Fair, 43–45
 wood engraving of, 39, 43, 44, 44
Metropolitan Museum of Art, 45–46,
  137, 138–39, 140, 174, 176, 177
Modern Chromatics (Rood), 126–27
Modern Painters (Ruskin), 62, 158
Monet, Claude, 127
Montclair Art Museum, 140
Moore, Charles Henry, 40

Moore, J. W., 61
Morgan Collection, 40
Morse, Jedidiah, 13, 14, 17
Mountain Stream, The (Kensett), 28
Mount Chocorua (Kensett), 70, 96–98, 97
Mount Lafayette (Kensett), 121, 122
Mount Washington from the Valley of
  Conway (Smillie), 67, 67
Murger, Henri, 22
Murray, Draper, and Fairman, 15, 16

Nahant Rock and Seashore (Kensett),
  165, 166
National Academy of Design, 22, 26,
  29, 35, 67, 122, 138, 153, 163, 174
 Kensett as member of, 37–40
 wood engraving of, 38, 40
National Gallery (London), 21, 51
"Nature" (Emerson), 62
Nazarene Brotherhood, 31
Negro Life in the South (Johnson), 40
Newbury, Sarah Kensett, 56
New England Scenery (Church), 70, 71,
  72
New Haven, Conn., map of, 13–14
New Haven Green (Rossiter), 16, 17
New Picture of London (Leigh), 25, 27
Newport (Kensett), 132
Newport Coast (Kensett), 108, 110
Newport Rocks (Kensett), 102, 137, 143,
  148, 168, 174–75, 176, 180
New York Daily Tribune, 156
New York Evening Post, 138
New York Gallery of Fine Arts, 35
New York Herald, 137–38, 145
New York Mirror, 62
Niagara Falls (Church), 83, 86
Niagara Falls (c. 1851–52) (Kensett),
  87, 89
Niagara Falls (c. 1852, pencil on buff
  paper) (Kensett), 87–90, 87
Niagara Falls (1852, pencil on paper)
  (Kensett), 87, 87, 90
Niagara Falls (1853–54) (Kensett), 86,
  86
Niagara Falls and the Rapids (Kensett),
  52, 86–87, 88
Niagara Falls from the Foot of Goat
  Island (Cropsey), 83, 86
Niagara Falls series, 86–91, 122
Notch of the White Mountains, The
  (Cole), 73, 74

October Day in the White Mountains (Kensett), 63, *68*, 70, 98
October in the Marshes (Kensett), *170*, 171, *173*, 177
Old Pine, Darien, Connecticut, The (Kensett), 148, *150*, 165, 175, 176
Olmsted, Frederick Law, 43
Olyphant, Robert M., 46, 138, 139
On the Beverly Coast, Massachusetts (Kensett), 108, *111*, 140
On the Coast (Kensett), 170
On the Coast of New Jersey (Richards), 118, *118*
Osborne, Sarah and Caroline, 27
Osgood, Samuel, 148, 149, 152, 157
Out of Money Club, 27
Outskirts of Windsor Forest (Kensett), 28
Overbeck, Friedrich, 31
Ox Bow, The (Cole), 73, *74*, 78

Paradise Rocks, Newport (Kensett), 122, *127*
Paris et ses environs (Parrott), 29
Parrott, William, 29
Passing Off of the Storm (Kensett), 170, 171, *172*, 175
Peep at Windsor Castle from St. Leonard's, A (Kensett), 59
Peep in Windsor Forest, A (Kensett), 28
Perkins, Jacob, 15
Perkins Stereotype Steelplate, 15
Picturesque America, 144
Pissarro, Camille, 127
Polk, James K., 62
Poore, Benjamin Perley, 27
Pre-Raphaelite Brotherhood, 29, 155
Putnam, George P., 45

Ranney, William, 40
Raven Hill, Elizabethtown, Essex County, N.Y.: A Study from Nature (Kensett), 91–93, *92*
Rawdon, Ralph, 14
repoussoir, 63
Richards, Frederick Debourg, 113
Richards, William Trost, 113–19
Rocks at Nahant (Haseltine), 119–20, *119*
Rocky Shore (Heade), *112*, 113
Rollinson, William, 16
Rome, art community in, 30–32

Rood, Ogden, 132–33
Roque, Oswaldo Rodriguez, 137–61
Rossiter, Thomas P., 16, 48, 49, 50, 52, 91
    as friend of Kensett, 17–18, 20, 22, 27, 40
Rousseau, Jean-Jacques, 55
Rowayton, Connecticut (Kensett), 133
Royal Society of British Artists, 29
Ruskin, John, 62, 158
Rutherfurd, Lewis, 132

Salt Meadow in October (Kensett), 176, *178*, 179, 180
Santy Lighthouse on Nantucket (Richards), 113–18, *118*
Scene on the Wye, England (Kensett), 28
Scènes de la vie de bohème (Murger), 22
Scientific American, 38, 40
Sea (Long Island Sound from Fisher's Island), The (Kensett), 148–49, *149*, 180
Seaport with the Landing of Cleopatra at Tarsus (Kensett), *51*, 52
Seaport with the Landing of Cleopatra at Tarsus (Lorrain), *51*, 52
Sea Shore (Kensett), 165, *167*
Self-portrait (Kensett), 23, *24*
Seurat, Georges, 127
Seymour, Horatio, 42, 43
Sheeler, Charles, 135
Sheepshanks, John, 52
Shelton, Charles, 14
Shelton and Kensett, 14
Shore of Darien, Connecticut (Kensett), 145, *145*, 149
Shrewsbury River (1856) (Kensett), 103, *103*
Shrewsbury River (1858) (Kensett) frontispiece, 52, 57, 99, 102, 132, 177
Shrewsbury River (1860) (Kensett), 103, *105*
Shrewsbury River, New Jersey (Kensett), 103, *104*
Shrewsbury River series, 102–3, 108, 121, 132, 133–35
Shrine—A Scene in Italy, The (Kensett), 52, 58–59, *60*, 99
Silliman, Benjamin, 17
Silva, Francis, 113, 163
Sketch Book (Irving), 62
Sketch Club, 36, 37

Smillie, James, 67
Society of British Artists, 30
Staigg, Richard Morrell, 33, 38
Standing Artist (Kensett), *58*
Standing Female Figure (Kensett), *31*, 33
Standing Monk Holding a Staff (Kensett), 57–58, *58*
Stolzenfels (Kensett), *56*, 57
Storm, Western Colorado (Kensett), *134*, 135
Story, William Wetmore, 32
Studio Reception, Paris A (Rossiter), *48*, 50, 52
Study for Dream of Arcadia (Cole), 166, *167*
Study from Nature: Rocks and Trees (Durand), 82, *82*
Study of Beeches (Kensett), 171, *171*
Summer Day on Conesus Lake (Kensett), 163, *169*, 170, 177, 180
Sun, Serene, Sinks into the Slumberous Sea, The (Blakelock), 152, *152*
Sunday Morning (Durand), *78*, 79
Sunset (Kensett), 175, *175*
Sunset on the Sea (Kensett), 118, 137, 148, 152, *154*, 160, 175, 176, 177
Sunset Sky (Kensett), 174, *174*, 176, 180

Taylor, Bayard, 121
Taylor, S., 59
Thackeray, William Makepeace, 25, 37, 121
Thoreau, Henry David, 62
Thorwaldsen, Bertel, 31
Time and Tide (Bricher), *119*, 120
Tintern Abbey (Kensett), *54*, 56
Titian, 52
Tocqueville, Alexis de, 67
Toppan, Charles, 14–15
Town, Ithiel, 17
transcendentalist philosophy, 62, 158–59
Tree Study, Catskill (Kensett), 94, *94*
Tree Study, Franconia Notch (Kensett), 94, *94*
Tuckerman, Henry T., 45, 155–56, 158
Turner, Frederick Jackson, 62
Turner, James Mallord William, 52, 158
Tuttle, Lucius, 13
Twilight in the Cedars at Darien, Connecticut (Kensett), 148, *160*, 161, 177
Twilight in the Wilderness (Church), 156

Twilight on Hunter Mountain (Gifford), 72, 73, *73*
Twilight on the Sound, Darien, Connecticut (Kensett), *162*, 166–68, 175, 177

Union League Club, 42–43
United States Capitol Extension, 40–42
United States Sanitary Commission, 43
Upper Mississippi (Kensett), *100*, 102, 103, 135

Van Dam, A. p., 21–22
Vanderlyn, John, 23, 25–26, 50, 86
van Goyen, Jan, 168–70
van Ostade, Adriaen, 52
van Valkenberg, Miss, 19
Vedder, Elihu, 158
veduta ideata, 58
Vernet, Horace, 40, 41
View from Cozzens' Hotel near West Point (Kensett), 57, 70, 90, 122, *128*, 135, 163, 166

View from Richmond Hill, (Kensett), 52, *53*, 56
View Near Richmond, England, A (Kensett), 28
View of Episcopal Academy at Cheshire, Connecticut, *12*
View of Gloucester Harbor (Lane), *109*, 113
View of Haarlem on the Haarlemer Meer (van Goyen), 168–70, *168*
View of Shrewsbury River (Kensett), *101*, 103
View of the Beach at Beverly, Massachusetts (Kensett), 52, 109, 113, *114*
View of the Grande Galerie of the Louvre, 22, 23
View on the Hudson (Kensett), 122, *126*, 135
vignette for a bank note (Kensett), *15*, 16
vignettes, engraved, 15
Vinit, Léon, 19, 21
Voyage of Life, The (Cole), 74

Waconsta Club, 18
Walters, William T., *153*, 156

Washington College, 13
Weber, Paul, 119
West Rock, New Haven (Church), 70–72, *71*
White Mountains—From North Conway, The (Kensett), 52, 63–73, *65*, 79, 82, 96, 102
White Mountain Scene (Kensett), 75, *75*, 79–82
Whittredge, Worthington, 42, 140
Wight, Peter B., 39
Willey, Benjamin, 66
Williams, Stevens, Williams, and Company, 176
Willis, Nathaniel Parker, 141
Wilson, Edmund, 161
Wilson, James Grant, 37
Windsor Castle from the Park (Kensett), 55, 56
Winter Sports (Kensett), 61, *61*
Wood, Fernando, 42
Woodland Waterfall, A (Kensett), 82–83, 84